D0205850

	U.S.S.R. TERRITORY IN 1938		U.S.S.R. OCCUPIED OR SATELLITE COUNTRIES
	U.S.S.R. ANNEXED SINCE 1938		OTHERWISE CONTROLLED BY U.S.S.R.

The Great Globe Itself

THE

Great Globe

Itself

A PREFACE TO
WORLD AFFAIRS

BY

WILLIAM C. BULLITT

Ambassador to the Union of Soviet Socialist Republics, 1933-36
Ambassador to France, 1936-40

NEW YORK
CHARLES SCRIBNER'S SONS
1946

ACKNOWLEDGMENTS

THE PUBLISHERS wish to acknowledge with thanks the permission of *The Saturday Evening Post* to reprint passages on pages 17–20 by Forrest Davis, and permission of Yale University Press to reprint passages from *The Real Soviet Russia*, by David J. Dallin, on pages 78, 80–84, and from *A History of Russia*, by George Vernadsky, on pages 32, 33, 58–60.

FOREWORD

"The cloud-capp'd towers, the gorgeous palaces,
The solemn temples, the great globe itself,
Yea, all which it inherit, shall dissolve
And, like this insubstantial pageant faded,
Leave not a rack behind."

SHAKESPEARE: *The Tempest.*

THE NIGHT before the invasion of southern France in August, 1944, by the American and French Armies, the officers at General Bethouart's mess talked not about the World War in which they were engaged, but about the next World War. They knew that all the Great Powers were working on the problem of utilizing atomic energy for slaughter, and they let their imaginations run on a future war of robot planes and rockets loaded with atomic bombs.

The General closed the conversation with a parable: "The end of the next World War? The human race is destroyed by atomic bombs. Two aviators remain alive chasing each other around the earth in jet planes. Over a forest in Africa, propulsive energy exhausted, first one, then the other, crashes at the foot of a high tree in the branches of which sit an aged chimpanzee and his mate. The old ape shrugs his shoulders, turns wearily to his wife and says: 'There you are, Ma; now we have to start it all over again.'"

Everyone laughed; but less than a year later, on August 6, 1945, an atomic bomb flattened Hiroshima. And the War Department in Washington, which is not an hysterical organization, included in its technical report on the atomic bomb the words, "a weapon has been developed that is potentially destructive beyond the wildest nightmares of the imagination; a weapon so ideally suited to sudden unannounced attack that a country's major cities might be destroyed overnight by an ostensibly friendly power. . . . Should a scheme be devised for converting to energy even as much as a few percent of the matter of some common material, civilization would have the means to commit suicide at will."

The atomic bomb is in its infancy—less developed than the airplane when the brothers Wright first flew at Kitty Hawk. No one yet knows if further research in the realm of atomic energy will permit the development of a bomb powerful enough to destroy "the great globe itself"—an unstable little planet—or if we shall have in hand merely a bomb capable of destroying all life within a radius of x miles. We do know, however, that the atomic bomb we now have in our hands would enable us to destroy any nation against which we should use it. We do know that other nations, probably within this generation, perhaps within a few years, will develop their own atomic bombs and that we thereafter shall live in the same jeopardy in which we now hold the rest of the human race. We, the people of the United States, today are uniquely secure and powerful; but our security is temporary, ephemeral. The tragic truth for us, as for all men, is: If we cannot abolish war, we may abolish mankind.

Is there the slightest chance that we may be able to abolish war? If so, how? What is to be done with this two-legged mammal who acts so often like an angry ape but sometimes like a son of God?

As Voltaire wrote, "the man who ventures to write contemporary history must expect to be attacked both for everything he has said and everything he has not said." Moreover, to strive to state exactly, in simple terms, the present plight of the human race is to attempt the impossible. There are too many unknown quantities and too many variables in the world equation. It is possible only to hope to come close to the truth, and, by an honest effort, however inadequate, to provoke more just appraisals and wiser proposals.

We have little time. "After the event even a fool is wise," wrote Homer in the *Iliad*. On all the statesmen and peoples of the world, but especially on us, the people of the United States, there is today a terrible obligation to be wise before the event. After the next World War . . . there may be no after.

The Great Globe Itself

I

MAN IS CAUGHT in a trap of his own invention. He has
acquired, and is acquiring each year, increased control
over the forces of inanimate nature; but he has not
acquired and is not acquiring any increased control
over the forces of his own nature. The sciences which
deal with inanimate nature, physics and chemistry, have
outstripped the sciences which deal with animate nature,
biology and psychology. In consequence the atomic
bomb is in the hand of a superficially civilized savage
who is somewhat restrained by the pressure of custom
and the teachings of religion. His forefathers on murder bent, had at most a stone, a club, a dagger, a sword,
a spear and a bow. Their intended victims had at least
legs with which to run away. There is no running away
from the atomic bomb. And there is no hope that
biology and psychology can produce adequate changes
in human nature—in time. Moreover, the influence of
religion on man's conduct is not increasing, and the
years from 1914 to 1946 have been a period of moral
decay in international customs, a period of de-civiliza-
tion.

1

If Christ's teaching: "Do unto others as you would they should do unto you," or its Confucian corollary, "Do not do to another what you would not have him do to you," had become the way of life of mankind before the discovery of methods to utilize atomic energy, the future would be bright with hope for all humanity. For atomic energy offers the physical means to make this earth a fairer habitation than man has ever dreamed. But the atomic bomb came first. And our problem is no less than this: To try to develop and integrate in the national and international customs of all peoples wisdom and character of the quality that hitherto has distinguished a few saints and sages.

To raise the level of some peoples is not enough. The world is studded with the wrecked remains of relatively civilized communities that fell before barbaric conquerors. To beat swords into plowshares while the spiritual descendants of Genghis Khan stalk the earth armed with atomic bombs, is to die, and to leave no descendants. Must we conclude, therefore, that the human race is an unsuccessful experiment which is nearing an unhappy end? Perhaps. But before embracing annihilation, we may at least examine every bar of the trap which holds us, try to remember how we got into it, and try to find a way out.

Let us begin our search by looking backward from our present situation to some events of the immediate past; then examine the facts that lie behind those events; then, if the facts permit us to draw any conclusions that offer hope of peace, try to look forward and chart a way out of our present predicament. It might be more logical to begin by a discussion of the development of such civilization as mankind possesses, then proceed to an examination of the fundamental aims and present objectives of the Great Powers, then assess the possibilities and draw conclusions. Such an approach to the problem would avoid the unpleasant obligation to state conclusions from time to time before examining the facts on which they are based. But the process of working backward from the fact of the atomic bomb, although less logical, has the virtue of corresponding to reality. The atomic bomb is the central fact in the minds of all men who attempt to think about their own future or the future of mankind. And we may as well face at once the question: What nation or nations do we fear may use the atomic bomb against us?

We do not fear Great Britain, or any member of the British Commonwealth of Nations. Great Britain and Canada participated with us in the production of the atomic bomb, and they know as much about it as ourselves. That disturbs no American, just as no British subject is disturbed because we have the atomic bomb. We expect our intimate relations with the British Empire to grow closer with each passing year.

We do not fear France. So long as France remains an independent nation in full control of her foreign policy, she will look to the United States as an old friend who in days of need may come to her aid as we came in 1917 and 1941. A puppet government in France, like a puppet government in England, might be forced to become hostile to us; but so long as the interests of the people of France control French policy, France will be our friend.

From disarmed Germany and Japan and exhausted Italy, we have nothing to fear for the foreseeable future. And so long as China is independent, with a government whose actions are based on the interests of the people of China and not on the interests of some foreign state, she will look to us for help and friendship. We certainly have no fear of any Latin American nation or of any people of Africa or the Near East. There is but one nation that we do fear may some day use the atomic bomb against us. We fear the Soviet Union.

Most Americans did not become acutely aware that the destruction of the military forces of Germany and Japan would not necessarily mean peace until October 2, 1945, when the representatives of the five Great Powers at the London Conference separated after agreeing on the single point that they could not agree about anything. But this conflict between the Russians on one side, and the Americans, British, French and Chinese on the other, had been latent in international relations for more than four years. President Roosevelt himself had stated the essential facts in two declarations.

On February 10, 1940, addressing the American Youth Congress, the President said:

The Soviet Union, as everybody who has the courage to face the fact knows, is run by a dictatorship as absolute as any other dictatorship in the world.[1]

On November 7, 1941, in decreeing the extension of Lend-Lease aid to the Soviet Union, the President declared:

I have found that the defense of the Union of Soviet Socialist Republics is vital to the defense of the United States.[2]

Both these statements by President Roosevelt were true. It was in the national interest of the United States to give aid to the Soviet Union, in spite of the fact that its Government was a "dictatorship as absolute as any other dictatorship in the world," because the Soviet Union was fighting heroically against Germany, and we had reason to believe that defeat of the Soviet Union and Great Britain by Germany would lead eventually to German attack on the Americas. We believed that Hitler would not stop but could only be stopped. We, therefore, gave ten billion dollars' worth of Lend-Lease aid to the Soviet Union.

But that did not alter the nature of the Soviet Government or its aims. In nature, it remained "a dictator-

[1] *The Public Papers and Addresses of Franklin D. Roosevelt*, 1940, p. 93.
[2] *New York Times*, November 8, 1941.

ship as absolute as any dictatorship in the world," which differed from the Nazi dictatorship most conspicuously in policy toward the Jews. Hitler slaughtered Jews—men, women and children—for no other reason than that they were Jews; whereas Stalin killed only those gentiles and Jews who displeased him.

The aims of the Soviet Government, we hoped, were not those expressed in the official Communist doctrine taught in the Soviet Union. We knew that according to the Lenin-Stalin version of the Communist creed, the supreme moral goal of mankind was the establishment of Communism in all nations. We knew that Lenin himself had considered this end as justifying the use of all means for its attainment; that he had written in Chapter 6 of his pamphlet, "The Infantile Sickness of 'Leftism' in Communism," first published in 1920: "It is necessary . . . to use any ruse, cunning, unlawful method, evasion, concealment of truth," and that he looked forward to wars with non-Communist states like the United States, which he called either "bourgeois" or "imperialist," before the ultimate world triumph of Communism. He had stated his views frankly: "We are living not merely in a state, but in a system of states; and it is inconceivable that the Soviet republic should continue for a long period side by side with imperialist states. Ultimately one or the other must conquer. Meanwhile a number of terrible clashes between the Soviet republic and the bourgeois states is inevitable." [3]

[3] Lenin, *Collected Works*, Vol. XXIV, p. 122, Russian edition.

We trusted that the actions of the Soviet Government would not follow Communist doctrine and that such wars might not be inevitable. We are a practical people and rightly believe in the truth of the maxim "actions speak louder than words." We hoped that Communist action would not live up to Communist words. But action followed.

When the Polish Army was staggering under the blows of the German Army on September 17, 1939, the Soviet Union attacked Poland and annexed all eastern Poland. Similarly, by threats of annihilation, the Soviet Union swallowed inch by inch the Baltic states: Estonia, Latvia and Lithuania. When the Soviet Union attacked Finland on November 29, 1939, however, that supposedly digestible morsel turned out to have much grit in it. "Everyone in Moscow from Stalin down thought the Red Army would be in Helsinki in a week after the attack started," wrote William Shirer in *Berlin Diary*. But the Finns fought superbly, and the public opinion of the world rose against the Soviet Union. President Roosevelt expressed that opinion later in the words: "It has invaded a neighbor so infinitesimally small that it could do no conceivable possible harm to the Soviet Union, a neighbor which seeks only to live in peace as a democracy, and a liberal forward-looking democracy at that." [4]

The League of Nations summoned the Soviet Union,

[4] *The Public Papers and Addresses of Franklin D. Roosevelt*, 1940, p. 93.

which was a member of the League, and the other members, to a session to consider the Soviet aggression against Finland. Molotov sent the reply, "The Soviet Union is not at war with Finland." The Red Army was killing Finns and seizing their country without declaration of war. The Soviet Union remained a member of the League—but not for long. On December 14, 1939, the Soviet Union was expelled from the League of Nations. Many members of the League sent supplies of arms to Finland. The United States gave financial aid. The Finns fought on against hopeless odds, and when peace was signed on March 12, 1940, the Soviet Union had to content itself with only a piece of Finland. And it had achieved the moral position of being the only nation ever expelled from the League of Nations for aggression.

Stalin's record as a breaker of solemn international agreements and treaties rapidly approached that of Hitler himself.[5] And it became the obvious duty of those who were charged with the defense of the interests of the United States, the chief of which was world peace, to ask themselves if after all, in spite of our hopes, the Soviet Government was not following Communist doctrine rather closely. Was the ultimate aim of the Soviet Government the establishment of Communist dictatorship throughout the earth? Was its immediate objective the subjection of neighboring na-

[5] See Appendix I, p. 219, *Comparison of Hitler's Breaches of International Agreements and Stalin's.*

tions to serve as springboards from which to leap further?

It was obvious in 1941 that the destruction of Hitler and the Nazis and the disarmament of Germany would bring mankind great gains: the mania of "racism" would be wiped from the earth; danger of German attack on any people would be eliminated; the peoples of Europe would be liberated from Nazi tyranny. But it was equally obvious that the states of Europe, after liberation from the Nazi yoke, might fall under Soviet dictatorship. Enslavement of Europe by Moscow might replace enslavement by Berlin. Stalin might mount Hitler's saddle.

Such a result of the war could not be considered satisfactory either by the peoples of Europe, who would be enslaved, or by Great Britain or the United States. The chief war aim of the American and British peoples was the establishment of lasting peace. No lasting peace could be based on the bondage of the once free peoples of Europe. Moreover, the British felt that they would be as menaced by Russian control of Europe as by German. And the vital interests of the United States, which led President Roosevelt to extend aid to the Soviet Union, might after a time be threatened by Russians instead of Germans.

The hostility of the people of the United States to Hitler's Germany, like our hostility to the Kaiser's Germany in the First World War, was based both on moral grounds and on the conviction that it was contrary to the vital interests of the United States to permit any power which might become hostile to us, to control the islands of the Atlantic, the west coasts of Europe and Africa, and the water gates to the Atlantic —that is to say, the North Sea, the English Channel and the Strait of Gibraltar. Hitler had been well on his way toward those objectives. If he had invaded England successfully in the summer of 1940, he would have been able to establish his power from Ireland to Dakar, unless we had first seized that great French port in West Africa. The Soviet Union represented no such immediate threat to the Americas. The Russians had a long way to go before reaching the Atlantic. The danger was not that the Soviet Union would swallow Europe at one gulp; but that the Soviet Union would bite such a large piece out of the body of Europe and incorporate it in her closed politico-economic system— the world's most colossal cartel—that the remainder of Europe, which temporarily would be free from direct Soviet control, would be unable to maintain orderly economic or political life, and eventually would be unable to resist Soviet economic, political and military pressure. The Russians could not swallow Europe in one gulp but might in two, unless Great Britain and the United States should establish a firm basis for the independence of all the European peoples—those of eastern and central Europe and the Balkans as well as those of western Europe.

The primary task of American military policy in

Europe was to sustain the powers that were fighting against Hitler. The primary task of American foreign policy should have been to make certain that the defeat of Germany would liberate fully from all foreign tyranny, Nazi or Soviet, the independent states which existed in Europe before Hitler began his career of conquest by seizing Austria in March, 1938.

A month after Germany's attack on the Soviet Union, which began on June 22, 1941, President Roosevelt sent Mr. Harry Hopkins to Moscow as his personal representative to confer with Stalin. The German armies were advancing into Russia and many who had no first-hand knowledge of the superb stamina of the Russian people considered the Russian position desperate. Mr. Hopkins decided rightly that the Russians would fight hard and well, and that it would be in our national interest to give them Lend-Lease aid.

In return for the offer of such aid he asked nothing. The vital interest of the United States in a free and independent Europe was not expressed, although the basis of all healthy dealing between great powers is give and take, and the position of the Soviet Union was so grave that Stalin could not have refused to give a written guarantee that at the end of the war he would respect the independence of all European states, and raise no objection to the formation of a European federation of democratic states.

To argue that Stalin might not respect, or would not respect, such a guarantee was to misunderstand the object of obtaining such a guarantee. That object had a positive side as well as a negative. The negative was to prevent Soviet subjugation of eastern, central and southeastern Europe. The positive was to clear the way for a constructive attempt by the United States to create a peaceful, democratic Europe which should be sufficiently strong and stable to defend itself from future aggression. We had a right, after all, to have an American foreign policy conceived in the interests of the people of the United States and world peace. If we had obtained from Stalin a written promise to keep his hands off Europe and he had respected it, all the world would have gained. If he had given such a promise with the intention of breaking it ultimately, he would at least have had to behave as if he had no intention of breaking it so long as he and his country were dependent for their lives on aid from the United States. If he had given his promise, Stalin could not have objected to a declaration of American aims in Europe by the President of the United States or to diplomatic and political moves designed to achieve those aims.

Prime Minister Churchill favored the creation of a Europe composed of independent democratic states joined in a federation, into which German states disarmed and democratized might eventually be admitted. Whether that formula or some other were to to be adopted—and there was room for honest difference of opinion with regard to the terms of such a formula— it was clearly in the interest of the United States and

Great Britain, and peace, that Europe should emerge from the war democratic, with its eastern boundary approximately that of August 23, 1939, when Stalin made his pact with Hitler.

No one knew better than President Roosevelt that President Wilson's failure to achieve the settlement in Europe that he desired at the close of the First World War was due to the fact that he had not used his power while he had it. He had not insisted on elimination of the Secret Treaties or specific acceptance of his specific projects by our allies, Great Britain, France and Italy, during the period when they were totally dependent upon us for their lives. He had waited until after the war, when his power over his allies had slipped from his hands. Repeatedly President Roosevelt was warned that at the close of the Second World War he would find himself in difficulties with his allies similar to those which confronted President Wilson at the Peace Conference in Paris. In 1941 and 1942 the President had the power to compel Great Britain and the Soviet Union to accept proposals designed to produce lasting peace. He might have enunciated, and forced written acceptance of, a program for peace in Europe and Asia even more clear and specific than the program contained in President Wilson's Fourteen Points, which had given the United States the moral leadership of the world. That leadership was conspicuously ours during the First World War and conspicuously not ours, or anyone else's, during the Second World War. Throughout the war Milton's great line remained true: "The hungry sheep look up, and are not fed."

War is not a prize fight. The winner does not go home from the ring and receive a purse. Military effort unaccompanied by equal political and moral effort produces no constructive result. Power in international affairs is a fleeting thing. The most justifiable use of power is to forward the growth of moral ideas. It was in the interest not only of the United States, but of all the allies and all the peoples of the world—the Russians included—that we should use our power to make certain, so far as humanly possible, that at the close of the war the peoples of Europe and Asia would find liberty and peace.

Mr. Hopkins' failure to demand of Stalin a specific written guarantee with regard to Europe was the first of many similar omissions which led finally to the conflict at the Conference of Foreign Ministers in London in October, 1945. The second brilliant opportunity to promote our interests, and those of Europe and peace, while aiding the Soviet Union, came—and was not seized—when Mr. Averell Harriman and Lord Beaverbrook conferred with Stalin from September 26 to October 1, 1941. Stalin then asked for an enormous quantity of war material of all sorts. Mr. Harriman accepted most of Stalin's demands, but did not ask for any commitment from Stalin with regard to Europe.

Mr. Harriman, however, was instructed by President Roosevelt to inform Stalin that the American press was attacking the Soviet Government's hostility to religion, and that the American public would be more disposed to give unlimited aid to the Soviet Union if the Soviet Government should make some mollifying gesture in the religious field. Stalin immediately suspended publication of the Soviet anti-religious propaganda magazine *Bezbozhnik*, The Godless. The President was delighted to have this assistance in handling the domestic political problem presented by the antipathy of Christian Americans to a government which had adorned the walls of Russia with the slogan "Religion is the opium of the people"; and Stalin no doubt was equally delighted by this evidence that the American Government had become interested in making the Soviet Government popular in the United States and might refrain from asking him for a written promise that might hamper his freedom of action in Europe.

The President and Prime Minister Churchill knew that their views with respect to the future of the world differed from those of Stalin, and one of their intentions when they drew up the Atlantic Charter on August 15, 1941, was to ask Stalin to adhere to it. The first three points in the Atlantic Charter read:

1. Their countries seek no aggrandizement, territorial or other.
2. They desire to see no territorial changes that do not accord with the freely expressed wishes of the peoples concerned.
3. They respect the right of all peoples to choose the

form of government under which they will live; and they wish to see sovereign rights and self-government restored to those who have been forcibly deprived of them.

The President and the Prime Minister feared they might have some difficulty in persuading Stalin to adhere to the Charter because it was difficult to square the Soviet Union's aggressions against Finland, Estonia, Latvia, Lithuania, Rumania and Poland, with the terms of the Charter. The German armies were driving the Russians from the territory which they had seized in those countries, and were engaged in installing Nazi tyranny where Soviet tyranny had flourished.

On January 1, 1942, the Soviet Union adhered to the Charter. There were those who believed that this meant the Soviet Union had reformed, finding it did not pay to be "the big bad wolf," and that the independence of the Baltic states and Poland henceforth was assured.

President Roosevelt stated his own opinions often in private to various advisers; but he never made them public except indirectly through the pen of Mr. Forrest Davis of *The Saturday Evening Post*. After the Teheran Conference, which closed on December 1, 1943, the President spent two hours describing his foreign policy to Mr. Davis, and after Mr. Davis had prepared his articles, the President personally corrected them. The account of what was in the President's mind ran as follows:

To the President, an ingrained optimist who believes in the efficacy of cross-the-table confabulation, the fact that he and Stalin were face to face was at least half his battle. It marked, as he saw it, a long step forward in the accomplishment of his "great design" for a peaceable, law-abiding world. . . .

It was at Teheran that the President most clearly exhibited his tough-minded determination to enroll the Soviet Union as a sincere and willing collaborator in postwar settlements. That determination, I am able to say, is at the center of his "great design."

The President had persevered, against discouragements, to bring Stalin across the table from himself and Churchill. The conference was occurring principally on his initiative. Throughout the sessions he was to make every endeavor to meet Stalin's mind, to understand his point of view and to assure the Russian of his own complete good faith. It seemed to him that the creation of a reciprocal spirit of confidence among the Big Three was more desirable than specific compacts. . . .

The President conducted at Teheran a seminar, for Stalin's benefit, in the good-neighbor policy. Tracing the improvement in inter-American relations since we abandoned dollar diplomacy and the Roosevelt (Theodore) corollary to the Monroe Doctrine, which we had used to justify meddling in the Caribbean republics, he stressed the advantages accruing to us as the only great power in the hemisphere. In proof, he cited the simultaneous declarations of war against the Axis by our weaker neighbors in December, 1941. Emphasizing the absence from our hearts of any hankering for the lands of our neighbors, the President recommended the policy for strong powers paramount in their regions, such as the United States in the New

World and the Soviet Union, presumptively, in Eastern and Northern Europe. . . .

At this point, the Marshal volunteered a sweeping declaration of his desire to conciliate his neighbors, saying flatly that he had no desire to own Europe. His country, he added, is only half populated and the Russians have plenty to do at home, without undertaking great new territorial responsibilities. The President, accepting the assurance with gratification, at once voiced his belief in the Marshal's good intentions.

The foregoing colloquy, which has not been, I believe, previously reported, provided one of the highlights of the Roosevelt-Stalin conversations. Signifying Roosevelt's solicitude for the small nations of Europe, it perhaps even more importantly afforded him an opportunity to avow his trust in Stalin's word. Since Teheran, the President and the Marshal have carried on a personal correspondence, exchanging hand-written, informal letters every three or four weeks, as well as more frequent personal cablegrams. Mr. Roosevelt's reliance on the Russian's bona fides as expressed at Teheran and subsequently in their correspondence furnishes a key to the Government's hopefully patient dealings with Moscow—bordering at times on what has been termed appeasement. . . .

In the interest of his objective, Mr. Roosevelt has avoided the slightest cause of offense to the Kremlin . . . The core of his policy has been the reassurance of Stalin. That was so, as we have seen, at Teheran. It has been so throughout the difficult diplomacy since Stalingrad. Our failure to renew our offer of good offices in the Russo-Polish controversies must be read in that light. Likewise our support, seconding Britain, of Tito, the Croatian Communist partisan leader in Jugoslavia. So it is also with the President's immediate and generous response to Stalin's demand for a share in the surrendered Italian fleet or its equivalent. Our bluntly reiterated advice to the Finns to quit the war at once without reference to Soviet terms falls under the same tactical heading. . . .

The President's Russian policy, although never explicitly defined, has drawn diversified criticism, chiefly on the ground of principle as well as risk. Agreeing with the objective, the critics question his methods. By allowing the Kremlin to take a unilateral course with Poland and Finland, unchecked by word from us, it is held that he has prejudiced the cause of peace by general agreement. The President's tacit acceptance of the transfer of East Prussia and other parts of Prussia to Poland in compensation for the loss of her eastern provinces alarms those who see in such forcible measures a violation of the Atlantic Charter's stipulations regarding territorial integrity. By giving ground, moreover, in the face of the Kremlin's independent assertions, such critics hold that the President has weakened in advance not only our influence in Europe, but the very principle of a co-operative peace. The arguments based on risk run something like this:

Suppose that Stalin, in spite of all concessions, should prove unappeasable, determined to pursue his own policy regardless of the west? What assurance does the Roosevelt approach hold that he may not capture all Poland, Finland, the Balkans and even Germany from within, as was the case with the Baltic states, once his armies occupy those countries and he can recognize his own Moscow-dominated undergrounds? A Europe dominated by the hammer and sickle, with the Baltic and Black seas Russian ponds, the Danube basin a Russian protectorate, and Soviet power on the Rhine, might suit this country's vital interests even less than the torn and distracted Europe of 1939. . . .

The risks are inherent in the situation. Once Germany falls, there will be no military power between the Russian border and the English Channel. Into this power vacuum neither English-speaking power can move permanently. We have had to face that risk since, in June, 1941, we resolved to help Russia resist Nazi invasion. Our historic interest, like England's, has demanded a European balance of power wherein no single nation commands all the Continent's resources and manpower to our potential disadvantage. Stripped to the bare essentials, we fought in 1917 and are fighting now to prevent the mastery of Europe by one aggressive power. Should Russia, as the sole European power, display tendencies toward world conquest, our vital interest would be again called into account.

Mr. Roosevelt, gambling for stakes as enormous as any statesman ever played for, has been betting that the Soviet Union needs peace and is willing to pay for it by collaborating with the west.

The two paragraphs at the close of this statement contain the gist of President Roosevelt's thought. Instead of attempting to fill the "power vacuum" in Europe by the creation of a federation of independent, democratic states, he chose to gamble on his ability to convert Stalin from Soviet imperialism to democratic collaboration. Hitler's invasion of Czechoslovakia on March 14, 1939, had convinced the President finally that Hitler was unappeasable. He still considered Stalin appeasable.

The means by which the President hoped to accomplish the conversion of Stalin were four:

(1) To give Stalin without stint or limit everything he asked for the prosecution of the war, and to refrain from asking Stalin for anything in return.
(2) To persuade Stalin to adhere to statements of general aims, like the Atlantic Charter.
(3) To let Stalin know that the influence of the White House was being used to encourage American public opinion to take a favorable view of the Soviet Government.
(4) To meet Stalin face to face and persuade him into an acceptance of Christian ways and democratic principles.

The epic bravery of the Red Army and the Russian people had prepared the field for propaganda in favor of the Soviet Government. The Russians, as always throughout their history, were fighting for their soil with magnificent tenacity, and their courage rightly had aroused the sympathy of the world. On this fertile ground, the power of the White House was used to sow a crop of propaganda. Mr. Joseph E. Davies, who had been Ambassador to the Soviet Union from November 16, 1936, to the spring of 1938, was encouraged to publish a volume entitled *Mission to Moscow* and to produce a motion picture with the same title. In his book and film Mr. Davies spread before the American people an alluring picture of the Soviet Union, and made many speeches throughout the United States in which his theme was "by the testimony of performance and in my opinion, the word of honor of the Soviet Government is as safe as the Bible." [6] A comparison of Mr. Davies' statements with Stalin's breaches of international agreements set forth in Appendix I is not without interest.

All Americans wanted to believe that the Soviet Union was what we wished it to be. Our hopeful wishes predisposed us to accept any laudatory lie and to discount every refractory fact. And all the agents of the Soviet Government in America, all the members of the Communist party, and all the dupes who are "fellow travellers," made hay with American public opinion while the Red Army fought heroically and the White House sun shone.

This systematic campaign for the bamboozlement of the people of the United States with regard to the nature and aims of the Soviet Government was highly successful, and on the surface Soviet-American relations were greatly improved. But Stalin still would not agree to meet the President face to face. Three times the President sought a conversation with Stalin and three times Stalin refused before agreeing to meet the President at Teheran. There, as we have seen, the President did his best to appease Stalin. When the question of Poland arose, the President declared himself out of the conversation, and let Prime Minister Churchill

[6] *New York Daily Worker*, February 25, 1942.

alone attempt to defend the rights of the Poles. The situation of Poland was so serious that it was obvious that only a united stand by Great Britain and the United States could save the Poles from enslavement. But the President washed his hands of the question.

Stalin insisted to Churchill that the Soviet Union must annex all eastern Poland as far as the Curzon line —one-third of the country—and that Poland must be compensated by annexing eastern Germany. Churchill argued that both these annexations contained seeds of future wars; but Stalin was adamant, and Churchill finally accepted his demands—and Roosevelt assented to the agreement. In justification, the President and Churchill argued that the vital question was not the boundary of Poland on the east, but the establishment of a completely free Polish state with an absolutely independent government uncontrolled by the Soviet Government. This they hoped they had bought at the price of paying Stalin one-third of Poland's territory. But the event proved that this price was not high enough. Stalin wanted to control all Poland, and by enlarging the boundaries of Poland to the Oder and the western Neisse rivers to control all eastern Germany as well. In the end, Stalin installed in Warsaw a Soviet puppet government which was completely under his control, and, when it had difficulty in subduing Polish patriots, he established seventeen Russian general headquarters throughout Poland with adequate troops to hunt down the remaining Poles who refused to admit that Poland must live in slavery.[7] Thus he extended the area controlled from Moscow to the Oder River.

President Roosevelt met Stalin again at Yalta in the Crimea on February 4, 1945. The weary President was on the verge of thrombosis but he was obliged to travel to Russia for the privilege of talking once more with the Soviet dictator. He was not at his best and, in a moment of weakness, gave the Kurile Islands and control of the Chinese ports of Port Arthur and Dairen to the Soviet Union and agreed to let Stalin slip into the proposed United Nations Organization as "independent states" the Soviet Ukraine and White Russia, which are less independent than the states of California and Massachusetts. And he made the agreement to recognize in the future a government of Poland satisfactory to the Soviet Government which President Truman later carried out. He also secured Stalin's signature to another joint declaration of noble principles which, like the Atlantic Charter, contained no specific, detailed commitments. It ran:

The establishment of order in Europe and the rebuilding of national economic life must be achieved by processes which will enable the liberated peoples to destroy the last vestiges of Nazism and Fascism and to create democratic institutions of their own choice. This is a principle of the Atlantic Charter—the right of all peoples to choose the

[7] *New York Times,* Oct. 16, 1945.

form of government under which they will live—the restoration of sovereign rights and self-government to those peoples who have been forcibly deprived of them by the aggressor nations.

To foster the conditions in which the liberated peoples may exercise these rights, the three governments will jointly assist the people in any European liberated state or former Axis satellite state in Europe where in their judgment conditions require (A) to establish conditions of internal peace; (B) to carry out emergency measures for the relief of distressed peoples; (C) to form interim governmental authorities broadly representative of all democratic elements in the population and pledged to the earliest possible establishment through free elections of governments responsive to the will of the people; and (D) to facilitate where necessary the holding of such elections.

The three governments will consult the other United Nations and provisional authorities or other governments in Europe when matters of direct interest to them are under consideration.

When, in the opinion of the three governments, conditions in any European liberated state or any former Axis satellite state in Europe make such action necessary, they will immediately consult together on the measures necessary to discharge the joint responsibilities set forth in this declaration.

By this declaration we reaffirm our faith in the principles of the Atlantic Charter, our pledge in the declaration by the United Nations, and our determination to build in co-operation with other peace-loving nations world order under law, dedicated to peace, security, freedom and general well-being of all mankind.

God was kind to President Roosevelt. He had always great confidence in his luck, and his luck held. He died before the actions of the Soviet Government in Poland, Hungary, Austria, Rumania, Bulgaria, Yugoslavia, the portion of Germany occupied by the Red Army, Iran, Manchuria and Korea, had forced him to admit that he had lost his gamble "for stakes as enormous as any statesman ever played for." Stalin had remained unconverted. The events of 1945 proved beyond shadow of a doubt that the Atlantic Charter and the Yalta Declaration had been to Stalin merely excellent ready-made suits of sheep's clothing which he could wear until he no longer needed a camouflage. Stalin had remained faithful to Lenin's teaching: "It is necessary to use any ruse, cunning, unlawful method, evasion, concealment of truth." The war was over but there was no sign of peace. The President's "great design" had failed. Stalin had won "stakes as enormous as any statesman ever played for." But the tired President was never forced to admit that he had lost, that not even he with all his genius could appease the unappeasable.

II

"Despotism tempered by assassination: that is our Magna Charta."

> A Russian nobleman commenting on the assassination of Tsar Paul I, 1801, quoted by Count Munster, Hanoverian Minister to St. Petersburg.

"The history of old Russia is the history of defeats due to backwardness. She was beaten by the Mongol Khans. She was beaten by the Turkish Beys. She was beaten by the Swedish feudal lords. She was beaten by the Polish-Lithuanian squires. She was beaten by the Anglo-French capitalists. She was beaten by the Japanese barons. All beat her for her backwardness, for military backwardness, for cultural backwardness, for governmental backwardness, for industrial backwardness, for agricultural backwardness."

> STALIN: *Speech to the First All-Union Conference of Managers of Soviet Industry, February 4, 1931.*

"They managed to get rid of the Tsar but not of Tsarism. They still wear the Tsarist uniform, albeit inside out."

> T. G. MASARYK (Founder of Czechoslovakia): *The Making of a State.*

WHY is Stalin unappeasable?

The peoples of the Soviet Union live in an enormously rich, sparsely inhabited, undeveloped area, so extensive that it includes one-sixth of the land of the entire earth.

They long for a higher standard of living, and some individual freedom, and peace. Now that Germany and Japan have been conquered and disarmed, no great power desires anything but friendship with the Soviet Union. These circumstances would lead any democratic government in the world to think of nothing but peace. Why does it remain tragically true that the Soviet Government still desires to impose its will on peoples beyond the frontiers of the Soviet Union and that Stalin, like Hitler, will not stop but can only be stopped?

The answer to this question is to be found in the sources of the mighty river of Soviet Imperialism. Some lie deep in Russian history, others in Communist doctrine. An engineer who has studied the countless streams that contribute to the Mississippi River understands its devastating floods. Those who have studied Russian history, and the works of Marx, Lenin and Stalin, and the practices of the Soviet dictatorship, and the Communist faith, and Soviet foreign policy, will not find it worth their while to read this chapter. Others may.

The Soviet Union is unique among great powers. It is not only a state but also the headquarters of an international faith. To understand it as a state is important. To understand the Communist creed is vital.[1] Let us

---

[1] The Trotsky version of Communist doctrine, and various other versions, differ from the Stalin version. Only the Stalin version is permitted in the Soviet Union. Parties outside the Soviet Union which call themselves Communist are obliged to adhere to the Stalin version of the Communist creed and obey orders from Moscow, under penalty of having themselves excommunicated and denounced as "Fascist dogs," etc., by Moscow. Any foreign Communist party which refuses to

begin by tracing the growth of Tsarist Russia, then examine the Russian revolution and the present Soviet State, and finally try to understand the Communist creed, and Soviet foreign policy which is one of its forms of expression.

The Growth of Tsarist Russia

The Russians entered history as inhabitants of the fertile prairies of the Ukraine and the less fertile forest belt of the Novgorod-Moscow area. Their land was all flat, unprotected by any natural frontier: an ill-defined, defenseless area in the vast plain that extends from Mongolia to Bordeaux.

Europe, in reality, is not a continent but a relatively small peninsula jutting westward from the vast continent of Asia. The Ural Mountains by which the old geographers marked the eastern boundary of Europe and the western boundary of Asia are, for much of their length, not mountains but hills like our own Berkshires. The passes are low and easy of access: that on the road from Sverdlovsk (Ekaterinburg) in Siberia to Molotov (Perm) rises only to 1,245 feet. There it is easier to pass from Asia into Europe than to go from Springfield, Massachusetts, to Pittsfield. In civilization, ideals

---

take orders from Moscow is at once denounced in violent language. The simple test of whether or not a Communist party is taking orders from Moscow is whether or not it is denounced by Moscow. The word "Communist" in this book is used to describe those who accept the Stalin version of the Communist creed and obey orders from Moscow.

and traditions, Europe is one with the Americas; but geographically Europe is a small part of Asia.

Over the long and fertile Asiatic-European plain, from the dawn of recorded history, tribe after tribe of savage nomads moved westward. The Russians themselves probably reached the lands where they settled by the same route. Against the savage hordes which followed them they had no protection except their own hands and weapons. They had other hostile neighbors on the north, south and west. They were often conquered. Their history is a tragic story of war, starvation, torture, rape, murder and slavery. In the hard school of experience they learned to regard a foreigner as a man who tries to kill you and take your land. From time to time the Russians achieved a temporary armistice with their neighbors and called it peace. But they have never known in all their history what we in America know so well: the peaceful existence of neighboring states side by side, with established boundaries accepted without question. Our conception of permanent friendly relations between states has no place in their historical experience.

We, living within well-defined and easily defensible boundaries, without strong neighbors, having our chief contacts with foreign nations through friendly international trade, regarding foreigners as possible immigrants and, therefore, as potential Americans, have become the most unsuspicious of all great nations. The Russians have been driven by the horrors of their his-

tory to become the most suspicious. To deal with foreigners with an outward show of good fellowship while
preserving a wary secretiveness, has become second
nature to them. To survive they had to practice the art
of deceit as well as the art of war. Centuries ago they
learned to say, "yes, of course," in such a way that no
one could be quite sure what thought lay behind their
ostensible assent. To them all foreigners are potential
enemies.

The Russians are amongst the toughest of all the major races of Europe. They had to be in order to survive.
And they came through their terrible sufferings with
their primitive energies unimpaired. They are strong
physically, intellectually and emotionally, and the Russian woman is even more durable than the Russian man.
The Russian male was often defeated on the field of
battle. The Russian female was never defeated. She
worked harder than her husband and produced children
besides. She still does. The Russians have often been
out-fought. They have never been out-bred.

Through all their history, except in moments of
approaching anarchy, the Russians have been ruled by
dictators. They have never known what it is to live in
ordered freedom. To an American, Russia under the
rule of the last of the Tsars, Nicholas II, was a land of
unendurable tyranny; but under his autocracy the Russians enjoyed greater liberty than they had ever known
before.

The despotic form of the Russian state was consolidated through the conquest of the Russians in 1240 by Batu, grandson of Genghis Khan, founder of the great Mongol Empire. For two hundred years the Russians lived under the rule of the Mongols. Such Russian princes as were left alive were forced to recognize their complete submission to the Khan of the "Golden Horde." As the historian Vernadsky writes:

Mongolian influence . . . found expression in many aspects of the Russian governmental and social structure. The most substantial effect was felt in the political thought of the Russian people. The Mongolian state was built upon the principle of unquestioning submission of the individual to the group, first to the clan and through the clan to the whole state. This principle was in the course of time impressed thoroughly upon the Russian people. It led to the system of universal service to the state which all without differentiation were forced to give. Under the influence of Mongolian ideas the Russian state developed on the basis of universal service. All classes of society were made a definite part of the state organization. Taken altogether, these ideas amount to a peculiar system of state socialism. The political theory developed into a finished plan later, in the Moscow Kingdom and the Russian Empire; but the basis of the idea of state service was laid down during the period of Tartar domination.

The Mongolians also introduced a new view regarding the power of the prince. The power of the Khan was one of merciless strength. It was autocratic; submission to it was unqualified. This view of the authority of the prince was transferred to the Grand Duke of Moscow when the rule of the Khans was weakened. When the last threads of

Tartar control were broken by Moscow, the dukes of Moscow openly regarded themselves as absolute monarchs, and considered their people completely subject to their will. All lands within the boundaries of his state were claimed by the duke to be devoted to the interests of the state. The current theory was that the prince was the sole owner of the land, and that all other persons merely had the tenure and use of it temporarily.[2]

From the time of the Mongols until today, the Russians have been inured to living in a totalitarian state under the tyranny of an absolute dictator.

The Mongol conquest of Russia affected the Russian Church no less than the Russian State. Christianity had reached Russia at a late date. In 987 Vladimir, heathen Grand Duke of Kiev, sent envoys to study the religions of the neighboring nations. According to Nestor, the chronicler, the envoys, reporting on the Bulgarians, who were then Moslems, said: "There is no gladness among them; only sorrow and a great stench; their religion is not a good one." The envoys found "no beauty" in the Catholic churches of the Germans. But when they reached Constantinople and beheld the incomparable beauty of the mass in St. Sophia, they said: "We no longer knew whether we were in heaven or on earth." Vladimir promptly chose the Greek Orthodox Church, had himself baptized in 988, married a sister of the Byzantine Emperor, converted his heathen subjects to Christianity, and thus gave the Russian people the

[2] George Vernadsky, *A History of Russia*, p. 56.

greatest source of consolation that they have had throughout their tragic history.

The Mongol Khans did not attempt to destroy the Church; but on the contrary acted as its patrons, guaranteeing the rights of the Church and the integrity of its property. Their rule was so savage, however, that many men desired to escape from the world of the flesh, and went into the forests to live as hermits. Gradually great monasteries grew up and became the chief centers of Russian cultural life. And everywhere, from the cities to the smallest villages, the Church became the symbol of human decency and hope in a world of horror.

The Russians became one of the most deeply religious of all Christian peoples, and their rulers speedily learned to use their religious emotions for political purposes. When the Turks captured Constantinople in 1453 and destroyed the Eastern Roman Empire, the Grand Duke of Moscow, Ivan III, began to propagate the idea that he had become the successor of Constantine, the only legitimate protector of the Orthodox Church, and that Moscow had become "the Third Rome." To lend color to this claim, he finally married the niece of the last Byzantine Emperor.

Thus originated the mystical Russian belief that "Moscow is the Third Rome," and that from Moscow must come the light and power to lead all men to righteousness. It is easy for any people to believe that it is superior to other peoples, and that it has a mission to bring light to those who live in darkness. And the deeply religious Russians became imbued with the idea that they were the instrument that God had chosen to save the world. Since the capture of Constantinople by the Turks, this messianic ideal has never been absent from the Russian mind. The Tsars used it to further their wars, not only against the Moslems but also against Christian nations, and even the anti-religious Communists use it to promote the aggressions of their state.

Thus, at the close of two centuries of Mongol domination, emerged two Russian habits of thought that are still vital forces in the Soviet Union:

(1) The idea that it is natural to live under a dictatorship in a totalitarian state.
(2) The idea that Moscow is destined to rule and save the world.

Ivan IV, "The Terrible," Tsar from 1544 to 1584, introduced into Russian life another idea embodied in a peculiar institution which has continued to exist until the present day: the secret political police. Ivan called the directing organ of this police the Oprichina and its members Oprichniki. Their duty was to ferret out unfaithfulness to him, and to punish it with the most savage cruelty. Their emblem was a dog's head and a broom, symbolizing their mission to sniff out disloyalty and to sweep away all enemies of the Tsar.

Ivan the Terrible was a sadist of great physical strength and energy. (He killed his own son with his own hands.) He was not popular with the Russian nobles, called "boyars" and he decided to "liquidate" them. This task he turned over to the Oprichniki, with full power to murder any boyars they pleased, rape their wives and seize their estates. The Oprichniki found the task congenial, and when there were not enough boyars left to keep them busy, turned their attention to priests and even whole cities. Thus St. Philip, Metropolitan of Moscow, was murdered for condemning the Oprichina as an unchristian institution; and the inhabitants of Novgorod, which had relatively democratic institutions of the type prevalent in the Hanseatic League, were slaughtered systematically until but few were left in the ruins of their town. In the Red Square in Moscow, Ivan the Terrible had hundreds who displeased him boiled and roasted alive for the edification of his subjects.[3] When that happened, Shakespeare was alive, Queen Elizabeth was on the throne of England, and the Magna Carta had been in force for three hundred and fifty years. Such is the time lag that separates the Russians from the ways of western civilization.

Ivan's institution of the Oprichina never disappeared from the apparatus by which the Russian Tsars ruled their subjects. Its name was changed—under the last Tsar it was called the Okhrana and it was much less cruel than the Oprichina—but its fundamental nature remained unchanged. The Soviet Government raised the power of this secret political police to heights worthy of

---

[3] *Ivan the Terrible*, by Stephen Graham, p. 225.

a super Ivan the Terrible. Under Lenin and Stalin it was called first the Cheka, then the O.G.P.U. and then the N.K.V.D. It remained the blood descendant of the Oprichina. It developed spying to a fine art, slaughtered men, women and children by the million, and made fear the dominant motive in Russian life. (Hitler's Gestapo, organized in imitation of the Soviet O.G.P.U., was also a lineal descendant of the Oprichina.) Ivan the Terrible for centuries was regarded as the embodiment of evil by Russians of all classes; but after Stalin began his great "purge" of 1936–38, his obedient historians began to white-wash Ivan, and the Russian young are now taught by books and movies that Ivan was a noble leader of the Russian people.

Ivan distributed the lands, towns and villages of his victims to his Oprichniki, and organized a new court composed of these efficient murderers. He assumed the title Tsar—that is to say Caesar—but he created a fantastic court in the semblance of a monastery, where the Oprichniki wore black robes, and interlarded violent and obscene debauch with prayers. The Oprichniki decided that their estates would be more profitable if the peasants who tilled them were forbidden to move to other estates. The freedom of the peasants had already been severely restricted, but Ivan obligingly decreed in 1581 that the peasants and their families must remain permanently on the soil they tilled—thus creating the complete institution of serfdom. This form of slavery differed from Negro slavery in the particular that the serfs were attached to the land but not to the proprietor. They could not be sold without the land. They were sold with the land.

Since the peasants composed the vast majority of the population of Russia at that time, most Russians became serfs. They were not liberated from this form of slavery until March 3, 1861—the day before Abraham Lincoln made his first inaugural address. Thus for 280 years, covering more than the whole period from the colonization of Virginia to the inauguration of Lincoln, the mass of the Russian people lived under conditions that were rarely better and often worse than those of the Negro slaves in America.

It was Ivan The Terrible, who started the Russians of his little Muscovite state on the career of conquest which made them rulers of one-sixth of the earth's surface. In the past four hundred years the Russians have conquered 168 different peoples and tribes. In 1935 the Soviet Union was issuing primary school books in 165 different languages and dialects.

In 1552 Ivan captured Kazan from the Tartar Khans, and in 1554 took Astrakhan, and for the first time the Volga became a Russian river. Then he conquered the Finnish and Tartar tribes between the Oka and Kama rivers. And in 1580 the Cossack Yermak entered Siberia with a band of about sixteen hundred followers and captured the realm of the Khan Kuchum in the Tobolsk area. Eighty years later a few Russians reached the Amur river and the Pacific.

Thus the human tide began to wash back over the long flat plain across which the Mongols had entered Europe. The establishment of complete Russian control over Siberia and the conquest of the Moslem peoples who inhabited much of southeastern Russia, the Crimea, the Caucasus, and Central Asia, was a long, slow process, but it was a steady process; and at last the Russians consolidated their hold on the northern shores of the Pacific Ocean.

In their attempts to move toward the Atlantic they met much tougher opposition. They ran into the outposts of western civilization; a higher civilization than their own in every phase of life. And they made little headway because of their "backwardness."

Peter the Great, an able Tsar, who ruled from 1689 to 1725, decided to end that "backwardness" by imposing European industry on his sluggish subjects. He visited western Europe and studied industrial techniques. The civilization of Europe was at an extraordinary height. Louis XIV was king of France, and from his palace of Versailles ruled a state that had reached a higher level of culture and well-being than men had known since the fall of the Roman Empire.

Peter was a man of great energy, intelligence, and ruthlessness—he had his own son tortured to death—and he was determined, whatever the cost, to Europeanize the economic life of Russia, in order to increase the war power of his state. But as the great Russian historian Klyuchevsky wrote:

His beneficent actions were accomplished with repelling violence. Peter's reform was a struggle of despotism with the people, with its sluggishness. He hoped through the threat of his authority to evoke initiative in an enslaved society, and through a slave-owning nobility to introduce into Russia European science, popular education, as the necessary condition of social initiative. He desired that the slave, remaining a slave, should act consciously and freely. The inter-action of despotism and freedom, of education and slavery—this is the political squaring of the circle, the riddle which we have been solving for two centuries from the time of Peter, and which is still unsolved.[4]

Stalin is still trying to solve it. Peter's plans were the forerunners of Stalin's Five Year Plan. And Peter, like Stalin, imposed them on his reluctant subjects by force and executions. Peter introduced certain industries, modernized his army and succeeded in creating the first Russian navy. Stalin introduced many industries, modernized his army and is creating a new navy. Like Peter, Stalin became "an apostle of civilization with a knout in his hands."

Peter sought, as a first step toward the west, "a window to Europe." He moved his capital from Moscow to the marshes which border the Neva River, and there on piles built St. Petersburg—which is now Leningrad. To hold and enlarge this "window to Europe" he had to defeat the Swedes. He did, and in 1721 he annexed In-

[4] Klyuchevsky, *History of Russia*, Russian edition, Vol. IV, pp. 292-3.

germanland, Estonia, Livonia, and parts of Karelia
and Finland.

Peter was less kind to the Church than the Mongol
Khans had been. When the Patriarch of Moscow, the
spiritual chief of the Orthodox Church, opposed his
reforms, he abolished the Patriarchate, and put in its
place a government agency subject to himself, called the
Holy Synod. Thus Peter brought the Church under his
control, just as Stalin has now brought the Church under his control by establishing the Committee on the
Affairs of the Orthodox Church, attached to the Council
of People's Commissars, the Chairman of which is a kind
of Soviet Commissar for God.

Peter's efforts to strengthen his despotism and his
armies by bringing European science and industry to
Russia, were continued by his successors, and the Russian court under Catherine the Great, 1762 to 1796,
had all the outward trappings of European life; but
behind that facade the Russian peasant continued to live
in filth, misery and serfdom.

Catherine longed for military glory. The Russian
autocrats have never had any difficulty at any moment
in making their subjects attack a neighboring state from
the days of Ivan the Terrible's attack on Kazan to the
days of Stalin's attacks on Finland and Poland, and
Catherine had none. She prepared in secret a daring
plan of aggression. Her first objective was to seize the
shores of the Black Sea, the Balkans and Constan-

tinople. She attacked Turkey and made large territorial gains, but did not get Constantinople. Her second objective was Poland.

Poland at that time was a country of about 11,000,-000 inhabitants, with wider boundaries than those of 1939. Poland had had a parliament called the Seym since 1493. And as early as 1505 the King of Poland was compelled to accept a statute which gave the Seym an equal voice with the Crown in all executive matters. Moreover, the King was elected by the Parliament. By these measures the Polish Parliament succeeded not in introducing democracy, but in making the executive too weak to organize the protection of the state. Even this extreme dominance of the legislative branch of the Polish government over the executive, did not satisfy the Polish gentry. They introduced into the Polish Constitution a fantastic provision called the *Liberum Veto*. The *Liberum Veto* provided that no measure could be passed by the Parliament except by unanimous vote. Each deputy had unlimited right to kill any measure proposed in the Parliament by announcing, "I disapprove." Moreover, the *Liberum Veto* was extended still further to give each deputy the right, by exercising his veto, to dissolve the Parliament, whereupon all measures previously passed had to be resubmitted to the next Parliament. Thus by 1700 the orderly conduct of public business was made almost impossible: foreign agents could nearly always bribe one member of the Parliament to veto out of existence any Parliament to which they objected. Repeatedly Polish patriots tried to eliminate these fatal clauses of their Constitution, but under threats of war by Russia, Prussia and Austria were always forced to abandon their efforts. The Polish gentry, by seeking an exaggerated personal freedom, had achieved not liberty, but only aristocratic anarchy under a powerless king, and the way was prepared for the destruction of their state by Russia, Prussia, and Austria. The Russian dictatorship, for all its horrors, had a survival value for the Russian people far greater than the weak Polish executive had for the people of Poland.

The *Liberum Veto* made easy the way into Poland for Catherine's agents and troops. As a precaution against war with Prussia and Austria, she made them partners in her crime, and together they partitioned Poland: First in 1772, again in 1793 and finally in 1795—after the Poles of all classes from peasants to princes, under the leadership of Kosciuszko, had fought heroically in defense of their freedom. The name of Poland was wiped completely from the map of Europe.

Russia took the greater part of the country. But Russia found Poland hard to digest. The words of the Polish national hymn: "Poland is not dead so long as we live," became the motto of every Pole. And Catherine the Great's grandson, Alexander I, was forced to deal with the demands of the Poles for a constitution. They had had a parliament for more than three hundred years, and it is difficult to govern men who have known even a little liberty by the system of tyranny invented by the Mongol Khans. Russia had no constitution, but speaking at Vilna in July 1814, Alexander said to the Poles: "Gentlemen, yet a little patience, and you will be more than satisfied with me." The next year he gave the Poles a constitution by which Poland was united to Russia in the person of the Tsar as a separate political entity, but the Poles had a parliament, liberty of the press and the right to use their flag.

The Russian subjects of the Tsar, however, resented the grant to Poles of rights which had not been granted to Russians. There was, indeed, a strange contradiction in the fact that the conquering Russians had no such rights as the conquered Poles. The Russians began to demand similar rights. In 1832, after a Polish uprising, the Russian autocracy solved this contradiction in a characteristic manner. Instead of granting its Russian subjects the same rights as the Poles, it took away the Constitution of the Poles! That made everything level; but on the Russian level—a lower level than the Poles had ever known.

As Sir Bernard Pares, dealing with the events of the year 1832, wrote with profound truth: "Poland fell entirely under Russian bureaucratic government. . . . It was as if Russia could only hold Poland by uncivilizing it."[5] In 1918 Poland regained her independence. In 1939 she was again wiped from the map by joint attack of the troops of Hitler and Stalin. The two totalitarian

[5] Sir Bernard Pares, *A History of Russia*, 4th edition, p. 326.

dictatorships embraced over her body, and Stalin tele-
graphed to Ribbentrop: "The friendship of the peoples
of Germany and the Soviet Union, cemented by blood,
has every reason to be lasting and firm." [6]

Today Russian troops occupy all Poland. A puppet
government, controlled from Moscow, is now installed in
Warsaw. And, unhappily, there is no reason to believe
that the Russians will be more inclined at present than
they were a hundred and fourteen years ago to accept
the contradiction of the grant to the Poles of rights
which have not yet been given to Russians. The Russians today live under a despotism whose authority is
based on secret police and firing squads. That secret
police and those firing squads dominate Poland today.
No Polish Government can eject them, except by taking
measures which the Russian dictator would call provo-
cative and anti-Russian. It is as true today as in 1832
that Russia can only hold Poland by uncivilizing it. And
the same is true of Estonia, Latvia, Lithuania, Rumania,
Hungary, Bulgaria, Yugoslavia, Austria, Czechoslovakia, and Germany. The relentless eye of the dictator
in the Kremlin can distinguish only serfs and enemies;
and the neighbors of Russia, if they do not wish to be
the one, must reconcile themselves to being considered
the other. The process of uncivilizing them, and reduc-
ing their standard of living and liberty to the level of
the Soviet Union, is now in full progress. We saved them

[6] Tass Telegram from Moscow published in *The Daily Worker*,
New York, December 26, 1939.

from our enemies. We have as yet made no serious attempt to save them from our Russian friends—who signed the Atlantic Charter.

The first outward sign that the Russians some day might perhaps become interested in political democracy and individual freedom came at the death of Tsar Alexander I in 1825. The Tsar had defeated Napoleon's invasion of Russia, and later the Russian armies had marched to Paris. In France and Germany, the Russian officers saw a standard of living, culture, freedom and happiness so much higher than their own at home that, when they returned to Russia, a number of the younger officers began to promote secret societies for political reform. The programs of all these societies included the abolition of serfdom; and that of the St. Petersburg society included a draft constitution, modeled on the Constitution of the United States.[7] They had a cogent argument: if the Poles can have a constitution, why can't we?

When the Tsar Alexander died in December 1825, a dispute with regard to the succession to the throne gave the conspirators an opportunity to act. They organized an uprising in St. Petersburg, but the military governor easily broke their forces with a few cannon shot. One hundred and twenty "Decembrists" as the conspirators were called, were placed on trial and received various sentences. Five were executed.[8] The Tsars of the nine-

---

[7] George Vernadsky, *A History of Russia*, p. 147.
[8] *Ibid.*, p. 149.

teenth century did not "purge" the families and friends of their opponents, in the manner of their predecessor Ivan the Terrible or their successor Stalin.

The democratic waves set in motion by the Decembrists in 1825 never subsided. Throughout the nineteenth century they rose and fell and rose again, approached tidal proportions in 1905, and finally submerged the Tsardom in 1917. During those ninety-two years Russia seethed with political, economic, intellectual and artistic ferment. Pushkin, Lermontov, Gogol, Dostoievsky, Turgeniev, Tolstoy, Chekhov, and Gorky brought a superb gift to the literary heritage of mankind. Glinka, Tschaikovsky, Moussorgsky and Rimsky-Korsakov made notable contributions in the field of music. The ballet was developed into a great art. Mendeleyev, Pavlov, and many other Russian scientists, did first rate original research. Railroads and industries began to transform Russia from an almost wholly agricultural country into a nation of factory workers as well as peasants. The population increased enormously, reaching one hundred and seventy million in 1914.

Only the Tsars seemed incapable of development. They clung to their autocracy, and such concessions as they made to the forces of change were always too little or too late. Indeed, they made concessions only when defeat in war had aroused their subjects to fury. Five hundred and fifty-six localized peasant revolts took place during the reign of Nicholas I, 1825 to 1855, but he could think of nothing better to do than to suppress all freedom of thought. At the close of his reign, however, he became engaged in the Crimean War against France and Great Britain, and he bequeathed to his successor Alexander II, 1855 to 1881, a resounding defeat. Alexander II, a wavering man of good intentions, under pressure of the patriotic rage and democratic energy engendered by this defeat, liberated the serfs in 1861. And in 1864 he established trial by jury—650 years after it had been established in England. He was assassinated.

Alexander III, 1881 to 1894, returned to repression as a policy, persecuted dissenting churches, muzzled the press and hunted down political reformers and revolutionists. He was succeeded by the last of the Tsars, Nicholas II, a weak little man, as incapable as a child of guiding the wild energies of the Russian people. Nevertheless, Nicholas announced to his subjects shortly after his accession to the throne: "Let all know that I intend to defend the principle of autocracy as unswervingly as did my father."

In 1905, the defeats that Russia had suffered in her war against Japan added patriotic resentment to all the other grievances of the Russian people. And finally, just as his predecessor Alexander II had been obliged to make concessions after the defeats of the Crimean War, Nicholas II was obliged to retreat a trifle from absolute autocracy. A general strike from one end of Russia to the other on October 10, 1905, forced him to

act, and on October 17 he granted his subjects a partial
bill of rights and a parliament called the Duma.

A wave of happiness rolled over Russia, and for a
moment it appeared that the anaemic Tsar might be
content to let his autocracy dissolve gradually into an
authority no greater than that of his cousin the King of
England. But the Tsar resented the mere existence of
the Duma, and the next twelve years were not years of
progressive and constructive approach to constitutional
monarchy, but of approach to revolution. They were,
nevertheless, the only years from prehistoric times to
this day in which the people of Russia enjoyed even a
tiny measure of ordered freedom—the eight months cov-
ered by the regimes of Prince Lvov and Kerensky being
a period of anarchic decay, rather than freedom.

The outbreak of the First World War united most
Russians briefly in a "Sacred Union." Hatred of Germany and all things German became so intense that the
Germanic name of the capital, St. Petersburg, was
changed to Petrograd. But the terrible defeats inflicted
on the Tsar's army by the Kaiser's army soon began,
like the defeats of the Crimean War and the Russo-
Japanese War, to arouse patriotic fury against the
criminal inefficiency and corruption of the Tsarist bureaucracy. In the summer of 1916, General Brusilov's
armies launched a superbly successful offensive against
the Austrians and Germans, but the Russian service of
supply broke down. The Russian soldiers often were

without food for three or four days, and always without proper medical care. Nevertheless, they continued to attack with magnificent heroism and stamina. When the offensive ended in September, 1916, Brusilov's armies had suffered a million casualties; and, as the wounded filtered back to the rear, a passionate resentment was aroused against the flaccid little Tsar, his Rasputin-ridden wife, and his corrupt bureaucracy.

Rasputin was murdered, and all who had access to the Tsar warned him that revolution was at hand. Grand Dukes, and even the ambassadors of his allies, urged him to remake his government and give wide powers to the Duma. Instead, on March 11, 1917, he discontinued meetings of the Duma, and had strikers demanding bread in the streets of Petrograd shot down.

The Russian Revolution

The next day the revolution began. On the morning of March 12, 1917, Petrograd was overrun by great masses of hungry, angry demonstrators, and three days later the Tsar abdicated. He and his family were exiled, and, after the Soviet Government came into power, they were murdered. Thus the title of Tsar was wiped from the pages of future Russian history. But under a different name Tsardom was revived—a much more efficient and unscrupulous Tsardom—the Tsardom of Lenin and Stalin.

The abdication of the Tsar was hailed throughout the world with joy as the beginning of an era of freedom for the Russian people. The Russians themselves embraced in the streets in ecstasy, and throughout the western world, which knew little of Russia or Russian history, it was assumed that the Tsar's vast empire would become a democratic republic, with a free parliament, freedom of speech, press, assembly, religion and all the other personal liberties guaranteed by the constitutions of western democracies.

The Provisional Government which succeeded the Tsar did its best to introduce a democratic regime. But it was a weak best. The Premier of the Provisional Government, Prince Lvov, was a Tolstoian who believed in "nonresistance to evil." Miliukov and Kerensky, and some of the other ministers were vigorous men. But from the outset the Provisional Government was more or less at the mercy of the Petrograd Soviet of Workers and Soldiers' Deputies, because the Soviet had far closer contacts with the Petrograd garrison and the masses of the city. The leaders of the Soviet, who at the outset were relatively moderate socialists, did not wish to seize power at once, because the Provisional Government was recognized as the governing authority of Russia by the army and the country as a whole, and rather than attempt to overthrow it, they preferred to maintain the Provisional Government in nominal authority, while imposing their will on it and undermining it.

The Petrograd Soviet was composed of varying numbers of workmen and soldiers—rising occasionally to as many as 2,500, chosen from the factories and battalions in the city—plus the leaders of the various socialist parties. All non-socialist parties were excluded from the Soviet, and at the outset the largest representation in it was held by the Socialist Revolutionaries, who claimed to represent the peasants. The Social Democratic Party, which was strong among the factory workers, was split between Mensheviks, who believed that socialism should be achieved by democratic methods and could not be established successfully in Russia until the country had been more industrialized, and the Bolsheviks, who wanted to introduce socialism immediately by any methods whatsoever. It was only after the German General Staff, knowing that Lenin was its bitter enemy, but estimating correctly that Lenin would take Russia out of the war, had sent the Bolshevik leader back to Leningrad in April 1917,[9] that the Bolsheviks began to call themselves Communists. They adopted the name Communist Party on March 18, 1918.

The Petrograd Soviet was too unwieldy a body to transact daily business in a revolution, and control of action was rapidly taken over by the Central Executive Committee of the Soviet Congress. Speedily a still smaller group—the Praesidium of the Central Executive Committee—seized the reins of authority. Lenin was incomparably superior to the other leaders in intelligence, will and political acumen, and gradually he and his followers began to dominate the Soviet. Thus, little by little, the so-called "dictatorship of the proletariat" began to be

[9] Wheeler-Bennet, *Brest-Litovsk, the Forgotten Peace*, p. 35.

transformed into a dictatorship over the proletariat, and everyone else in the Russian Empire, by the leader of the Communist Party.

Without Lenin there might well have been no Bolshevism and no Communist Party. Son of middle-class parents, with a big head, short legs, a sense of humor, and immense personal charm, the lines of his life were staked out for him when his elder brother, Alexander Ulianov, was caught in a plot to assassinate Tsar Alexander III. Lenin loved his elder brother deeply and admired him profoundly, and his brother was hanged. Thereafter, in hard moments, Lenin was always able to find within himself a flinty ruthlessness totally at variance with his usual personal kindliness and broad human sympathies. Neither danger, nor reason, nor pity could break the hard core that had been put in him by the hanging of his brother. Alexander Ulianov had been nourished on the writings of Herzen and Bakunin; and, like his brother, Lenin never shrank from using murder as a final argument. "In principle we have never renounced and cannot renounce terrorism. It is an act of war . . . indispensable at a certain point of the struggle," he wrote in *Iskra* in 1901. And his basic attitude toward Russia was expressed in Herzen's words:

We lack all the riches and all the inheritance of the West. We have no heritage from Rome, from antiquity, from chivalry, from feudalism, nothing Catholic, hardly anything bourgeois in our tradition. Therefore no regrets or relics, no respect for the past can hold us back.

Lenin's acts are more important for an understanding of the Soviet Union than his words; but some of his words became realities of the present day. In 1900 he left Russia, and, with several associates, founded in Munich an organ of the "Workers Social-Democratic Party," called *Iskra*—The Spark.

His first article in that paper contains the germ of the present day Communist Party. He wrote, "We must educate men who devote to the revolution not only their free evenings but their whole lives. . . . The struggle with the political police demands special qualities, professional revolutionaries. . . . When we have detachments of revolutionary workers specially prepared by a long training (of course 'in all the arms' of revolutionary warfare), no police in the world will be able to master them. . . . Rigorous secrecy, a minutely careful selection of members, and lastly complete fraternal confidence among revolutionaries. . . . What we need is a military organization."

Lenin succeeded in building such a "military organization" based on "a minutely careful selection of members" and "rigorous secrecy"; and to the end of his life treated the members of the inner circle or "general staff" of this "military organization," which finally he named the Communist Party, with "fraternal confidence." They criticized him freely and he criticized them. In personality and will he was so superior to these intimate associates that almost invariably he won his arguments. But there were arguments. Stalin, whose prestige was less than Lenin's, could get agreement only by "liquidating" those who disagreed with him and, in the end, "purged" nearly all Lenin's old associates.

The rank and file of Lenin's party were, of course, not admitted to meetings of this inner circle, just as G.I.s are not admitted to meetings of the Joint Chiefs of Staff. They were told only so much as they had to know to carry out their orders effectively. Persons outside the ranks of the party were treated merely as human material to be used to achieve the objectives of the party. As Gorky wrote after the Communists had come into power in Russia: "The government . . . treats the Russian workman as a log; it sets light to the logs to see if the flame of European revolution can be kindled on the Russian hearth." [10]

Lenin's "military organization" was a much more efficient instrument than the loosely knit political parties of his opponents, and shortly after his return to Petrograd on April 16, 1917, he turned its power to undermining the Provisional Government. He advocated "All power to the Soviets," immediate peace, seizure of the land by the peasants and the factories by the workmen. By such slogans as "Loot the looters" and "Peace in the village huts, War against the palaces," he began to stir up class warfare.

Russia desperately needed peace; but the Russian Government was bound by treaties with its allies not to make a separate peace with Germany, and Kerensky,

[10] Boris Souvarine, *Stalin*, p. 196.

who had become Minister of both War and Marine in the Provisional Government, prepared an offensive to be launched in July 1917. Lenin bitterly opposed the proposed offensive. On May 15, 1917, the Petrograd Soviet issued a manifesto calling for "peace without annexations or indemnities on the basis of the self-determination of peoples."

Kerensky started his offensive on July 1, 1917, and at first it was surprisingly successful. Most of the soldiers of the Petrograd garrison and sailors of the Kronstadt garrison, however, were resolved not to be sent to the front. They were weary of war, and on July 17 many of them participated in a demonstration organized by the Communists against continuance of the war and against the Provisional Government. Simultaneously news reached Petrograd that a German counter-offensive had routed the Russian Army. Patriotic rage turned against the Communists. Lenin fled to Finland. Trotsky and other intimate associates of Lenin were arrested.

Kerensky became Premier of the Provisional Government. The Communists pleaded with him, in the name of socialist solidarity and democratic freedom of speech, to release the Communist leaders. He did. Lenin returned from Finland. (After Lenin came into power, those who opposed him, socialists and non-socialists alike, were arrested or shot by the Communist secret police.)

The Russian Army began to disintegrate in the summer of 1917, and the economic life of the country began to slip into anarchy. In October, Trotsky was elected President of the Petrograd Soviet, and on October 29 the Petrograd Soviet created a Military Revolutionary Committee. The next day the regiments of the Petrograd garrison unanimously adopted a resolution reading:

The Petrograd Garrison no longer recognizes the Provisional Government. The Petrograd Soviet is our Government. We will obey only the orders of the Petrograd Soviet through the Military Revolutionary Committee.

Thus, through Trotsky, Lenin gained control of the Petrograd garrison, which was the only remaining prop of the Kerensky regime in the capital.

The second Congress of Soviets had been summoned to meet on November 7. Lenin decided to confront that Congress with an accomplished revolution, and ordered his forces to attack on that day. Kerensky, who knew what Lenin was planning, sneaked out of Petrograd on the morning of the 7th to try to find an army to support him. He failed to find one. Lenin and Trotsky had organized thousands of Red Guards by arming workmen of their party, and expected a stiff fight for power. But to defend the Provisional Government there remained only a pathetic group of cadets and women in uniform. A few shots—and all was over. Thus the Provisional Government, which wanted to bring western democracy to Russia, slithered into oblivion. And the day, November 7, was fixed as the date on which the Red Army parades in the Red Square in Moscow before the dictator standing on Lenin's Tomb.

The Congress of Soviets met at once and the Communists, who had armed force at their disposal, rode rough-shod over the other socialist parties. A government was formed under the title of "Council of Peoples Commissars" with Lenin as President, Trotsky as Commissar for Foreign Affairs; and at the end of the list: "Chairman for Nationalities: I. V. Djougashvili (Stalin)." [11]

The Soviet Government moved quickly to establish its authority throughout Russia. After a week of conflict, it crushed its opponents in Moscow, then began to extend its control to the smaller cities and villages. There was much opposition. And on December 20, 1917, Lenin revived the old instrument which Ivan the Terrible had used so effectively and horribly to crush opposition to his will: The Secret Political Police: The Oprichina. Lenin called his Oprichina the Extraordinary Commission for the Suppression of Counter-Revolution—the Cheka. The Chekists set to work as ruthlessly as had the Oprichniki, and gradually worked up to a "Red Terror" which reached fantastic heights. As the historian Vernadsky writes:

. . . The atrocities which were committed in its name during this period were not accidental abuses of authority. The "Red Terror" was a recognized and integral element in the process of subjecting the nation to the Bolshevik

[11] John Reed, *Ten Days that Shook the World*, p. 139.

will. Lenin himself declared, "No dictatorship of the Proletariat is to be thought of without terror and violence." Officially the activities of the Cheka were directed at the bourgeoisie alone. "We are not waging war against separate individuals; we are exterminating the bourgeoisie as a class," said Latsis, one of the leaders. As a matter of fact, however, the Cheka exterminated without discrimination all of those suspected of opposing the Soviet Government. The victims were not confined to the upper or middle classes but included peasants and occasionally even workers as well. The Cheka moved without compunction and ruthlessly. The taking of hostages from the non-communist groups of a community was a favorite method. In the event of an uprising against the Government—and especially if an attempted assassination of communist leaders occurred —the hostages, who were commonly non-political people who themselves had done nothing to oppose state authority, were shot without hesitation. Nor was the Cheka unwilling to resort to torture to obtain confessions or information which it considered necessary. Besides the executions ordered by the Cheka, individual Bolshevik groups in the provinces not infrequently took the law into their own hands and dealt death where they felt it warranted—as in the case of the collective execution of officers in Sevastopol in the spring of 1918. The active period of the "Red Terror" was a bloody one in which the normal processes of justice were supplanted by an all-powerful organization operating on a system of suspicion and summary judgment. Thousands suffered for the crime of opposing the dictatorship and more thousands completely innocent of any political activities suffered with them. . . .

. . . Using to the utmost the Cheka, the Red Army, and whatever other instruments they could bend to their will, the Bolsheviks succeeded during the winter of 1917–18 in entirely subjecting the governmental machinery to their control.[12]

The dream of all Russian democrats since the revolt of the Decembrists in 1825 had been that some day the people of Russia might be allowed to vote for members of a Constituent Assembly, which would draw up a democratic Constitution. The Provisional Government had set up the machinery for holding such elections, and they were held on November 25, 1917, eighteen days after the Communists had seized power in Petrograd. Out of 703 deputies only 168 Communists were elected. The deputies to the Constituent Assembly met in Petrograd on January 18, 1918. Immediately the Communists arrested all non-Socialist deputies. But the Socialist Revolutionaries still had a majority in the Assembly, and elected as President, Chernov, an opponent of the Communists. On January 20, Lenin sent troops with rifles and machine guns to the Constituent Assembly and disbanded it. Thus disappeared all shadow of hope for democracy in Russia. Thenceforth, the Government of the Soviet Union was a manifest dictatorship by the leader of the Communist Party. The old system of government by despot, clamped on the Russian people by the Mongol Khans, still held them in its merciless grip. As Masaryk wrote: "They managed to get rid of the Tsar but not of Tsarism. They still wear the Tsarist uniform, albeit inside out."

[12] George Vernadsky, *A History of Russia*, p. 259.

The practical problems which faced Lenin were great. They were rendered stupendous by his profound conviction that mankind could find salvation only through Communism, and that his mission was not merely to establish a Communist state within the limits of the Tsar's empire, but also to try to bring the blessings of Communist government to all states of the entire world. His immediate objectives were, therefore, not only to communize Russia, and to prevent the destruction of the Soviet Government by its domestic and foreign enemies, but also to promote revolutions in Europe. He was confident that socialist revolutions would sweep many European countries—especially Germany. In the sixth of his Twenty-one Theses, he wrote, on January 20, 1918: "That there will be a Socialist Revolution in Europe there is no doubt. All our hopes in the final triumph of Socialism are based on this certainty which is in the nature of a scientific prediction."

But this European revolution did not develop. The only Communist government installed in any European state for more than a brief period was the Bela Kun Government of Hungary, which held power from March 21, 1919, to August 1, 1919. Lenin did his utmost to help this government to survive, sending funds and jewels by secret couriers, and giving constant advice and directions to Kun by radio. But the Soviet Union had no common frontier with Hungary, and could not give direct military aid to Kun. In the absence of direct land communications, the Hungarian Soviet government collapsed. Its chief achievement, indeed, was to teach the Soviet Government that it would find it difficult to sustain successfully Communist revolutions in countries which were not Russia's immediate neighbors, and that it was strategically advisable to try to extend the area controlled from Moscow by conquering regions adjacent to the Soviet Union, before trying to control more distant areas.[13]

To save the Soviet Government from destruction by the Kaiser's Army, Lenin concluded an armistice with Germany on December 15, 1917, and a separate peace with Germany on March 3, 1918—despite the treaties which Russia had signed with her allies promising not to make a separate armistice or peace. To save his regime from overthrow by hungry mobs, Lenin sent his Red Guards and Chekists to take grain by force from the peasants and bring it to the starving cities. He distributed bread on ration cards in such a way as to make it the most potent of political weapons. The Chekists, Red Guards, members of the Communist Party, and factory workmen, received meagre but adequate rations;

[13] This lesson later was applied brilliantly in China. In 1930, the first Provisional Soviet Government of China was organized in southeastern China, in the Kiangsi Province. In 1934 Chiang Kai-shek assembled forces sufficient to crush the Communists, and began to surround them. The Provisional Soviet Government of China was in intimate relations with the Soviet Government of Russia, and it moved itself and its army from southeast China to northwest China, where it could be supplied easily from adjacent territory controlled by the Soviet Government. The Chinese Communists marched in a body more than a thousand miles to the northwest, and established their capital at Yenan close to the Soviet Union. There, until this day, they have maintained their government, and are resisting the Chinese Government with weapons and munitions turned over to them by the Soviet Government.

government employees received barely enough to keep them alive; craftsmen and unemployed got enough to starve slowly. All others—men, women and children— were declared "unproductive elements" and got no rations. Since "black market" food was almost unobtainable, the food ration cards were permits to live. And the Communists controlled the cards.

These measures, which Lenin took to save his dictatorship, did in the end save it, but provoked immediate reactions that almost extinguished it. The peasants were so enraged by the seizure of their grain that they began to resist the Chekists and Red Guards with arms. All democratic elements in Russia had already been infuriated by the disbanding of the Constituent Assembly, and by the systematic starvation and murder of all whom the Soviet Government considered its opponents. A civil war began.

Moreover, Lenin's separate peace with Germany had aroused violent hostility to his government in all the allied countries, because it released great German forces which the Allies feared would be used against the French, British and American armies fighting the Kaiser's army on the Western Front. Huge stores of arms and ammunition, sent by the Allies to be used by the Russian Army, had been stocked in Murmansk and Archangel, and in the Pacific port of Vladivostok. The Allies were determined not to let these supplies fall into the hands either of the Germans or of the Soviet Government. In April 1918, small forces of allied troops landed at Murmansk, and later at Archangel and Vladivostok. The Allies made no attempt to march to Leningrad and Moscow. Nevertheless, Russian forces under various leaders, having half-hearted support from some of the Allies, attacked the Communist forces with such success that, for a brief period in the winter of 1918–1919, the Soviet Government controlled little more of Russia than the territories of Ivan the Terrible.

The position of the Soviet Government appeared to be so desperate that on March 14, 1919, the Soviet Government handed to an emissary of the American Government in Moscow a written offer, good until April 10, 1919, to make peace on the basis of the *status quo* at the fighting fronts, and not to attempt to overthrow by force the anti-Communist governments which then controlled more than three-fourths of the area of the Russian Empire.[14]

This offer was not accepted by the leaders of the allied governments assembled at the Peace Conference in Paris. They were under the illusion that the Soviet Government would soon lose control even of Moscow and Leningrad, and that a democratic government would be set up in Russia. Although the leaders of the allied governments were not willing to make peace with the Soviet Government, they were equally unwilling to send troops to intervene decisively against it. As Lenin said

[14] U. S. Senate Document, 106, 66 Congress, 1st Session 1919, p. 1248.

later: "A few hundred thousands of the army of millions of the Entente could have crushed us by military force." [15] That force was not used, and after hideous conflicts between Russians, in which torture, murder, starvation and disease, as well as war, took a monstrous toll of lives, the Soviet Government defeated its Russian opponents, and established its authority over all the Tsar's Empire except Finland, Estonia, Latvia, Lithuania, Bessarabia, and Poland.

Throughout all this period Lenin made no attempt to hide the fact that the world Communist movement was being directed by the Soviet Government. He was President of the Council of Peoples Commissars of the Soviet Government; but he participated openly in Congresses of the Communist International, "the Comintern"—and was its revered leader. The summons to the First Congress of the Communist International, the avowed function of which was to organize and direct world revolution, was in fact sent out by radio by the Soviet Commissariat for Foreign Affairs.

From that day to this the Communist parties of the world have been agencies of the Soviet dictatorship. But after Lenin's death, on January 21, 1924, when the Soviet Government, deeply conscious of its weakness, was attempting to make non-aggression pacts with its neighbors, it was embarrassed by the manifest fact that it was directing "Fifth Columns," in the form of Com-

[15] Boris Souvarine, *Stalin*, p. 237.

munist parties, in the States with which, for the moment, it wanted peace. Stalin, after a fierce struggle with Trotsky, installed himself as dictator. His power over the Soviet Government, the Communist Party, the Secret Police and the Comintern became absolute. He participated in Congresses of the Comintern and dominated them completely. It could not be denied that he had anything to do with the Comintern. The fiction was, therefore, invented that he had nothing to do with the Soviet Government! It was maintained by the Soviet Government until May 6, 1941, when Stalin openly took the post of Chairman of the Council of People's Commissars.

No government in the world was actually fooled by this fiction. And the reluctance of democratic governments to admit the right of the Soviet dictator to direct fifth columns on their territories, was a potent factor in delaying recognition of the Soviet Government. The government of the United States refused to recognize the Soviet Government for sixteen years. But in September 1933, President Roosevelt decided that, if the Soviet Government would pledge itself in advance to cease to direct the American Communist Party and would permit religious freedom to Americans in the Soviet Union, he would recognize the Soviet Government.

On November 16, 1933, Litvinov, on behalf of the Soviet Government, signed the following pledge in the White House:

My dear Mr. President:

I have the honor to inform you that coincident with the establishment of diplomatic relations between our two Governments it will be the fixed policy of the Government of the Union of Soviet Socialist Republics:

1. To respect scrupulously the indisputable right of the United States to order its own life within its own jurisdiction in its own way and to refrain from interfering in any manner in the internal affairs of the United States, its territories or possessions.

2. To refrain, and to restrain all persons in government service and all organizations of the Government or under its direct or indirect control, including organizations in receipt of any financial assistance from it, from any act overt or covert liable in any way whatsoever to injure the tranquility, prosperity, order, or security of the whole or any part of the United States, its territories or possessions, and, in particular, from any act tending to incite or encourage armed intervention, or any agitation or propaganda having as an aim, the violation of the territorial integrity of the United States, its territories or possessions, or the bringing about by force of a change in the political or social order of the whole or any part of the United States, its territories or possessions.

.   .   .   .

4. Not to permit the formation or residence on its territory of any organization or group—and to prevent the activity on its territory of any organization or group, or of representatives or officials of any organization or group —which has as an aim the overthrow or the preparation for the overthrow of, or the bringing about by force of a

change in, the political or social order of the whole or any part of the United States, its territories or possessions.

In the summer of 1935, the Seventh All-World Congress of the Communist International, met in Moscow. Not only were American Communist leaders prominent in the Congress, but directions were issued to the American Communist Party with regard to the methods it should use to achieve capture of the American Government by "Trojan Horse" tactics. The American Ambassador in Moscow was then ordered by President Roosevelt to present a note to the Soviet Government stating:

As I have pointed out to the People's Commissar for Foreign Affairs when discussing earlier violations of the undertaking of November 16, 1933, the American people resent most strongly interference by foreign countries in their internal affairs, regardless of the nature or probable result of such interference, and the Government of the United States considers the strict fulfillment of the pledge of non-interference, an essential prerequisite to the maintenance of normal and friendly relations between the United States and the Union of Soviet Socialist Republics.

The Government of the United States would be lacking in candor if it failed to state frankly that it anticipates the most serious consequences if the Government of the Union of Soviet Socialist Republics is unwilling, or unable, to take appropriate measures to prevent further acts in disregard of the solemn pledge given by it to the Government of the United States.

I may add that it is a source of regret that in the present international situation the development of friendly relations between the Russian and American peoples will inevitably be precluded by the continuance on territory of the Union of Soviet Socialist Republics, in violation of the promise of the Government of the Union of Soviet Socialist Republics, of activities involving interference in the internal affairs of the American people.

Stalin paid no attention to this protest, refused to honor the pledge he had given to President Roosevelt, and continued to direct both the Soviet Government and the Comintern—including the American Communist Party. President Roosevelt, because of the threat to world peace by Hitler, decided that it was in the interest of the United States to ignore temporarily this violation of Stalin's pledge to him and continue to maintain diplomatic relations with the Soviet Union. The President, however, never admitted the right of the Soviet dictator to direct the American Communist Party, and when the Soviet Government was doing everything possible to produce the illusion that the Soviet Union was a "peace loving democracy," on May 22, 1943, the Comintern was ostensibly abolished. The American Communist Party, on May 20, 1944, changed its name to the Communist Political Association, and supported President Roosevelt in the 1944 election. The Profintern and other channels through which the Communist Parties of the world could be efficiently directed from Moscow had long been established; and Stalin, while abolishing the form, preserved the substance of his control over the world Communist movement.

Victory in the civil war had left the Soviet Government in full possession of one-sixth of the land surface of the globe—a vast expanse of mineral riches and superb agricultural country inhabited by 169 vigorous peoples and tribes. But the whole economic system of this huge empire had been so disrupted by the First World War, the Communist Revolution and the Civil War, that Lenin faced a gigantic task of reconstruction. Industrial production in 1920 was only one-eighth of what it had been in 1913. Car loadings in 1920 were one-third of the 1916 figure. The 1919 harvest amounted to only 30 million tons of grain against 74 million in 1916. "We are in a condition of such poverty, ruin, and exhaustion of the productive powers of the workers and peasants," said Lenin to the 10th Convention of the Communist Party in March 1921, "that everything must be set aside to increase production."

Under the pressure of these circumstances Lenin introduced a New Economic Policy, which involved a strategic retreat from the Communist economy which had been introduced in 1917. The Soviet Government had been taking from the peasants all their grain harvest in excess of a small amount for their personal needs. In consequence, the peasants had ceased to produce much more than enough for their own needs. To provide incentive for the peasants, Lenin decreed that after the government had taken a certain proportion of their grain as a tax, they could sell the remainder freely in the domestic market. The Soviet Government's full monopoly of all foreign trade was maintained. At the same time State management of industry was replaced by a system of state-controlled "Trusts," the State retaining control of large productive units, but permitting some small units to be owned and run by private individuals. Foreign capital was offered concessions, and in 1921 a State Bank was opened. (The economic regime introduced by the Soviet Government, acting through the satellite governments it has set up in Poland, Rumania, Bulgaria and Yugoslavia, is strikingly similar to the regime set up in the Soviet Union by the New Economic Policy.)

All these measures were temporary expedients to increase production. But many ignorant foreigners regarded them as the return of Russia to the capitalist system. Neither Lenin nor any other Communist, however, considered them as anything but a strategic retreat from a position which could later be retaken. How determined Lenin was to subordinate all individuals and organizations in Russia ultimately to the State may be judged from the fact that in 1920 the Ninth Convention of the Communist Party resolved that "the trade unions . . . must gradually be transformed into auxiliary agencies of the proletarian State. The tasks of the trade unions lie chiefly in the field of economic organization and education." Thereafter, the Trade Unions became not organs of the workmen for struggling against their employers, but organs of the State to keep the workmen obedient and submissive. That is their role to this day, although they now have the additional international tasks of convincing genuine Trade Unions outside the Soviet Union that there are genuine Trade Unions in the Soviet Union, and of influencing foreign Trade Unions through international Trade Union organizations. Similarly, the Peasants Cooperative Societies were transformed from organs controlled by the peasants into agencies of the State, and in 1920 became mere sections of the People's Commissariat of Food Supply.

"Retreat on the economic front" as the Communists described the New Economic Policy, was accompanied by a corresponding retreat on the foreign political front. The extreme weakness of the Soviet Union required an exceedingly prudent foreign policy. That did not change the underlying aim of the Soviet Government in foreign affairs any more than the New Economic Policy changed its underlying aim in domestic affairs. And it was certain that when the Soviet Government again felt strong enough to resume Communist advance at home and abroad, the Soviet Government would return to attack.

The New Economic Policy was so successful that production in both agriculture and industry rose steadily, until in 1927 it reached the level it had reached in 1913 under the Tsar. Stalin decided that the time had come to revert to attack on the domestic "front," to collectivize agriculture, and to direct all the industrial production and development in the Soviet Union in accordance with a Five Year Plan.

Only a dictatorship abundantly equipped with secret police and firing squads could have imposed on even the most patient and enduring of peoples the suffering which followed. A democratic government must maintain a decent standard of living for the voters or be defeated at the next election. A dictatorship can impose an extraordinarily low standard of living on its people, and use in any way it may choose all their production above a subsistence minimum. Stalin chose to turn the productive forces of his nation not to production of consumers' goods, for which the peasants were clamoring, but to basic industries necessary for war. The production of consumers' goods was held down to a minimum, while huge investments were made in iron and steel plants and armament and munition factories. Stalin's Five Year Plans were the forerunners of Goering's slogan: "Guns instead of butter."

As Five Year Plan succeeded Five Year Plan, the Soviet Union was transformed from an overwhelmingly agricultural country to one in which only half the population was engaged in agriculture. To collectivize agriculture, it was necessary to wipe out the millions of small farms which were the most characteristic feature of Russian life, and to consolidate them in large socialized units. Some of the poorest of the peasants favored this process. The more successful opposed it. Many of the successful had been soldiers in the Red Army during the civil war. That did not save them. They were stigmatized by the name of Kulak. Their farms and possessions were confiscated. If they objected—and millions did—they were either shot or sent to forced labor in Siberia.

The first consequence of this "attack on the agricultural front," was to produce famine. Between 1929 and 1933, the number of horses in Russia dropped from 34 million to 16 million, cows from 68 million to 38 million, sheep and goats from 147 to 50 million, hogs from 20 million to 12 million.[16] And in the winter of 1932–33 the government took so much grain away from the protesting peasants of the Ukraine and the Kuban, that between three and five million of them died of government organized starvation. But at this frightful cost Stalin managed to socialize agriculture and, by 1939, the individual peasant farmer had virtually ceased to exist.

Thus, before Stalin made his pact with Hitler on August 23, 1939, all traces of Lenin's New Economic Policy had been eliminated from Russia. "The function of compulsion inside the country has ceased, has withered away," Stalin announced in 1939, "The exploiters are no more and there is no one to suppress anymore." No individual or group economic interest possessing the slightest independence against the State remained in the Soviet Union. All men, women and children were at the mercy of the dictator for their daily bread. That did not conduce to independence of speech in the Soviet

[16] George Vernadsky, *History of Russia*, p. 348.

Union. But thought is irrepressible. And the thought was everywhere: Why if "there is no one to suppress anymore" is it necessary to maintain the secret political police at a higher pitch of efficiency, armament and numbers than ever before? Ivan the Terrible's Oprichina, had become the Okhrana of the Tsars, then Lenin's Cheka, then Stalin's O.G.P.U., then his N.K.V.D. Its name had changed. Its task remained unchanged: to smell out and sweep away ruthlessly all opposition to the dictator. Its ear was everywhere. And every Russian lived in fear of its knock on his door in the night. It had its own army of 250,000 men, better paid, housed and fed than the Red Army, its own artillery and airplanes, its own prisons and cellars for executions. Its budget in 1937 was 3,000,000,000 rubles.[17] To what height its budget now has risen we do not know; but it has been reported that the N.K.V.D. Army now numbers 600,000.

Even the Red Army is subjected to control by the N.K.V.D. through officers and men whose duty it is to report to the "Special Division" of the N.K.V.D. on all that the Army is saying and thinking. Every apartment house, every factory and every collective farm, every scientific society, every theatre has N.K.V.D. agents in it to listen for a critical word. Every member of the Communist party is obliged to report to the N.K.V.D. on everything he hears that may interest its insatiable suspicion. And hundreds of thou-

[17] David S. Dallin, *The Real Soviet Russia*, pp. 241-2.

sands of men and women who are not Communists are
driven to serve it under the threat that, if they do not,
they will hear its knock on the door in the night. In its
prison camps for the past fifteen years there have probably never been less than ten million men and women,
working in semi-starvation, often in the Arctic north,
where the average expectation of life is six years.

Foreign ambassadors, no less than Soviet Commissars
and generals, have the ear of the N.K.V.D. in their conversations. It even dared to put a two-faced dictaphone
in the wall between Ambassador Davies' bed and the
desk where he dictated his confidential telegrams. All
ambassadors are followed, day and night, by four of its
agents, and all who dare to speak to foreigners are
obliged to report at once on the conversation. The
N.K.V.D. keeps a searchlight directed on the residence
of the American Consul in Vladivostok, and a white face
peers from a window across the street day and night to
see what person may dare to set foot in this tiny diplomatic ghetto. None does. Aside from ballet girls, and a
few other N.K.V.D. agents, who are ordered to establish
contacts with the diplomatic corps, all Russians know
that it is not healthy to speak too often to foreigners
and, if they do, they disappear. The N.K.V.D. has succeeded in making fear the dominant emotion in Russian
life, and wherever its ear and hand reach beyond the
borders of the Soviet Union—there also is fear. The
N.K.V.D. is the living mockery of "Freedom from
Fear." It is the pillar of Stalin's state.

Fear of punishment and hope of reward are the emotions used by circus trainers in teaching tricks to animals. Fear of the N.K.V.D. and hope to rise to high official position by becoming an obedient member of the Communist Party are the emotions used by Stalin to bend able men to his will. In the fields of science and art it is possible for a man of ability to rise to a position of distinction without being a member of the Communist Party so long as he praises the dictatorship and carries out the orders of the N.K.V.D. But in all other fields membership in the Party greatly increases chance of promotion, and no man is ever promoted to a position of real economic or political power in the Soviet State unless he is a member of the Party. There is, of course, but one Party in the Soviet Union—all others have been "liquidated." Lenin established this "principle." He is said to have expressed it jokingly on one occasion by declaring that there could be any number of parties in the Soviet Union on one condition: that the Communist Party must be in power and all others in jail.[18] Stalin expressed the same thought less humorously in *Pravda* on November 26, 1936: "In the Soviet Union there is no basis for the existence of several parties, or, consequently, for the freedom of parties. In the Soviet Union there is a basis only for the Communist Party."

Stalin adheres to the formula laid down by Lenin in 1901—the formula that the Party must be not a political party in our sense of the word, but a "military

[18] William Henry Chamberlin, *The Russian Enigma*, p. 139.

organization." "The party is the fighting staff of the proletariat. . . ." "The party must lead the proletariat into the offensive—and must direct the retreat if circumstances demand it." On another occasion he described the "military organization" of the Party thus: "Three or four thousand men of the high command—the generals of our party. Then 30 to 40 thousand intermediate commanders: these constitute the officers corps of our party. And further, 100 to 150 thousand of the leading elements of our party—these are, so to speak—the subaltern officers of our party." [19] The remainder of the party, which now numbers about six million, takes its orders and obeys.

The leader of a political party in a democratic state has to meet the demands of the electorate—if not, the voters go to another party. In the Soviet Union, party members have no place to go. There is no other party. "Elections" consist merely of voting for a single party list, the members of which have been chosen by the dictator. They are not in fact elections, but demonstrations called for by the government. Hitler modeled his single party state on the Soviet single party state, and in both totalitarian states a normal "election" was one in which 90 per cent at least of the so-called electorate was afraid not to register its dictated approval of the dictator.

So long as the dictator controls both the machine

[19] David J. Dallin, *The Real Soviet Russia*, pp. 225-6.

of the Communist Party and the N.K.V.D., he can not be overthrown except by a revolt of the Army. Marshal Stalin is Generalissimo of the Army. And the generals and other officers of the Army are watched so closely and constantly by the N.K.V.D. that the slightest criticism of the dictator, even in conversation between military comrades, is apt to lead to permanent silence. Moreover, the officers of the army are so well treated in comparison with the lower classes of the Soviet Union that they have little physical cause for complaint. They belong to the Soviet aristocracy. They do not enjoy being spied on by the N.K.V.D.; but all Russians have become so habituated to living with the hand of the secret police behind their necks, that deprivation of personal liberty of the sort that exists in democratic countries does not drive them to revolt. Nothing is more incomprehensible to the Russians than the attitude toward human life expressed in Patrick Henry's words: "Give me liberty or give me death." An American feels that the preservation of individual liberty is the justification of the State. The ruling class of the Soviet Union fears that, without dictatorship and absolute control over the thoughts and acts of the individual, there might be no coherence in the Soviet State, which is composed of 169 peoples and tribes, and that the Soviet Union could not face on equal terms stable democratic states like Great Britain and the United States. One reason why there is so little liberty in the

Soviet Union is that the Russians of the ruling class fear that liberty would destroy their State.

The social structure of the Soviet Union under Stalin's dictatorship has been described with remarkable accuracy by Dr. David J. Dallin, in his book *The Real Soviet Russia* published in 1944 by the Yale University Press. At the bottom of the social pyramid is an enormous class which was small in the days of the last of the Tsars, Nicholas II—the class of those working in penal servitude under the guns of the secret police. In 1913 under the Tsar there were 32,757 such prisoners, among them 5,000 political prisoners. In 1940, according to the most authoritative estimates, there were at least 10,000,000 of these slaves of the N.K.V.D. working at forced labor.

Dr. Dallin's comparison of the social pyramids of the Tsar's Empire of 1914 and Stalin's Empire of 1940 appears on the next page.[20]

In commenting on this change in class structure Dr. Dallin writes:

The distinction between the social structure of 1914 and 1940 may be reduced to the following points:

First, the Soviet pyramid is lower, never having attained the upper limits of the social structure of old Russia. There are no millionaires of the old type, there is no court, there are no magnates of the old industry, and even

[20] David J. Dallin, *The Real Soviet Russia*, p. 97, *et seq.*

the highest elements of Soviet society enjoy a standard of living lower than that of former capitalists of the middle category.

Second, the Soviet pyramid begins at a lower social point. Its lowest class—forced labor—lives on a very much lower level than did the least secure elements of the old order.

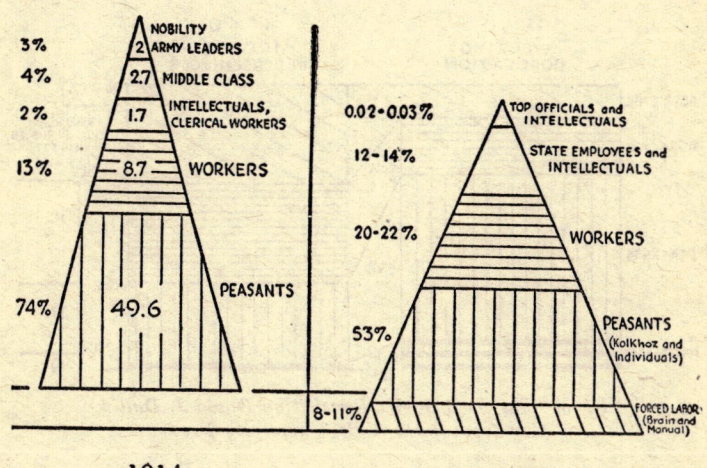

1914   1940

From "The Real Soviet Russia" by David J. Dallin
Courtesy of the Yale University Press

Third, the upper classes of the Soviet pyramid are greater numerically than all the higher classes of old Russia put together. The Soviet Union has more government employees than the entire number of nobles, capitalists, state employees, and intellectual workers of old Russia.

But the picture of the social structure of Soviet Russia viewed with regard to national income is quite different.

The highest class, comprising from 12 to 14 per cent [21] of the population, receives from 31 to 35 per cent of the national income (that is of products distributed and not retained for the state's various needs). The share of the workers is about the same, despite the fact that they number almost one quarter of the population. The peasants,

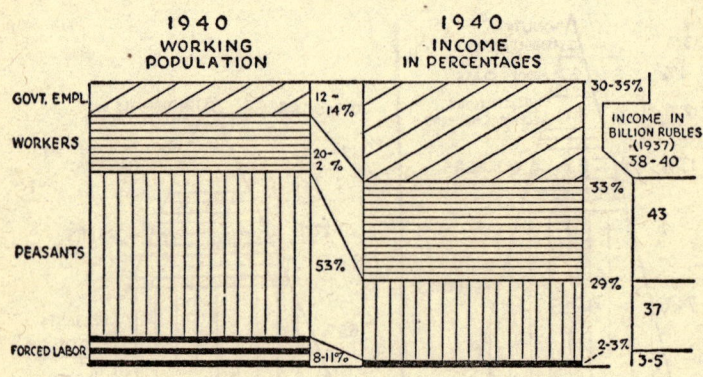

From "The Real Soviet Russia" by David J. Dallin
Courtesy of the Yale University Press

who comprise over half the population, receive a share less than that allotted to the employee class. The least secure, of course, is the class of forced labor, whose share in the national income is insignificant, although its place in the national economy is extremely important.[22]

[21] There are an additional 2,000,000 employees, or 3 per cent of the working population, who cannot be included either in the intelligentsia or in the ranks of manual labor; these are minor employees. The total number of government employees on the eve of the war was therefore between 12,000,000 and 13,000,000, or 17.5 per cent of the working population.

[22] The above figures, as well as the diagrams, are based on the available material, and are drawn with all possible objectivity; however, they must be regarded as rough estimates. Although Russia has an income tax and account is taken annually of the income of the

The proud assertion then of Paragraph 4 of the Soviet Constitution that "exploitation of man has been wiped out in the U.S.S.R., because private ownership of the instruments and means of production has been abolished" is unconvincing indeed. To be sure there is no private ownership; but how can it be asserted that the system as it has developed in Soviet Russia, with its social extremes, is devoid of the elements of exploitation, particularly in the Communist-Marxist sense of the term?

. . . . .

The methods of "exploitation" used are as old as the world, and the Soviet system has added nothing new to hoary experience. These methods are; first, wage labor; second, an unfree peasantry; third, slave labor. What is new in the Soviet system, distinguishing it from capitalism, is the universal application of these methods by the state. There are no slave owners, industrial magnates, feudal landlords in Russia. But the state is the employer of the free workers, as well as the slave owner and feudal lord. Only the state has the right to use all the historical methods of exploitation, while distributing the product as it sees fit.

The system differs radically from capitalism, and Soviet

---

various classes, the results are kept a strict state secret. Information divulged by official sources concerning the class structure of the country likewise leaves many questions unanswered. In 1937, for example, official sources reported that the peasantry comprised 61 per cent of the population; in 1939 these sources placed the figure at 46 per cent. The official sources failed to explain the discrepancy.

Official statistics do not, of course, mention the category of forced labor. The workers of this category sometimes appear in the column "workers," and thus add to the numerical strength of free labor, or they do not appear at all. For these reasons the actual numerical strength of the different social classes as given above does not necessarily coincide with the figures of the official statistical tables.

economists are unquestionably right when they emphasize this distinction. Whether it is a better system for the people is another question.

Under Stalin, however, as under the Tsars, the Russian people are continuing to breed with phenomenal rapidity. Their burgeoning biological urge enables them to recuperate from war, famine, epidemics and "liquidations" with astonishing speed. The population of the Tsar's Empire in 1914 was approximately 170,000,000. Losses in the First World War and in populations freed from Russian domination after the First World War, amounted to approximately 26,000,000 people. But in 1939 the population of the Soviet Union again was approaching 170,000,000. And it was rising to that figure in spite of the losses in the Civil War of 1918 to 1920, the famine of 1921 to 1922, the "liquidations," the famine of 1932 to 1933, and the enormous mortality among the millions of slave laborers of the O.G.P.U. and N.K.V.D.

If the population of the Tsar's Empire had continued to grow at its normal rate of increase without war, Communist revolution, famine or "liquidations," it would have been approximately 250,000,000 at the present time. Today it is probably less than 170,000,000—excluding territories annexed since 1939. And the estimates of highly competent specialists in population growth which indicate that (without counting new annexations) by 1970 the Soviet Union will have a population of 251,000,000 are perhaps too high [23]—just as similar estimates that the United States in 1970 will have a population of only 150,000,000 are perhaps too low. Nevertheless, it is clear that population growth is so much faster in the Soviet Union than in the United States that, under conditions of peace, within approximately thirty years the Soviet Union (without new annexations) is likely to contain approximately 100,000,000 more human beings than the United States.

The figures with regard to population changes in the Soviet Union, Great Britain and France are far more startling, and seem to point toward an overwhelming preponderance of young man power in the Soviet Union. They indicate that in 1955 the Soviet Union will have 36,900,000 men between the ages of 15 and 34; and in 1970 will have 43,300,000: Great Britain in 1955 will have 6,900,000; and in 1970 only 5,700,000: France in 1955 will have 6,100,000; and in 1970 only 4,800,000.[24]

If the Soviet Government is permitted to continue to control the huge areas in Europe and Asia over which it has extended its authority since August 1939, and now controls, either by annexation or the installation of puppet governments or occupation by the Red Army, there will be added to its human resources the following populations:

[23] *The Future Population of Europe and the Soviet Union*, by Frank W. Notenstein and others, League of Nations, Geneva, 1944, p. 312.
[24] *Ibid.*, p. 134.

EUROPE:

Poland	35,000,000
Eastern Germany	25,000,000
Rumania	20,000,000
Yugoslavia	15,700,000
Hungary	10,000,000
Bulgaria	6,300,000
Lithuania	2,000,000
Latvia	2,000,000
Estonia	1,000,000
Albania	1,000,000
Total	118,000,000

ASIA:

North China (Area held by Chinese Soviet Red Army)........	75,000,000
Manchuria	45,000,000
North Korea	10,000,000
Total	130,000,000

In addition the following European countries are today under partial control by the Soviet Government, and threatened with complete control by the Soviet Government:

Czechoslovakia	15,000,000
Austria	7,000,000
Finland	3,800,000
Total	25,800,000

If the Soviet Government should be permitted to consolidate its control over these 118,000,000 Europeans and 130,000,000 Asiatics (leaving aside the other 25,-000,000 Europeans it now controls partially), the man-power in the hands of the Soviet dictator would be far more than doubled. He would rule 418,000,000 people. In addition, the industrial power of the Soviet Union would be increased by the Silesian industrial area, which produced 30 per cent of the industrial output of Germany, the Manchurian industrial area, which produced 70 per cent of the industrial output of China, and the oil fields of Rumania.

Even if all these areas should escape from control by the Soviet Government, Stalin, or any other Soviet dictator who may succeed him, will have at his disposal many more vigorous young men than any democratic leader will have for defense of his country. Moreover, they will be young men educated to believe most fantastic lies about all non-Communist states. The Soviet Government has increased greatly the number of Soviet subjects who can read and write, and the scientific education it gives them is good; but it is careful to see to it that from books, radio and movies, the young receive only propaganda favorable to Communism and the dictator, and unfavorable to all non-Communist states. In consequence, the Russian young have in their heads a series of grotesque lies masquerading as facts.

Moreover, while decreasing the intellectual illiteracy of its subjects, the Soviet Government has vastly increased their moral illiteracy. Many more of them know how to read and write than under the Tsar: many fewer know how to distinguish between right and wrong. They are encouraged to believe that the end justifies the means, and that religion is an old wives' tale, quite unworthy of belief by a fine young komsomol. The original slogan under which the Soviet Government in 1917 attacked religious belief was: "Religion is the opium of the people." Since then violent persecutions of the church have alternated with periods of relative tolerance. But by 1940 there were in Russia 90 per cent fewer Orthodox priests than in 1917, and of the 46,475 Orthodox churches which existed in 1917, only 4,225 remained.[25] Only one Roman Catholic priest is permitted to celebrate the Mass in the whole 1939 area of the Soviet Union—a sixth of the earth's surface. In many sparsely populated regions the young have never seen a church. In Ruthenia and other newly annexed territories where there were many Catholics and many priests, the destruction of the independence of the Church is now proceeding rapidly.

The main purpose of all these persecutions was to break the power of the Orthodox Church and reduce it to an obedient agency of the Soviet Government. The religious persecutions which began in 1917, continued to rise in violence until 1923. Then, feeling in foreign countries, particularly England, became so aroused that persecutions began to interfere with foreign policy. They were moderated, and the churches which remained

[25] David J. Dallin, *The Real Soviet Russia,* p. 61.

open were permitted to function. The Union of the Militant Godless, however, continued to distribute antireligious propaganda with government assistance and direction; and Stalin did not bother to conceal his own views. He expressed them to an American Labor delegation on September 9, 1927, thus: "The Party can not be neutral towards religion, and it does conduct anti-religious propaganda against all and every religious prejudice. . . . Have we suppressed the reactionary clergy? Yes, we have. The unfortunate thing is that it has not been completely liquidated. Anti-religious propaganda is a means by which the complete liquidation of the reactionary clergy must be brought about. Cases occur when certain members of the Party hamper the complete development of anti-religious propaganda. If such members are expelled it is a good thing because there is no room for such 'Communists' in the ranks of the Party." [26]

In 1929 religious persecutions were resumed, priests were exiled, thousands more churches were closed. But in 1934 when the Soviet Government began to try to obtain support of the western democracies against Germany and Japan, the massive persecutions were diminished. Christmas trees and Easter lilies were again permitted. The new constitution of 1936, however, contained the clause: "Freedom of religious worship and

[26] *Stalin Interviews with Foreign Workers Delegations,* New York, International Publishers, 1927, pp. 32–33.

freedom of anti-religious propaganda is recognized for all citizens." Propaganda in favor of religion was still forbidden.

At the end of 1937, another violent persecution of religion was begun: priests were arrested, exiled and executed; approximately ten thousand churches were closed. By 1939, the spirit of most of the clergy had been crushed. Few priests who would not bow down to Stalin remained alive. Many were too broken and hopeless to refuse to become agents of the Soviet Government. Little by little the broken-spirited leaders of the Church moved toward a pact with Stalin.

When Hitler attacked the Soviet Union on June 22, 1941, the deal was consummated. The highest dignitary of the Church, Sergius the Metropolitan of Moscow, on June 29, prayed for the success of the Russian armies, and on November 7, 1941, hailed Stalin as "the divinely appointed leader of our armed and cultural forces leading us to victory."

Stalin needed all the force of religion, as well as all the force of patriotism, to draw from the peasants the last measure of sacrifice in the war against Germany. And from the Metropolitan Sergius he got what he wanted. In return Stalin permitted Sergius to be elected Patriarch and accorded him an audience. The next day the Patriarch carried out his first international political task, but not his last, for the dictator. He demanded a second front in Europe, saying to the allies of the Soviet Union: "We Russians are the world's most patient people, but the cup of our patience is over-flowing."

A government Committee on the Affairs of the Ortho-dox Church was set up to direct the actions of the 75-year-old Patriarch. Thus, having reduced the Church to the status of an agency of the Government, Stalin began to make it an efficient instrument. The training of new priests, which had been forbidden, was permitted. The establishment of an Orthodox Theological Institute was allowed. That was a far cry from the days when the Communists had placarded the walls of Russia with the slogan: "Religion is the opium of the people."

Which has won—the Church or the Communist Party? Stalin controls the Church and uses it as an instrument of national and international policy. But the Church teaches Christ crucified and risen. And whatever compromises its political leaders may make, it contains a small, clean core of priests whose faith has carried them through all sufferings and persecutions, as it carried thousands of their fellows to martyrdom. They teach the doctrine of the fatherhood of God and the brotherhood of man—the brotherhood of all men, every-where. Between that teaching and the Stalin creed of class warfare, international warfare, dictatorship main-tained by secret police and firing squads, hypocrisy, lies and hatred, there is no final compromise.

The Church is in Stalin's hands. He can recommence persecutions whenever he wishes. But there are no longer many illusions among the 164,000,000 Russians who are not members of the Communist Party as to the moral and spiritual quality of their State. And when the Christians among them meet in the streets or on the roads on the morning of Easter Day they greet each other with the words: "Christ is risen!" The Church in Russia is weak. But the word of God is strong. And religion has a way of outlasting dictators and persecutions. In the long run—if there is to be a long run on this earth for the human race—the gates of the N.K.V.D. will not prevail against it.

The Communist Creed and Soviet Foreign Policy

The Soviet Government believes in a Communist Creed, which it teaches to all its children, for which it prepares them to live, and, if need be, to die. That is the Marx-Lenin-Stalin creed which denies God and claims to be based on scientific fact; but is based on the improbable assumption that the establishment of Communist dictatorship throughout the earth and the abolition of private ownership of the means of production will end all war, civil and international, and so improve the nature of all men in all nations that, in Lenin's phrase, "the state will wither away" and all men will live without a state in perfect freedom and happiness. As Engels, the collaborator of Marx, envisioning a Communist world, wrote, "the machine of the state is put into the museum of antiquities, along side of the spinning wheel and the bronze axe."

Lenin, a man of immense human sympathies, intellect and courage, justified by this creed the creation of dictatorship in Russia. He believed that the state, whether in his hands or in the hands of a "bourgeois government," was an instrument of violence; but that, while living under Communist dictatorship, men could be prepared for perfect freedom. "While there is a state," he said, "there is no freedom. When there is freedom there will be no state."

The mysticism of this belief is perhaps the reason why it has evoked as great devotion and self-sacrifice as many religious creeds. The Communist true-believer offers his life as gallantly as an early Christian. He believes that he is fighting for the emancipation of all humanity from all evil. He thinks he serves eternal truth. The Communist Party, to him, is a union of the faithful. His old testament is the books of Marx and Engels; his new testament, the works of Lenin and Stalin. In his idolatry he is profoundly religious. The Soviet Union is to him the Church Militant.[27]

Since the highest moral goal, according to the Communist Creed, is to achieve the destruction of the state, following the establishment of Communist dictatorship throughout the earth, the highest moral duty of man is to serve to promote such dictatorship. This supreme moral end, the Communist believes, justifies all

[27] In the Communist parties outside the Soviet Union there is a far greater proportion of Communist true-believers than in the Russian Communist Party. The Russian Communists have to live in the reality which includes the N.K.V.D.; foreign Communists can still believe in the paradise which exists only in Soviet propaganda.

means for its achievement, including war, murder, character assassination, the pledged word given and broken. In the words of Lenin: "It is necessary . . . to use any ruse, cunning, unlawful method, evasion, concealment of truth." [28] The restraints imposed by moral scruples on democratic governments, which the Communists call "bourgeois" or "capitalist" or "imperialist," therefore, play no part in the decisions of the Soviet Government.

The Communist creed requires that the aim of the foreign policy of the Soviet Union, and all other Communist-controlled governments, should be to establish Communist dictatorship throughout the earth. That aim is unchanging and unchangeable. The strategy and tactics employed by the Soviet Government to achieve its aim are altered in accordance with its estimate of the world situation. Its aim is never altered. It is, and will remain, the conquest of the world for Communism. No one will have the slightest difficulty in understanding the foreign policy of the Soviet Union if he will think of it, as the Communists do, in military terms. It is the expression of the strategy and tactics of an army that attacks always if its Supreme Commander considers victory possible, and retreats only when it faces defeat.

Four short statements of Lenin and Stalin contain the fundamental theses on which Soviet foreign policy is based:

1. We are living not merely in a state, but in a system of states; and it is inconceivable that the Soviet republic

[28] Lenin, *The Infantile Sickness of Leftism in Communism,* 1920.

should continue for a long period side by side with imperialist states. Ultimately one or the other must conquer. Meanwhile a number of terrible clashes between the Soviet republic and the bourgeois states is inevitable.

> Lenin, *Collected Works*, vol. XXIV, page 122, Russian Edition. (Quoted with approval by Stalin in his book *Problems of Leninism.*)

2. From the time a Socialist government is established in any one country, questions must be determined . . . solely from the point of view of what is best for the development and the consolidation of the Socialist Revolution which has already begun. The question whether it is possible to undertake at once a revolutionary war must be answered solely from the point of view of actual conditions and the interest of the Socialist Revolution which has already begun.

> Lenin, *Twenty-One Theses*, January 20, 1918.

3. It is necessary . . . to use any ruse, cunning, unlawful method, evasion, concealment of truth.

> Lenin, *The Infantile Sickness of Leftism in Communism*, 1920.

4. The Comintern is the holy of holies of the working class.

> Stalin, Speech on the American Communist Party, May 6, 1929.

The Soviet Government knows what it intends, and, therefore, believes that wars are inevitable between the Soviet Union and the non-Communist states which it calls "bourgeois" or "capitalist" or "imperialist"—that is to say, states like the United States, Great Britain,

Canada, Australia, New Zealand, France, Belgium, the Netherlands, Switzerland and the Scandinavian states. Peace to the Soviet Government is not peace as we understand peace but an armistice in which to prepare attack.

On February 9, 1946, Stalin in his radio broadcast from Moscow, which set the present "Party line" not only for the Russian Communist Party but also for all other Communists, again reiterated his belief that wars are "inevitable" so long as the "capitalist system"—that is to say the system of all the democratic states, including the United States—exists. He attributed the Second World War not to the Nazis, not to the Fascists, not to the Japanese militarists, but to "capitalist world economy," saying: "It would be incorrect to think that the war arose accidentally or as a result of the fault of some of the statesmen. Although those faults did exist, the war arose in reality as the inevitable result of the development of the world economic and political forces on the basis of monopoly capitalism. Our Marxists declare that the capitalist system of world economy conceals elements of crisis and war, that the development of world capitalism does not follow a steady and even course forward, but proceeds through crises and catastrophes. . . . Thus, as a result of the first crisis in the development of the capitalist world economy arose the First World War. The Second World War arose as a result of the second crisis." [29]

[29] *New York Times,* February 10, 1946.

In the same address Stalin announced as an objective of the forthcoming Five Year Plans the development of a steel production of 60,000,000 tons a year. This represents three times the Soviet steel production of 1940, and is greater than the combined steel production of Germany, Japan and Great Britain in 1940. Moreover, Stalin now controls the steel production of Silesia, Manchuria, Czechoslovakia, Austria and Hungary. Steel production is the basic measure of industrial capacity to make war.

Since the Soviet dictator continues to believe, as he has always believed, that only the destruction of the democratic "capitalist" states and conquest of the world for Communism can produce peace, and since he knows that such a conquest cannot be achieved except by the Soviet Union making war successfully on the democratic states, or bringing about Communist revolutions in the democratic states, and since he has ordered this colossal increase in steel production at a time when all the people of the Soviet Union are in desperate need of consumer's goods, no doubt remains as to his determination to persist in his policy of aggressive Soviet Imperialism.[30]

Those who complain that the foreign policy of the Soviet Union is inconsistent and unpredictable confuse

---

[30] Just as most Americans did not take the trouble to read Hitler's book *Mein Kampf* until after his seizure of Czechoslovakia, just so most Americans today will not take the trouble to read the works of Lenin and Stalin. A few excerpts from one of Stalin's books, *Problems of Leninism,* will be found in Appendix III.

strategy and tactics with objectives. The Soviet Government progresses steadily toward its goal but changes its strategy and tactics like a good general staff, concealing its plans, shifting its forces. It judges carefully its own strength and weakness and the strength and weakness of the non-Communist states which occupy the rest of the earth. When it feels that it can strike successfully, it strikes. It knows what it wants and what it intends: hence Lenin's statement "a number of terrible clashes between the Soviet Republic and the bourgeois states is inevitable."

The establishment of Communist dictatorship throughout the earth, according to Communist teaching, may be achieved by two means:

(1) Class warfare—that is to say revolution within states which are not Communist, and "liquidation" of all classes except the proletariat.

(2) Conquest by the Soviet Union of non-Communist neighboring states, followed either by annexation or the installation of puppet governments directed from Moscow.

In its capacity as general staff of the Communist world army the Soviet Government, therefore, employs as offensive weapons not only the enormous military, political and economic power of the Soviet Union, but also "Fifth Columns" in all nations where it is permitted to install them. It issues its orders to these "Fifth Columns" and they obey. In democratic countries, the

Soviet Fifth Column is in the habit of camouflaging itself as a political party usually called the Communist Party. It uses all the democratic liberties, including freedom of speech, of the press and of assembly, to attempt to destroy from within the democratic state which protects it.

The sudden changes in strategy and tactics of these Soviet "Fifth Columns" are dictated by the Soviet Government. Since the control of the Soviet Union by the Communist dictatorship is the chief source of strength of world Communism, the interests of national Communist parties outside the Soviet Union are subordinated to the interests of the Soviet Union. They are often ordered to change their strategy and tactics and to take positions which render them ridiculous—just as a battalion of an army is often ordered to sacrifice itself for the benefit of the army as a whole.

The American Communist Party, for example, has been obliged to turn intellectual somersaults so often in following faithfully the strategic and tactical changes in Soviet foreign policy that only those who are ignorant of its actions can regard it as anything but a Soviet Fifth Column, the members of which are loyal to the Soviet Union, not to the United States, and are prepared to support the Soviet Union against the United States even in case of war. The American Communists are potential traitors, and would be ashamed if they were not. Their somersaults from July 1939 to October 1945 are recorded in their official organ *The Daily*

Worker, of New York, excerpts from which will be found in Appendix II.

As conquest of the earth for Communism is the objective of the Soviet Government, no nation lies outside the scope of its ambitions. Those countries which lie close to the Soviet Union are more immediately menaced than those which lie farther away for the simple reason that they are easier for the Red Army to get at. Wherever the Soviet Union can advance with impunity it advances. Wherever aggression is difficult or dangerous, it stops. Its appetite is unlimited. Its behavior resembles on a mammoth scale that of the amoeba—the microscopic unicellular animal, consisting of a nucleus surrounded by protoplasm, which has no mouth but takes in its food at any point on its surface. The amoeba constantly extends portions of its protoplasm, and if one touches something digestible, the amoeba flows around it and digests it; but if an indigestible grain of grit is encountered the protoplasm withdraws, and the amoeba extends another bit of protoplasm seeking a fresh victim in another direction. Similarly, from the nucleus of Moscow the Soviet Government constantly tests areas around the Soviet Union in search of victims. If it encounters serious resistance, it withdraws and tries another area. If it finds a digestible victim, it flows around it and digests it.

The Soviet Union's powers of digestion are greater than those of any other nation because its digestive processes are unrestrained by any considerations of humanity or morality. In areas which it controls completely it either murders immediately or deports to certain death at slave labor all its political opponents of all classes, including farmers and factory workers, and all highly educated persons whom it cannot terrorize into becoming its agents. By continuing, day after day and month after month, to murder and deport all who criticize, it finally reduces its victim to a terrorized mass of despairing individuals whom it then compels to go to a booth and "vote" for a Soviet-picked candidate under penalty of losing their bread-cards, which are nothing less than permits to live. By this process it has already digested Estonia, Latvia, Lithuania and Eastern Poland.

Before the Communists seized control of the Russian Government on November 7, 1917, they had the world to win and only class warfare as a weapon with which to win it. After November 7, 1917, they had, in addition, the power of a great state and a mighty people. They could use international warfare as well as class warfare. The use they have made of these weapons has depended solely on their military estimate of the world situation. Of one thing they are sure: that they will never cease trying to conquer the world for Communism. Their warfare against "bourgeois states," therefore, cannot end until they have imposed Communism throughout the earth. Peace treaties, non-aggression agreements, they regard as instruments which they sign merely because at some moment they consider it in their interest to sign them; and they sign with every intention of breaking such agreements when they feel strong enough to do so with impunity.[31]

In accordance with its estimate of the changing world situation the Soviet Government has changed its international strategy and tactics six times since November, 1917:

I. 1917–1920. Based on the estimate that Communist revolutions might sweep all Europe, the Soviet Government conducted an all-out offensive with its weapon of class warfare, while fighting defensively against its opponents in the Russian Civil War.

II. 1920–1933. Based on the estimate that the Soviet Union was desperately weak compared to non-Communist states and might be attacked by them, the Soviet Government conducted a manoeuvre of strategic retreat, signing non-aggression pacts with many of its neighbors: Turkey 1925, Germany 1926, Lithuania 1926, Iran 1927, Afghanistan 1931, Poland 1932, Finland 1932, Latvia 1932, and Estonia 1932. The Soviet Government continued to denounce the League of Nations as a capitalist conspiracy directed against it; but sent Litvinov to Geneva to advocate total international disarmament in March, 1928.

(The rôle of manoeuvre in Soviet foreign policy is strikingly displayed by the fact that while

[31] See Appendix I.

Litvinov was proposing total disarmament at Geneva, the 6th Congress of the Communist International meeting at Moscow adopted the following resolution:

"The overthrow of capitalism is impossible without violence, i.e., without armed uprisings and wars against the bourgeoisie. In our era of imperialistic wars and world revolution, revolutionary civil wars of the proletarian dictatorship against the bourgeoisie, wars of the proletariat against the bourgeois states and world capitalism, as well as national revolutionary wars of oppressed peoples against imperialism are unavoidable.") [32]

III. 1934–1939. Based on the estimate that the Soviet Union was in danger of a two-front attack by Germany and Japan, the Soviet Government attempted to reach agreement with Hitler. When Hitler rejected Stalin's approaches, the Soviet Government conducted another strategic manoeuvre for the purpose of mobilizing "bourgeois states" against Germany and Japan. It entered the League of Nations in 1934, signed treaties of alliance with "bourgeois states" (France and Czechoslovakia, in 1935), and ordered its Communist agents abroad to create "popular front" and antifascist movements in order to obtain support for the Soviet Union against Germany and Japan.

IV. August 23, 1939, to June, 1940. Based on the

[32] W. H. Chamberlin, *The Russian Enigma,* p. 193.

estimate that the Hitler-Stalin Pact of August 23, 1939, would produce a long and exhausting war between Germany, France and England, that the Soviet Union would have nothing to fear from Germany for the duration of that war, and that the misery produced by the war might enable the Soviet Union to establish Communism throughout Europe, the Soviet Government reverted to aggressive attack. It violated its treaties with Finland, Estonia, Latvia, Lithuania, Poland and Rumania, and annexed parts of Finland, all the Baltic States, and parts of Poland and Rumania.

V. June, 1940–1944. Based on the estimate that the rapid collapse of French and British resistance to the German armies on the continent of Europe might place the Soviet Union in danger of a two-front attack by Germany and Japan, the Soviet Government attempted to maintain its association with Germany and entered into a non-aggression agreement with Japan on April 13, 1941. When Germany attacked the Soviet Union on June 22, 1941, the Soviet Government adopted defensive strategy and tactics at home and abroad, doing everything possible to obtain the support of "bourgeois states" like the United States. It ostensibly abolished the American Communist Party and the Communist International (Comintern). This manoeuvre may be judged in the light of the fact that Stalin stated to the American Commission of the Presidium of the E.C.C.I. on May 6, 1929, "The Comintern is the holy of holies of the working class." [33] It signed the Atlantic Charter and all other general expressions of good intentions proposed to it by Great Britain and the United States. The American Communist Party, which temporarily was camouflaged under the name of the Communist Political Association, supported President Roosevelt in the 1944 election.

VI. 1945–1946. Based on occupation by the Red Army, or control by Moscow-directed puppet governments, of Estonia, Latvia, Lithuania, Poland, Rumania, Bulgaria, Hungary, Yugoslavia, Albania, parts of Austria and Czechoslovakia, and Germany as far as the Elbe River, and on the occupation of Manchuria and North Korea, the Soviet Government engaged in aggressive efforts to subject these vast areas to complete control, and used its Fifth Columns in France, Italy and Greece and other European countries to prepare the ground for its control of those countries.

The present foreign policy of the Soviet Government is based on the military consideration that it must have time to consolidate its power in the huge areas outside the 1939 boundaries of the Soviet Union which it now controls, and must cap-

---

[33] *Stalin's Speeches on the American Communist Party*, published by Central Committee, Communist Party, U. S. A., p. 15.

ture from within by Trojan horse tactics coun-tries of western Europe, and must rebuild its internal economy and develop for itself atomic bombs, before risking war with the United States. It must, therefore, not come into armed conflict with the United States immediately. It may, how-ever, permit itself to test the resistance of war-weary Great Britain and the United States at various points; and, if resistance is weak, subject new lands to its control: for example, Iran, Turkey and North China; but it must recoil be-fore any decided stand by either Great Britain or the United States, since it does not, for the mo-ment, dare to risk war with the United States, and fears that the United States would not permit it to conquer Great Britain.

Any attempt to judge Soviet foreign policy on the basis of its short-term strategy and tactics leads to ludicrous conclusions. Soviet foreign policy from 1917 to 1921, when the Soviet Government was trying to spread class warfare throughout Europe, was diametri-cally opposed to Soviet foreign policy from 1934 to 1939, when the Soviet Government was trying to obtain support of "bourgeois states" against Germany and Japan. Soviet foreign policy from 1921 to 1933 when the Soviet Government, in view of the physical weakness of the Soviet Union, feared attack by "bourgeois states" and made non-aggression treaties with its neighbors, was diametrically opposed to Soviet foreign policy from August 23, 1939, to June 1940, when the Soviet Union felt strong enough to attack the same neighboring states—and committed aggressions against many of them.

But there is no mystery in Soviet foreign policy. Stalin with reason says: "Our policy is simple and clear." The aim of Soviet foreign policy is constant: to establish Communist dictatorship throughout the earth. To achieve this objective its chief weapons are:

1. Class warfare conducted by the Communist Parties throughout the world.
2. Force, threats of war, or war.

The exact use to be made of these weapons is determined on military grounds by the Soviet Government, which adapts its strategy and tactics to the changing world situation. In the eyes of the Soviet Government, the Soviet Union is always engaged in warfare, open or concealed, with the non-Communist states of the world. And when the Soviet Government embraces in friendship any non-Communist government, it is always with the ultimate intention of driving a dagger into its back. That is why Stalin is unappeasable. That is why President Roosevelt's "great design" was foredoomed to failure. That is why for our own self-preservation we must face the unpleasant fact that Stalin, like Hitler, will not stop but can only be stopped. Does that mean that the Communists are right in their belief that wars between the Soviet Union and non-Communist states are inevitable? No!

The Soviet dictator has at his disposal the physical strength of the Soviet Union, the burgeoning growth in numbers of its peoples, the faith of the Communist true-believers, the old Russian tradition of Tsarist imperialism, the mystical belief that Moscow is the "third Rome" destined to rule the world, the aid of the puppet governments he has set up in Europe and Asia, the devotion of the Fifth Columns which, under the name of the Communist Party, he has installed in all nations, the assistance of the "fellow travelers," and dupes, and tired liberals, who despair of solving the problems of human life by Christian principles and democratic methods and like weary children have tossed themselves on his breast.

This is a formidable array of force in the hands of a dictator more absolute than Hitler, whose creed makes his aim the conquest of the world for Communism. A policy of appeasement of the Soviet Government will surely lead to war. Some day the Soviet Government will overstep the limits of appeasement, as Hitler overstepped the limits when he attacked Poland. But Soviet policy is as frankly based on military considerations to-day as it was when Lenin wrote: "The question whether it is possible to undertake at once a revolutionary war must be answered solely from the point of view of actual conditions and the interest of the Socialist Revolution which has already begun." [34] Lenin did not hesitate to retreat when he felt that he faced superior forces. Stalin will not make war if he feels that he faces superior forces. The most legitimate use of force on earth is to gain time to permit the growth of moral ideas. It will take some time for moral ideas to grow in the Soviet Union. There is no way to prevent the Soviet Union from conquering non-Communist states during that time except the hard way of keeping it constantly confronted by superior force.

Today all governments, except the Soviet Government, and its puppet satellite governments, are working for peace. The Soviet Government is working for conquest. It naturally prefers to make conquests without war, and impose its dictatorship throughout the world without having to fight. The peoples of the democratic states desperately desire peace. But they have not lost all instinct of self-preservation; and their governments, however reluctantly, will be obliged to build up national forces and international security organizations with sufficient power to enforce peace against all potential aggressors—including the Soviet Union.

[34] Lenin, *Twenty-One Theses*, January 20, 1918.

III

"Though a man escape every other danger, he can never wholly escape those who do not want such a person as he is to exist."

DEMOSTHENES: *De Falsa Legatione.*

"A brave world, sir, full of religion, knavery and change! We shall shortly see better days."

APHRA BEHN: *The Roundheads,* 1682.

THIS LITTLE EARTH, shrunk by the airplane and threatened by the atomic bomb, has emerged from the Second World War with only five states powerful enough to have obtained permanent seats on the Security Council of the United Nations: the United States, the Soviet Union, Great Britain, France and China. War has become a conflict of massed machines. And, at the moment, only three of these five Great Powers—the United States, the Soviet Union and Great Britain— are capable of producing the masses of machines necessary to wage war effectively. France, systematically pilliged by the Germans for five years, has not yet had time to recover her strength. Her army is admirable but small, and many of her industries require rebuilding. China has never had the industries necessary to produce modern machines of war. Her richest province, Manchuria, which contains nearly seventy percent of her industrial strength, was controlled by the Japanese from

1932 to 1945 and is now in large part controlled by the Soviet Union and the Chinese Soviet army. Her might lies in the intelligence, endurance and numbers of her people. She may recover Manchuria and she may become a great industrial nation. She is not now.

Our three chief enemies and one of our most faithful allies lie prostrate. Germany, split into four zones of occupation, her eastern industries controlled by the Soviet Union, her western industries paralyzed, her whole economy in chaos, is suffering some of the miseries she so lavishly inflicted on the other states of Europe; and, as she has not even a government, is not for the moment any sort of a power. Japan, stripped of her fleet and air force, is moving dazedly away from militarism under the wise guidance of General MacArthur. Italy, having learned that the paths of fustian Fascist glory lead to the grave, is struggling to keep body and soul together. Our ally Poland, devastated and starving, her government controlled by the Kremlin, has been reduced to the status of a suffering satellite of the Soviet Union. Her men will be used in the great industrial area of Silesia to produce arms for Communist armies, and, like the men of the other Soviet satellite states, may be used by the Soviet Government to fight in a cause which is not theirs; but Poland, in truth, has ceased to be an independent power.

The other states of Europe, and all the states of the Near East, Asia, Africa, and Latin America, however high may be their level of culture and their future possibilities, have not today the industrial strength necessary for a war of massed machines. Immediate striking power of the first dimension is held exclusively by the Soviet Union, Great Britain and the United States. This does not mean that the Soviet Union, Great Britain and the United States should attempt to dictate to the rest of the world; but it does mean that no major war can be carried on today without the assent and participation, open or camouflaged, of either the Soviet Union or Great Britain or the United States.

What are the vital interests of these three Great Powers, and where, if anywhere, do they conflict?

Both the Soviet Union and the United States are free from the basic worry which underlies all vital interests of Great Britain. The Soviet Union and the United States produce enough food and raw materials for their essential needs. Great Britain does not. To the Soviet Union foreign trade is a dispensable luxury. To the United States foreign trade means the difference between prosperity and hard times. To Great Britain foreign trade is a matter of life and death.

In 1815, when Wellington defeated Napoleon at Waterloo, the population of Great Britain—excluding Ireland—was approximately 12,000,000. Today the population of the same area is approximately 46,000,-000. The feeding, clothing and housing of this vastly increased population was made possible by the development of a complex system of trade and business with all the world. The rapid development of British industry and coal mining after the Napoleonic wars, the earnings of the British merchant marine, insurance companies, banks, foreign investments, and a host of export businesses, made it possible to pay for the imports without which the increased population of Great Britain could not live—and can not live. The primary vital interest of Great Britain is, therefore, to keep open the seaways to her ports, and the second is to earn abroad by exports, or services, or other means, the money to pay for essential imports.

To make certain that the seaways would be kept open, Great Britain developed the world's largest navy and in the nineteenth century established the "Two Power Standard"; that is to say, maintained a navy larger than any other two navies in the world. After the sinking of the German Navy at the close of the First World War, British sea communications seemed secure. The magnitude of British concern with regard to this vital interest was promptly demonstrated, however, by British anxiety about the growth of the American Navy. Lloyd George, the British Prime Minister, went so far as to say that "Great Britain would spend her last guinea to keep a navy superior to that of the United States or any other power." [1] And Lord Robert Cecil expressed the feelings of nearly all the inhabitants of the British Isles when, on April 8, 1919, he wrote to Colonel House, American delegate at the Peace Conference in Paris, "The position is undoubtedly complicated

[1] *The Intimate Papers of Colonel House,* Vol. IV, p. 180.

by the British sentiment about sea power. It has been now for centuries past an article of faith with every British statesman that the safety of the country depends upon her ability to maintain her sea defence, and like all deep-rooted popular sentiments it is founded in truth. Not only have we dominions scattered over the face of the world, each of which requires protection from the sea, but the teeming population of the islands of the United Kingdom can only be fed and clothed provided the avenues of sea traffic are safe. We import four-fifths of our cereals, two-thirds of our meat, the whole of our cotton and almost the whole of our wool. If we were blockaded for a month or less we should have to surrender at discretion. That is not true of any other country in the world to the same extent. Least of all is it true of the United States, which could, as far as necessaries of life are concerned, laugh at any blockade." [2]

In spite of the depth of this sentiment, Great Britain accepted the equality of the American Navy at the Washington Conference in 1922. This decision was based not only on the fact that the United States had the means to build a larger navy than the British Navy, but also on the wise conclusion that it was extremely improbable that the American Navy would ever be used to blockade Great Britain. There was, in point of fact, small risk in this British gamble on American friendship. The British and the American people shared so many basic customs, including the common custom of

[2] *The Intimate Papers of Colonel House,* Vol. IV, p. 418.

using the English language, and had so many common interests, including their mutual interest in Canada, and were so linked by a common heritage of liberty, democracy and Christian ideals, that it was difficult to conceive of any event which might turn their friendship into hostility—however much they might criticize each other, their quarrels would remain family quarrels without divorce. It was natural that the maintenance of close friendship with the United States should become the first axiom of British foreign policy.

The American Navy was not built up to parity with the British Navy until after Pearl Harbor. But construction in the United States thereafter was so rapid that today the American Navy is far larger than the British. That does not worry the British. The help given the British Navy by the American Navy, both before Pearl Harbor and after, made the British regard the American Navy as one of the great guarantors of the safety of their sea communications.

This British confidence in the United States is not matched by any similar confidence in any other nation. Today the United States and Great Britain together hold a world monopoly of sea power. Little remains of the once powerful French fleet, and the Soviet Union has not yet undertaken seriously the task of constructing a navy. Soviet naval construction is shrouded in secrecy. We know that the Soviet Union has built many submarines; and before the outbreak of the Second World War, various Soviet officials, including President

Kalinin, talked as if the Soviet Union were about to construct a huge navy. But as yet a large Soviet Navy is not visible on the high seas, and warships are not easy to conceal. If the Soviet Union should begin to construct a navy which threatened to become as powerful as the British Navy, the same reaction would occur in Great Britain as occurred when the German Kaiser, Wilhelm II, pushed the construction of his navy. Great Britain would feel obliged to consider such a Soviet Navy a threat to her primary vital interest of keeping open the seaways to her ports. But the Soviet Union has no vital interest in the possession of a large navy. She holds today more than a sixth of the surface of the earth; she is more completely self-sufficient than any other nation in the world, and she has no overseas possessions to guard. She does not need a large navy for defense. She could use one only for aggression. There is, therefore, no clash in the naval sphere between a vital British interest and a vital Soviet interest.

In the days of the Spanish Armada and the fleets of Louis XIV and Napoleon, control of the surface of the sea by the British fleet assured the safe arrival in port of British merchantmen. The submarine and the airplane have complicated enormously the problem of protecting the British life lines. German submarines in both the First and the Second World War brought Great Britain close to disaster—and the airplane has now become an even greater threat to merchant shipping than the submarine. A foretaste of future perils was given the British by the Germans in World War II when they based both submarines and airplanes on Western France and greatly increased thereby sinkings of merchant ships. The German planes thus employed were few in number; but enough to demonstrate that a large number of modern planes based on the Continent from Norway to Western France would present a deadly threat to British shipping and that at all costs Great Britain must prevent control of Western Europe by a possible enemy.

The English Channel at the Straits of Dover is only twenty-two miles wide. Some sixty miles from Dover lies London. The invention of robot planes, rockets and atomic bombs has raised Great Britain's vital interest in a friendly Western Europe to a new dimension. Anyone who considers British anxiety with regard to Western Europe exaggerated, has only to remember the V1s and V2s which fell on London during World War II, and imagine the serenity of New Yorkers if rockets loaded with atomic explosives were to be placed by an enemy in the country around Philadelphia and pointed toward Manhattan Island. Distance is no final guarantee against rockets. But distance decreases accuracy and gives time to employ counter-weapons. The further away from the coasts of England rocket bases lie, the greater will be the chance that the rockets may be stopped.

The rocket, the airplane and the atomic bomb have given a terrible urgency to the maintenance of the old British policy of preventing the domination of the continent of Europe by any one great power. Four centuries ago the British became convinced that if any power should control all Europe, Great Britain would not be strong enough to withstand attack by that power, and that, in consequence, it was vital to Great Britain to prevent such domination of Europe. For their own preservation, therefore, the British throughout four centuries persistently strove to strengthen the weaker states of Europe against the strongest state of the continent. If peaceful means proved insufficient to prevent domination of Europe by a single state, the British supported their continental allies by force of arms. Philip II of Spain, Louis XIV of France, Napoleon, William II of Germany, and Hitler, all had to be stopped by war; and if a Soviet dictator should attempt to follow in the footsteps of these dead aggressors, Great Britain, after exhausting the resources of appeasement, would again have to resort to war.

The Soviet Union has no vital interest in control of Europe. Its territory is already so vast that the distance by air from Odessa to its eastern limit at the Bering Strait is as great as the distance from Odessa to Boston, Massachusetts. It is an underpopulated country, a land of huge open spaces with few inhabitants. If the peoples of the Soviet Union controlled their government and could impose their will upon it, they would react like normal human beings and turn their energies to the development of their own country, and the raising of their own low standard of living, and the Soviet Union might enter a period of peaceful internal construction, comparable to the period of American development from 1864 to 1914. But unfortunately the peoples of the Soviet Union do not control their government. They are controlled by it. And the Soviet Government is obsessed by the belief that its duty is to conquer the world for Communism. This belief conflicts with every real vital interest of the peoples of the Soviet Union; but it dominates Soviet policy, and the peoples of the Soviet Union are tools in the hands of the Soviet dictator. The fact that the Soviet Union has no vital interest in attempting to dominate all Europe, therefore, does not mean that the attempt will not be made. Such an attempt would threaten the vital interests of Great Britain, and the British would feel obliged to fight.

The Soviet Union has already cut deeply into the body of Europe. It has annexed Estonia, Latvia, Lithuania, Eastern Poland and portions of Finland, Czechoslovakia and Rumania. It controls, through satellite governments, Rumania, Bulgaria, Yugoslavia, Albania and Poland. It controls, through the Red Army, Eastern Germany and much of Central Germany, and Hungary, and half of Austria, and has a dominant influence on the policies of Czechoslovakia and Finland. The British have met this advance westward of Soviet imperialism until the present time by the same policy of appeasement with which they met Hitler's aggressions until he attacked Poland. Appeasement of Stalin has been no more successful than appeasement of Hitler.

If, or when, Stalin will overstep the patient limits of appeasement, as Hitler did, remains to be seen. No vital interest of the Soviet Union compels him to go on. The Communist Creed does.

To earn abroad by exports, or services, or other means, the money to pay for the imports without which the population of the United Kingdom can not live, is in the long run as vital to Great Britain as the protection of the seaways to her ports. War disrupts international trade. Export industries must be transformed into munition plants and their products consumed on the field of battle, not exchanged for imports. Customers for exports, especially those in the actual battle zone, have their purchasing power destroyed. In the years of World War II, Great Britain was obliged to sacrifice the greater part of her export trade, and, therefore, to use a large portion of the foreign investments of British subjects, and to incur foreign debts, in order to pay for essential imports.

In order to earn the money to pay her debts and to purchase essential imports, Great Britain will be obliged to export much more than she imports for many years to come. Her people will have to live at a low level of consumption, without luxuries, and work as hard as they can. The blood and tears of war are over momentarily for the British, the sweat remains.

A way out of this hard path has tempted many British politicians. The British Government might try to close the Empire and various other nations permanently within a sterling bloc, and attempt to make British purchases, in so far as possible, within the area of London-managed currency. Such action would have serious effects on the export trade of the United States. The United Kingdom and the Empire are by far the greatest customers of the United States. If their peoples should be unable to purchase in the United States because they were forbidden to exchange their pounds sterling for dollars, the reduction of American exports might make the difference between prosperity and hard times in America. The area to which it is possible to make exports normally from the United States has already been reduced by the Soviet Monopoly of Foreign Trade. No individual in the Soviet Union is permitted to buy anything abroad. All purchases are made by the Soviet Government itself. It buys habitually not the consumer's goods its people want but articles needed to strengthen its war machine. And it uses its control over imports and exports as a political weapon, and turns off or on the spigot of trade in accordance with its political designs. Every new area subjected to Soviet domination is included sooner or later within the wall of the Soviet Monopoly of Foreign Trade. Every time the Soviet Union extends its power over another area or state, the United States and Great Britain lose another normal market. If the British Empire through a permanent sterling bloc should close itself to the normal trade of the United States, as the Soviet Union has closed itself through its Foreign Trade Monopoly, the consequences would be serious to American economic life. To avoid this contingency the American Government, subject to Congressional approval, has proposed to lend Great Britain $3,750,000,000 at 2 percent interest—payment of interest and amortization to begin in 1951. This amount has been calculated as the minimum number of dollars needed by Great Britain for dollar purchases within the next five years. And the British and ourselves have agreed that we will work out an accord for the reduction of all trade barriers. There is some hope, therefore, that normal international trade may be restored throughout most of the world. But the abundant sixth of the earth's surface within the Soviet Union will be permanently lost to normal trade so long as the Soviet Foreign Trade Monopoly exists. Europe has always been Great Britain's best customer and, since the extension of control by the Soviet Union over an area removes it from normal trade, it is important to British exporters that the Soviet Union should not extend its control further westward in Europe. For reasons of trade, therefore, as well as vital military and naval interests, the British are opposed to the extension of Soviet control in Western Europe.

The British Empire includes nearly one quarter of the land surface of the earth and its total population is more than 500,000,000, of which India provides at least 350,000,000. It is in itself an extraordinary league of nations and races, held together in part by common customs, traditions and sentiments, and in part by British armed force.

The great bulk of the Empire lies close to the Indian Ocean in an immense semi-circle that sweeps from South Africa to India and thence to Australia. The short route from Great Britain to the Indian Ocean runs by way of the Mediterranean, and that sea has rightly been called the lifeline of the Empire. It is to the British Empire what the Trans-Siberian railroad is to the Soviet Union. To protect her communications through the Mediterranean, Great Britain holds Gibraltar, Malta and Cyprus, and maintains forces in Egypt to guard the Suez Canal, which connects the Mediterranean and the Red Sea—the thin northwestern arm of the Indian Ocean.

When oil became the basis of fuel for ships, automobiles and airplanes, the eastern end of the Mediterranean developed a new and intense importance for Great Britain. There was no oil in the British Isles. And the greatest undeveloped fields of oil in the world lay in Iran, Iraq and Saudi Arabia. Through the Anglo-Iranian Oil Company, which was controlled by the British Government itself, Great Britain obtained concessions for the development of oil in southwestern Iran. Another important field was developed in northeastern Iraq. But Ibn Saud, King of Saudi Arabia, preferred Americans to British and gave the concessions for the development of the oil fields in his country to an

American corporation. In 1943 our Navy Department and our Interior Department became seriously concerned about the exhaustion of oil fields in the United States. Their experts estimated that all our oil reserves would be completely exhausted in less than twenty years. Our economic life is so dependent on cheap oil and gasoline that President Roosevelt, after a careful study of the question, decided that the people of the United States had a vital interest in the preservation of American interests in the oil of Saudi Arabia. He set up the Petroleum Reserves Corporation, with Secretary Ickes of the Interior Department as President, and instructed the Secretary to devise ways and means to insure the interests of the United States in the oil reserves of Saudi Arabia. The President was warned that this meant an extension of American Government interest to an area remote from the United States; but he decided that the exhaustion of our oil reserves was so grave a threat to American economy in peace and war that our Government must take an active interest in the security of these American oil concessions in the Near East. Secretary Ickes on September 24, 1945, in London signed an agreement with the British Government covering the development and utilization of the oil of the Near East which is now before the Senate for ratification. Thus for the first time the Government of the United States asserted its direct interest in the security of the Near East.

The security of the Near East is today threatened by

the Soviet Union. Indeed, the Soviet Government has already begun its thrust against this oil-filled bastion of the British route to India. Northwestern Iran has already been detached from control of the Iranian Government and placed in the hands of Soviet agents. And the Iranian Government has appealed for protection to the United Nations. The sovereignty and integrity of Iran was formally guaranteed by the Soviet Union and Great Britain in January 1942 by an agreement which contained the additional promise that both Great Powers would withdraw their armed forces from Iran within six months after the end of World War II. And at the Teheran Conference, on December 1, 1943, Premier Stalin, Prime Minister Churchill and President Roosevelt all pledged their countries to the maintenance of the territorial integrity of Iran in the following words: "The governments of the United States, the U.S.S.R. and the United Kingdom are at one with the Government of Iran in their desire for the maintenance of the independence, sovereignty and territorial integrity of Iran."

The Soviet Government broke these agreements as soon as it became convenient to do so. The armed forces of the Soviet Government were not withdrawn from Iran by March 2, 1946, as promised. Behind the lines of the Red Army in northwestern Iran a Communist-controlled movement was organized, led by Iranians trained in Moscow. Arms were given to all who were ready to become Soviet agents. This movement was camouflaged under the name "Democratic Party" and a revolt "spontaneously" broke out in northwestern Iran. The Iranian Government sent troops to suppress the revolt. The Red Army with tanks and guns prevented the Iranian troops from entering northwestern Iran, and a local government under Soviet control was set up in the area.

On January 19, 1946, the Iranian Government appealed to the United Nations. After a tense meeting of the Security Council of the U.N. in New York—marked by strong support of the Iranian position by Secretary Byrnes, and by a spectacular gesture on the part of the Soviet delegate, Ambassador Gromyko, who walked out of the Security Council meeting of March 27—an agreement was reached in Teheran between the Soviet and Iranian Governments. By that agreement the Soviet Government obtained the right to establish a joint Soviet-Iranian oil company to exploit the oil resources not only of northwestern Iran but also northern and northeastern Iran—the Soviet Government to hold a majority of the shares of the company. On its part, the Soviet Government promised to withdraw its troops from Iran within six weeks after March 24, which promise supplemented its unfulfilled pledge to withdraw its troops on March 2. The fact that the Soviet Government changed its tactics in Iran does not indicate that it has abandoned its aim to control Iran. It does show that, when faced by American opposition, the Soviet Government will not dare to persist in overt and blatant aggressions; but will use subtler tactics, which, in their turn, will have to be countered.

The fate of the northwestern portion of Iran, called Azerbaijan, remains undetermined. It is still controlled by a Soviet puppet government, whose forces have been armed by the Soviet Union and contain a large proportion of Soviet agents. The Soviet Government may try to use northwestern Iran as a base from which to conquer all Iran politically. Stalin can, if he wishes, send a solid block of Soviet-controlled deputies from northwestern Iran to the Iranian Parliament; Soviet agents have formed Communist cells in all Iran; many Iranian politicians are weak in character; and the Red Army will remain on the Iranian frontier ready for action. It is not, therefore, improbable that Stalin may be able to gain control of the Iranian Government by methods less crude than seizure of the country by the Red Army. At the southeastern frontier of Iran lies India. In southwestern Iran lie the Anglo-Iranian oil fields and the huge British refinery at Abadan. The southern ports of Iran lie on the Persian Gulf, which is a finger of the Indian Ocean. If the Soviet Union should bring the whole of Iran under her political control, she would be in position to strike a mortal blow at the British Empire.

In spite of the emphasis on oil in the Soviet Government's latest agreement with the Iranian Government, Soviet interest in the Near East is not primarily an interest in oil. The Soviet Union already has within her boundaries the world's greatest oil reserves. The Soviet

Encyclopedia, an official publication of the Soviet Government, in 1939 stated: "As far as oil reserves are concerned the Soviet Union occupies the first place, possessing 67.2 percent of the world's reserves." In addition the Soviet Government has now acquired the vast reserves of northern Iran. No urgent need for oil drives the Soviet Union. The Soviet Government's primary interest in the Near East is an interest in political control—an interest in the acquisition of another springboard from which to leap further. Soviet interest in the Near East, therefore, differs greatly from American and British interest. American interest in Saudi Arabia has nothing to do with political control; it is purely an interest in oil, and the only special political interest we have in Saudi Arabia is in the maintenance of sufficient peace and security to permit the orderly extraction of oil. Great Britain's interest in the Near East is double: an interest like our own in the maintenance of sufficient peace and security to permit the orderly extraction of oil and an interest in maintaining the independence of the states of the Near East in order to prevent the Soviet Union from acquiring bases for attack on her route to India.

The Soviet establishment of a puppet government in northwestern Iran threatens not only Iran but also Iraq and Turkey. Through this puppet government the Soviet Government now controls the portion of Iran which lies just across the border from the rich oil fields of Iraq. These fields produce approximately a fifth of the present output of Near Eastern oil. They are controlled by the Iraq Petroleum Company in which British, French and American interests participate—the Americans receiving 23.75 percent of the oil produced. Northwestern Iran is, therefore, close to the producing oil fields of both Iraq and Iran. Since British forces in the area at the moment are weak in comparison with Soviet forces, the Red Army is in position to overrun rapidly the oil fields of Iraq as well as Iran, and to begin the conquest of the Arab world. Any such aggression by the Red Army would, of course, be resisted by the small British forces in the area and World War III would begin.

The installation of a Soviet puppet government in northwestern Iran doubles the length of the eastern frontier that Turkey will have to defend in case of Soviet attack. Soviet threats against Turkey are at the moment secondary to Soviet action in Iran, but Soviet imperialism is no less dangerous to Turkey than to Iran, and the vital interests of the British Empire are no less engaged in the fate of Turkey than in the fate of Iran.

Russian attacks on Turkey are no new thing. The Russians by war took from the Turkish Sultans the Crimea, the Southern Ukraine, Bessarabia and the Caucasus. And among the wars caused by Russian pressure on the Turks are those of 1711, 1769–84, 1809, 1828, the Crimean War 1855–56, and the war of 1877–78. The ultimate goal of Russian aggression against Turkey has always been the possession of Constantinople and the adjacent waters which connect the Black Sea with the Mediterranean—the Bosphorus, the Sea of Marmora and the Dardanelles. Under the rule of the Tsars this aim was often sanctified by calling it a duty to drive the Moslems from the city of Constantine and to raise the Cross once more on St. Sophia. Under the Anti-Christian Communists it is explained by the formula "Russia needs a warm water port." The religious argument of the Tsars was less of a hoax than the physical argument of the Communists. Odessa, the great port of the Soviet Union on the Black Sea, a city of more than 600,000 inhabitants, is a warm water port. Ice, easily broken by small ice breakers, forms on the sea at Odessa only two or three weeks on average each winter. The port is never closed to navigation. In addition, the Soviet Union has now annexed the great East Prussian port of Koenigsberg on the Baltic. And the plea that "Russia needs a warm water port" is mere bait to hook the sympathies of persons who do not know the facts of Soviet geography.

No less specious is the argument that the Soviet Union must control the Turkish straits in order to insure her access to the open oceans. The Soviet Union already has direct access to the Atlantic by way of the great Arctic port of Murmansk, through which, winter and summer, she received such an enormous proportion of our lend-lease supplies during the Second World War. And on the Pacific, the Soviet Union already has not only the great port of Vladivostok which is kept open all winter by ice breakers, but also, through the secret agreement signed in Yalta on February 11, 1945, by Roosevelt, Churchill and Stalin, acquired the large Chinese naval base of Port Arthur and "preeminent interests" in the Chinese commercial port of Dairen, both of which are open all year.

Moreover, control of the Turkish straits would in no way give the Soviet Union "access to the open oceans." Soviet ships leaving Odessa for the Atlantic and the Pacific must, to be sure, pass through the Bosphorus and the Dardanelles, but they must also pass through either the Dodecanese Islands or the Cyclades, which are populated by Greeks. Then, if bound to the Pacific, they must pass through the Suez Canal and the Red Sea and the Indian Ocean, and either the Straits of Malacca or the Torres Strait, north of Australia. If bound for the Atlantic they must pass Malta, Bizerte and Gibraltar. Thus Stalin cannot control the exits from Odessa to the Atlantic or the Pacific without conquering vast areas in addition to Turkey, and it is clear that his threats to Turkey are not based on any question of a warm water port, which he already has at Odessa, or of access to the open oceans, but on his determination to control the Near East in order to break the back of the British Empire.

Under the terms of the present Straits Convention, signed at Montreux on July 30, 1936, Soviet merchant vessels from Odessa and the other Russian Black Sea ports pass freely through the Bosphorus, the Sea of

Marmora and the Dardanelles to the Mediterranean, in time of peace and in time of war. These straits split Turkey into two unequal parts, as New York State is split by the Hudson River. The Turks have fortifications on the Bosphorus and the Dardanelles, and while foreign warships are permitted to pass through the straits in time of peace, belligerent foreign warships are not permitted to pass through the straits in time of war. This is an elementary national precaution, as Constantinople lies at the point where the Bosphorus empties into the Sea of Marmora, as New York lies at the point where the Hudson empties into the Atlantic; and the Turks can no more risk having foreign naval battles at Constantinople than we could risk having foreign naval battles in the harbor of New York. Moreover, they cannot risk bombardment and seizure of Constantinople by passing armadas. There is no restriction whatsoever on the passage of Soviet shipping through the straits except the restriction that the Soviet Black Sea fleet cannot in time of war use them, if the Soviet Union is a belligerent. This restriction also applies to the warships of all other nations, so that the fleets of enemies of the Soviet Union in time of war cannot use the straits to get into the Black Sea and attack the Soviet Black Sea fleet or ports.

The possession of Constantinople and the straits would give the Soviet Union access to the Eastern Mediterranean for its Black Sea Fleet in time of war, and would afford a superb base for airplane attack on shipping in the Eastern Mediterranean; and the British line of communication to India, through the Mediterranean and the Suez Canal, would be most gravely menaced. The British, on October 19, 1939, signed a treaty of alliance with Turkey which obliges them to go to war on the side of Turkey if Turkey is attacked by any European power, including the Soviet Union. And it is difficult to believe that, if the Soviet Union should attack Turkey, Great Britain would dishonor her signature and sacrifice not only Turkey, but also her own interests in the Mediterranean route to India. The Turks, who are among the most courageous and honorable of peoples, would certainly resist Soviet aggression with such arms as they possess. A Soviet attack on Turkey would, therefore, almost certainly produce World War III.

The peoples of the Soviet Union have no vital interest in seizing Turkey. Nor have they the slightest vital interest in two other areas now being claimed by the Soviet Government. Stalin has demanded control under trusteeship of Tripolitania, the Italian colony in North Africa, and a base in Eritrea, the Italian colony at the lower end of the Red Sea. The Soviet Government knows as well as every other Government that it can not achieve these demands except by victory in war. A Soviet base in Eritrea would cut the British line of communications through the Suez Canal and the Red Sea to the Indian Ocean. And Soviet control of Tripolitania would not only threaten British communications through the Mediterranean but also the security of Egypt and the whole of French North Africa.

Another port that attracts the Soviet Union is Salonika in Northeastern Greece. It would be economically unprofitable for the Soviet Union to use this port instead of Odessa. But it would make an excellent base for Soviet sea and air attack on British communications through the Mediterranean. At the present time the Soviet Union, through satellite governments, controls Rumania, Bulgaria, Yugoslavia and Albania. But it is not easy to make Balkan mountaineers accept Communist dictation, and the Soviet Government does not dare put into effect at once its full Communist program. It is, however, striving to consolidate Yugoslavia, Albania and Bulgaria in a single federal state— a state which would have as one of its objectives the seizure of Salonika from Greece. A successful attack by such a South Slav satellite state on Greece would give the Soviet Union any rights or controls in Salonika it might wish to have. And, since the Soviet Union, like all other permanent members of the Security Council of the United Nations, has an absolute veto on any action by the U.N., the U.N. would be unable to act to protect Greece. Once again the burden of protecting a small country menaced by Communist imperialism would fall on Great Britain.

Today the British are backing the resistance of Greece, Turkey, Iraq and Iran to the advance of Soviet imperialism. The Soviet Union is thrusting daily against this resistance. Yet in this entire area the Soviet Union has no vital interest engaged. And it is difficult to escape the conclusion that the acts and threats of the Soviet Union are based on a decision that the next step toward the conquest of the world for Communism should be the demolition of the British bastion in the Near East and the cutting of the British life line to the Indian Ocean.

Afghanistan, which lies to the east of Iran, between the Soviet Union and India, is not at the moment being threatened by the Soviet Union. And at no other point in Asia does the Soviet Union approach closely areas of vital British interest. British interests in China are largely in the Hongkong-Canton area and the Shanghai area, and before reaching those areas Soviet forces would find themselves colliding with interests of the United States.

Peace is essential to Great Britain for the rebuilding of the war-shattered fabric of her international trade. Without rebuilding that trade she cannot, in the long run, live. In a sense, therefore, peace is the greatest of British interests. But abandonment of her vital interests in the Near East and Europe would produce for her a swifter death than the slow strangulation of her trade. She is obliged to oppose all Soviet attempts to drive her from the Near East and to control Western Europe. At no point do vital Soviet interests compel the Soviet

Government to attack vital British interests. But the Communist Creed does require such an attack—unless it seems too dangerous.

We Americans also have vital interests, although we usually feel so secure that we forget they exist. They may be summarized in three simple doctrines: 1. The Monroe Doctrine: that any attempt by a European power (or Asiatic) to extend its political system to the American Hemisphere would be dangerous to the peace and safety of the United States. 2. The Atlantic Doctrine: that control of the Atlantic coasts of Europe and Africa and the islands of the Atlantic, and the water gates to the Atlantic—the North Sea, the English Channel and the Straits of Gibraltar—by any power which might become hostile to the United States would be dangerous to the peace and safety of the United States. 3. The "Open Door" Doctrine: that an attempt by any power to destroy the independence of China and control the future development and actions of China, would be a threat to the peace and safety of the United States.

These are the primary vital interests of the United States in defense of which, reluctantly, we have been ready to go to war in the past and for which we shall, presumably, be ready to go to war in the future. We have many other important interests, like our interest in the security of the American oil concessions in Saudi Arabia, which we may be ready to defend by war or may not, depending on circumstances; but none of these interests is comparable in importance to our vital interest in the Western Hemisphere, in Western Europe, Western Africa, and the islands of the Atlantic, and in China.

The chief motive that lay behind the enunciation of the Monroe Doctrine was the fear that the United States and our system of democratic government would be endangered if the reactionary great powers of Europe, leagued in the Holy Alliance and devoted to the divine right of kings, should increase their influence in the Western Hemisphere by colonization, war or intrigue.

In 1821 Tsar Alexander I, originator of the Holy Alliance, issued a ukase prohibiting Americans, and citizens of all other nations except Russia, from navigating or fishing within 100 Italian miles of the Pacific coast of North America, from the Bering Strait to the 51st parallel of north latitude. American protests were fruitless. Then the Tsar and his fellow autocrats of the Holy Alliance, seeking "to put an end to the system of representative government," began to consider the desirability of extinguishing the young democracies newly founded in the former Spanish colonies in the Americas.

Thereupon President Monroe, on December 2, 1823, stated the doctrine which bears his name. The essential passages of his message are the following:

. . . The American continents, by the free and independent condition which they have assumed and maintained, are henceforth not to be considered as subjects for future colonization by any European powers . . . The political system of the allied powers is essentially different from that of America. This difference proceeds from that which exists in their respective governments. And to the defense of our own, which has been achieved by the loss of so much blood and treasure, and maintained by the wisdom of their most enlightened citizens, and under which we have enjoyed unexampled felicity, this whole nation is devoted.

We owe it, therefore, to candor and to the amicable relations existing between the United States and those powers, to declare that we should consider any attempt on their part to extend their system to any portion of this hemisphere as dangerous to our peace and safety. With the existing colonies or dependencies of any European power we have not interfered and shall not interfere. But with the governments who have declared their independence, and maintained it, and whose independence we have, on great consideration and on just principles, acknowledged, we could not view any interposition for the purpose of oppressing them, or controlling in any other manner their destiny, by any European power, in any other light than as the manifestation of an unfriendly disposition toward the United States. . . .

It is impossible that the allied powers should extend their political system to any portion of either continent (North and South America) without endangering our peace and happiness; nor can anyone believe that our Southern brethren, if left to themselves, would adopt it of their own accord. It is equally impossible, therefore, that we should behold such interposition, in any form, with indifference.

In antique language, this message of President Monroe contains modern ideas which apply to the present world situation. The Soviet Government desires to extend its political system to the Americas, and has agents working to that end in every country of North and South America. The Soviet Government is far more powerful and ruthless than the government of the Tsar Alexander I, and it is building up its own unholy alliance of Communist states in Europe and Asia, dedicated to the divine right of Communist dictators, which is as hostile to democracy as the Tsar's Holy Alliance, and far more dangerous. It is by no means certain that the Monroe Doctrine, which was invented to counter the projects of one Russian autocrat in the nineteenth century, may not have to be used to counter the projects of another in the twentieth. No vital interest whatsoever compels the Soviet Union to try to extend its political system to the Americas. The Communist Creed does.

Our Atlantic Doctrine is to be found not in a single document, but in scores of declarations and hundreds of actions of the American Government during the First and Second World Wars. President Roosevelt, for example, in his radio address to the nation on National Security—delivered on December 29, 1940, when we were neutral and the Soviet Union was Germany's associate, and only Great Britain, Greece and China were fighting against the Axis—said:

. . . Never before since Jamestown and Plymouth Rock has our American civilization been in such danger as now . . . The Nazi masters of Germany have made it clear that they intend not only to dominate all life and thought in their own country, but also to enslave the whole of Europe, and then to use the resources of Europe to dominate the rest of the world . . . At this moment, the forces of the states that are leagued against all peoples who live in freedom are being held away from our shores. The Germans and the Italians are being blocked on the other side of the Atlantic by the British, and by the Greeks, and by thousands of soldiers and sailors who were able to escape from subjugated countries. In Asia, the Japanese are being engaged by the Chinese nation in another great defense. . . .

Some of our people like to believe that wars in Europe and in Asia are of no concern to us. But it is a matter of most vital concern to us that European and Asiatic warmakers should not gain control of the oceans which lead to this hemisphere. One hundred and seventeen years ago the Monroe Doctrine was conceived by our Government as a measure of defense in the face of a threat against this hemisphere by an alliance in Continental Europe. Thereafter, we stood on guard in the Atlantic, with the British as neighbors. There was no treaty. There was no "unwritten agreement." And yet, there was the feeling, proven correct by history, that we as neighbors could settle any dispute in peaceful fashion. The fact is that during the whole of this time the Western Hemisphere has remained free from aggression from Europe or from Asia. Does anyone seriously believe that we need to fear attack anywhere in the Americas while a free Britain remains our most powerful naval neighbor in the Atlantic? Does anyone seriously believe, on the other hand, that we could rest easy if the Axis powers were our neighbors there? If Great Britain goes down, the Axis powers will control the continents of Europe, Asia, Africa, Australasia, and the high seas—and they will be in a position to bring enormous military and naval resources against this hemisphere. It is no exaggeration to say that all of us, in all the Americas, would be living at the point of a gun—a gun loaded with explosive bullets, economic as well as military. We should enter upon a new and terrible era in which the whole world, our hemisphere included, would be run by threats of brute force. To survive in such a world, we would have to convert ourselves permanently into a militaristic power on the basis of war economy. Some of us like to believe that even if Great Britain falls, we are still safe, because of the broad expanse of the Atlantic and of the Pacific. But the width of those oceans is not what it was in the days of clipper ships. At one point between Africa and Brazil the distance is less than from Washington to Denver, Colorado—five hours for the latest type of bomber. And at the North end of the Pacific Ocean America and Asia almost touch each other. Even today we have planes that could fly from the British Isles to New England and back again, without refueling. And remember that the range of the modern bomber is ever being increased. . . .

Germany has said that she was occupying Belgium to save the Belgians from the British. Would she hesitate to say to any South American country, "We are occupying you to protect you from aggression by the United States"? Belgium today is being used as an invasion base against Britain, now fighting for its life. Any South American country, in Nazi hands, would always constitute a jumping-off place for German attack on any one of the other Republics of this hemisphere. Analyze for yourselves the future of two other places even nearer to Germany if the Nazis won. Could Ireland hold out? Would Irish freedom be permitted as an amazing pet exception in an unfree world? Or the Islands of the Azores which still fly the flag of Portugal after five centuries? You and I think of Hawaii as an outpost of defense in the Pacific. And yet, the Azores are closer to our shores in the Atlantic than Hawaii is on the other side. There are those who say that the axis powers would never have any desire to attack the Western Hemisphere. That is the same dangerous form of wishful thinking which has destroyed the powers of resistance of so many conquered peoples. . . .

Democracy's fight against world conquest is being greatly aided, and must be more greatly aided, by the re-armament of the United States and by sending every ounce and every ton of munitions that we can possibly spare to help the defenders who are in the front lines. It is no more unneutral for us to do that than it is for Sweden, Russia and other nations near Germany, to send steel and ore and oil and other war materials into Germany every day of the week . . . We must be the great arsenal of de-mocracy.

In the introduction which he wrote for the 1940 volume of his Public Papers and Addresses, President Roosevelt defined still further his conception of the Atlantic Doctrine:

. . . We have learned how narrow the oceans which separate us from the wars abroad have become. The speed of modern bombers and their ability to fly untold distances without refueling, have brought home to us how near the coasts of Africa, and the Cape Verde Islands, and the Azores are to our own shores. . . .

Modern warfare has given us a new definition for that word "attack." There was a time when we could afford to

say that we would not fight unless attacked, and then wait
until the physical attack came upon us before starting to
shoot. Modern techniques of warfare have changed all that.
An attack today is a very different thing. An attack today
begins as soon as any base has been occupied from which
our security is threatened. That base may be thousands
of miles away from our own shores. The American Government must, of necessity, decide at which point any threat
of attack against this hemisphere has begun; and to make
their stand when that point has been reached.

President Roosevelt never defined publicly the points
in Europe occupation of which by a power that might
attack the Western Hemisphere would compel the
United States "to make their stand." He was deeply
conscious that improvements in all forms of airborne
weapons might make it desirable to place those points
further and further away from our coasts. He, therefore, never stated the Atlantic Doctrine in public in a
brief formula; but often in private conversation he
stated it in the simple terms that the United States
could not afford to permit any nation, which might in
future attack either North or South America, to control
the west coasts of Europe and Africa, or the waterways
to the Atlantic or the islands of the Atlantic. That, in
essence, is today our Atlantic Doctrine. It applies with
equal force to any nation that we have reason to believe
may become hostile to us. We applied it to Germany in
the First and Second World Wars. And unless we have
lost all sense of self preservation, we shall apply it with
equal impartiality to the Soviet Union, if that totalitar-

ian state should attempt to extend its conquests to Western Europe.

President Wilson was never obliged to face the issue of our Atlantic security as bluntly as was President Roosevelt. From the time the French Army defeated the German Army at the battle of the Marne in September 1914, until we entered the First World War in April 1917, the complete defeat of the French and British armies in France never seemed probable. But there was not the slightest doubt in President Wilson's mind as to the effect on the United States of a German victory. As early as August 30, 1914, President Wilson said to Colonel House that "if Germany won it would change the course of our civilization and make the United States a military nation." In consequence, he interpreted our rights and duties as a neutral in a manner favorable to the Allies. Great Britain and France floated large loans in the United States, and the United States became in some measure "the arsenal of democracy." Moreover, President Wilson insisted on the right of American merchant ships to travel unmolested through the war zone. And it was the sinking without warning of American merchantmen in the war zone that led the Congress to declare on April 6, 1917, that a state of war existed between ourselves and Germany.

Both President Wilson and President Roosevelt hoped that a policy of neutrality favorable to Great Britain and France would enable the United States to avoid actual fighting. There is no truth whatsoever in the Nazi propaganda story that in 1939 President Roosevelt promised England or France or Poland or any other nation to bring the United States into the war. President Roosevelt, like President Wilson, hoped that, by supplying the nations that were defending themselves against Germany, the United States could remain both neutral and safe. But such was the strength of Germany that both Presidents felt obliged to go further and further in order to prevent German victory.

In June, 1940, from the stocks of the American Army, President Roosevelt sold Great Britain for $43,000,000 equipment which had been purchased at the close of World War I, at a cost of $300,000,000.[3] This equipment consisted of 895 pieces of 75 millimetre field artillery; 1,115,000 rifles; 85,000 machine guns, together with millions of rounds of ammunition, and some newly produced aircraft. In September 1940, the President gave Great Britain 50 destroyers, in exchange for the lease of bases in the Caribbean area. And after the passage of the Lend-Lease Act on March 11, 1941, the President gave the British, and later the Russians, everything they needed that we could produce—although we were "neutral." And on October 8, 1941, although we were still "neutral" the President ordered units of our Atlantic fleet to engage in convoy duty in

---

[3] *The Public Papers and Addresses of Franklin D. Roosevelt,* 1940, p. 673.

the Atlantic, and to destroy any German or Italian sea or air forces encountered. And they did.[4]

In both World Wars our attempt to remain both neutral and safe failed. In both we preferred our safety to our neutrality. Slowly we recognized that our safety depended on our preventing the conquest of the friendly democracies of Great Britain and France, which, by controlling the west coasts of Europe and the exits to the Atlantic, protected us. Our instinct of self preservation gradually broke through the crust of our desire to live in peace and ease. And, however great our desire for peace may seem to be, our instinct of self preservation, in the future as in the past, will in the long run compel us to act in accordance with President Roosevelt's statement: "An attack today begins as soon as any base has been occupied from which our security is threatened. That base may be thousands of miles away from our shores. The American Government must, of necessity, decide at which point any threat of attack against this hemisphere has begun; and to make their stand when that point has been reached." [5]

Our "Open Door" Doctrine with regard to China was expressed on July 3, 1900, by the Secretary of State, John Hay, in the following words:

The policy of the Government of the United States is to seek a solution which may bring about permanent safety

---

[4] *Testimony of Admiral Harold R. Stark,* Pearl Harbor Investigation, January 3, 1946.

[5] *The Public Papers and Addresses of Franklin D. Roosevelt,* 1940, p. XXXI.

and peace to China, preserve Chinese territorial and administrative entity, protect all rights guaranteed to friendly powers.

The objectives of the United States in adopting this doctrine were twofold: 1. To prevent the closing of China to our foreign trade. 2. To prevent the domination of China by any foreign power which might eventually mobilize the man power of China for war against us.

Only two great powers have threatened to dominate China—Japan and Russia—and the United States has opposed whichever of these powers was momentarily the stronger aggressor.

At the time of the Boxer Rebellion in 1900, Russia sent large bodies of troops into Manchuria, savagely suppressed Chinese opposition, took control of the area, and extorted from the Chinese Government an agreement promising her control of Southern Manchuria. Under pressure from the United States, Japan and Great Britain, Russia consented to modify this agreement and to withdraw her troops gradually from Manchuria. Russia, however, found excuses for delaying the withdrawal of her troops, and demanded from China compensations which would have strengthened her hold on Manchuria. Japan, backed by Great Britain and the United States, tried to get Russia to carry out the promised evacuation of her troops. When Russia delayed, Japan went to war in February, 1904. After the Japanese Army and Navy had inflicted sensational defeats on the

Russian Army and Navy, President Theodore Roosevelt offered his good offices to arrange an armistice. And peace between Russia and Japan was signed at Portsmouth, New Hampshire, on September 5, 1905. But the result of the war—in spite of the treaty of November 1908 between Japan and the United States, in which the "independence and integrity of China" was promised—was the substitution of Japan for Russia in Southern Manchuria. Thenceforth, until the Japanese attack on Pearl Harbor, December 7, 1941, the Government of the United States attempted to prevent, by methods short of war, Japanese dismemberment and domination of China.

The present situation in Manchuria, which is now the richest province in China and contains approximately seventy percent of her industries, resembles in many respects the situation after the Boxer Rebellion. The Soviet Union has promised to withdraw her troops from Manchuria and to restore the province to China. But such Soviet troops as have been withdrawn, have been replaced by Soviet-armed units of the Chinese Red Army. It was Japan, backed by the friendly neutrality of Great Britain and the United States, which drove the Russians from Manchuria in 1904. At the present time only the United States has the physical power to force the Russians to withdraw. And the Soviet Union has a Chinese satellite Communist government in North China. When President Roosevelt secretly at the Yalta Conference, gave the Kurile Islands and control of the Chinese ports of Dairen and Port Arthur to Stalin, and undertook to make Generalissimo Chiang Kai-shek accept this sacrifice, the plea of the American Government to the Chinese Government was that Soviet demands for further control of Manchuria would be eliminated. The event has proved that in this case, as in so many others, President Roosevelt was deceived by Stalin. The Soviet Government is doing its utmost to ensure its permanent control of Manchuria. There is no longer any balance of power in the Far East between the Soviet Union and Japan. And unless the United States is ready to back the Chinese Government, headed by Chiang Kai-shek, with force, the dismemberment and domination of China by the Soviet Union, using the Chinese Communists as agents, is to be expected.

We fought World War II to prevent the domination of China by Japan, and to prevent the domination of Europe by Germany. We now face the possibility that the result of our sacrifices and victory in World War II will be the domination of China by the Soviet Union and the domination of Europe by the Soviet Union. The vital interests expressed in both our Open Door Doctrine and our Atlantic Doctrine are threatened by Soviet Imperialism. For this strange and bitter fruit of victory the people of the United States have to thank those who based American foreign policy on appeasement of Stalin.

IV

"The United States at this minute stand at the summit of the world. I rejoice that this is so. Let them act up to the level of their power and responsibility—not for themselves but for all men in all lands—and then a brighter day may dawn on human history."

WINSTON CHURCHILL: August 16, 1945.

"The American people have a genius for splendid and unselfish action, and into the hands of America God has placed the destinies of afflicted humanity."

POPE PIUS XII: *Christmas*, 1945.

"We shall nobly save or meanly lose the last, best hope of earth."

ABRAHAM LINCOLN: Dec. 1, 1862.

PRESIDENT TRUMAN inherited an American foreign policy in bankruptcy. President Roosevelt had gambled on his ability to convert Stalin from the aim of imposing Communist dictatorship throughout the earth to the aim of establishing a world collaboration of independent states. He had lost his gamble. Stalin had remained unconverted and was striving to dominate vast portions of Europe and Asia as springboards from which to leap further. Moreover, the foundation of the United Nations had been laid on the gamble that the Soviet Union, Great Britain, China, France and the United States could be trusted not to attempt to extend their control over independent peoples, and, in consequence, deserved an absolute veto on any action by the United Nations. The U.N. as finally organized in San Francisco was powerless to act against an aggressor among the Big Five or an aggressor supported by any one of the Big Five: a bandit Great Power could veto all action by the police. Insofar as the U.N. was concerned, the Soviet Union would be free not only to subject permanently the once independent peoples over whom it had established control in Europe but also to grasp new areas— and its fingers obviously were itching for Iran, Turkey and Manchuria.

By the autumn of 1945 it was clear, except to those who did not wish to see, that the Soviet Union had replaced Germany as the embodiment of totalitarian imperialism, and that the foreign policy of the United States had been based on wishful thinking. The American people's dream of world peace turned into a nightmare of atomic bombs. President Truman faced a time for greatness.

Power was in the hands of the people of the United States such as no people had ever held before. Our air force was incomparably superior to any other; our navy was larger than the combined navies of the rest of the world; our army was a superb fighting force at the peak of its efficiency; our industrial plant, by far the greatest in the world, was intact—and we alone had the atomic bomb which guaranteed the speedy destruction of any nation that might dare to risk conflict with us. We had wasted the political opportunities which were ours when our allies were dependent on us for their lives; but power was in our hands to enforce our will. We wanted peace and we could have used our power to move toward peace. We did not know how to use it. The most eminent men in the world turned to us for wise leadership. But we stood like the most powerful creature that ever lived, the carnivorous dinosaur Tyrannosaurus Rex, who had a body the size of a locomotive, teeth a foot long—and a brain the size of a banana. He perished from the earth. We too shall perish from the earth if we can not understand our present predicament and act in accordance with our own vital interests, which are the vital interests of all humanity—the Russian people included—since they are the interests of freedom and peace.

Let us try to understand, knowing well the limitations of human intelligence, the present situation of mankind on this planet; then attempt to formulate some policies worthy of the statement: "into the hands of America God has placed the destinies of afflicted humanity."

Let us begin by remembering some elementary facts that, in the welter of daily events, we are apt to forget:

First: Civilized life accrues from long-established customs which help men to survive and to live in ordered freedom. The rise of humanity from primitive savagery to civilization has depended on the gradual accumulation of a vast mass of custom which surrounds each infant like the air he breathes. He does not have to discover for himself all the human race has learned through a hundred centuries of painful trial and error. He accepts unconsciously the customs into which he is born. Those customs spring from the struggle for existence. The primary task of life is to live, and whether life exists in the form of a unicellular organism like the amoeba or in the form of man, it exists under the pressure of immediate needs which must be satisfied—like the need for food. Need unsatisfied brings pain, pain produces action to satisfy the need. If such action fails, another action is tried. If it succeeds, it is repeated; and eventually produces habit in the individual and custom in the group. The hunger, fear, hatred, vanity and love that well within all men are channeled by long-established customs into forms of expression that have a survival value for the individual and the group to which he belongs.

Human life is very largely controlled by such customs, and when a form of behavior has become a long-established custom it is not lightly abandoned. As Cicero wrote, "custom produces a kind of second nature." Cannibalism, for example, is banned by long-established custom, and men revert to cannibalism only under extreme and unusual provocation. On the other hand, new modes of conduct which have not had time to become long-established customs are discarded lightly. For example, the custom of sparing noncombatants in time of war which became widely prevalent in Europe in the eighteenth and nineteenth centuries was discarded in the twentieth century. All belligerents in the Second World War bombed noncombatants.

Second: One of the long-established customs that have helped men to survive has been the custom of excluding murder as a method of deciding disputes within a family. Before the dawn of history, the family became a peace group. Gradually the tribe and finally the nation became a peace group. But the youth, and comparative instability, of the custom of treating the whole nation as a peace group is indicated by the frequency of civil wars.

Never in history has it become custom for all nations to treat one another as a single peace group. Many philosophers have dreamed of world peace, and some statesmen have striven to achieve it, but none has succeeded. The closest approach to world peace was attained by the Romans, who nearly two thousand years ago established and maintained peace within their vast Empire for two centuries. The custom of treating all nations within the Roman Empire as a single peace group became well established, and the Empire contained all there was of western civilization at the time. But the Roman Empire included only a small portion of the whole world, and it was destroyed by the invasions of barbarians sweeping westward over the Asiatic-European plains. The Roman peace was peace within western civilization, not world peace.

Shared customs as well as force held the Roman Empire together. And to hold together in a peace group states which share the same basic customs is less difficult than to preserve peace between states whose basic customs differ. In spite of all other customs shared by the southern states and the northern states of the United States, war between them was produced by the single unshared basic custom of human slavery. Conversely, one reason why our relations with Canada are so brotherly is the fact that we share so many customs.

Since the year 180 A.D. statesmen have never even been able to persuade the nations within the community of western civilization to treat one another as members of a single peace group. And until it becomes world-wide custom for all nations to treat one another as a single peace group, and until that custom has been long established, we shall have no reason to believe that wars between nations have been banished permanently from the earth.

Third: Changes for the better in long-established customs usually are produced by great religious leaders or statesmen of extraordinary wisdom and character. The ethical teachings of religion have done far more than any other influence to lift men from savagery to civilization. Moses, Buddha, Confucius and Mahomet, each in his own way and on his own level, led men toward the light. And in the teachings of Christ the light itself was present. All nations that have achieved a civilization worthy of the name have been influenced profoundly by some equivalent of the Ten Commandments and the Sermon on the Mount. Without certain elementary qualities of human character no civilization is possible, without certain rarer qualities no high civilization can exist. Honesty, respect for the pledged word, courage both physical and moral, kindness, courtesy, a devotion to truth, justice and beauty, and a lively sense of the fatherhood of God and the brotherhood of man, mark the civilized man at his best. And the level of a country's civilization is determined by the degree to which these qualities are fostered by its long-established customs, and compose the atmosphere in which its children are raised.

Fourth: Our own civilization, like the civilization of Western Europe and the British Isles and Dominions, is derived from three main sources: the customs of the Athenian democracy which flourished during the fifth century before Christ; the customs of the Roman Empire; and the teachings of Christ. We are a part of western civilization, and such specifically American behavior patterns as we have developed are the consequence of the impact of frontier life on immigrants from the British Isles and Europe, the leadership of our great statesmen Washington, Jefferson and Lincoln, and the influence of the Christian Churches.

In the sixth and fifth centuries before Christ, the Greeks developed for the first time in history the idea that men could live together for the common good of all without a dictator king, under a democratic government chosen by the people. Their ideal was a man, fully developed in body, mind, and soul, living in freedom a life of courageous beauty. From the beginning, the young democracies of the Greek city states had to withstand both internal and external attacks. Many times they were overthrown by armed bands under a leader who installed himself as tyrant. But always the novel idea of democracy revived, and during the fifth century before Christ the Athenian democracy produced a way of life so free, so delightful and so releasing to the human spirit that one small city gave sustenance, in little more than a century, to an outburst of genius such as the world had never known before and has never known since: The dramatists Aeschylus, Sophocles, Euripides and Aristophanes; the historians Herodotus, Thucydides and Xenophon; the architects Ictinus and Callicrates; the sculptors Pheidias and Praxiteles; the painter Apelles; the philosophers Socrates, Plato, and Aristotle; the statesmen Themistocles and Pericles; and a host of others of almost equal rank.

In Herodotus we may read the beginnings of the struggle between the young European idea of democracy and the old Asiatic idea of tyranny, which in those days was represented by the great kings of Persia. That struggle has lasted twenty-five hundred years and is not yet over—indeed the world of western democracy confronts today the same menace of Asiatic tyranny that confronted the Athenians, and later, the Roman Empire.

The Roman Empire drew its structure from the

Roman Republic and Roman law, and its cultural inspiration from the art, literature, drama and democracy of Athens. Its civilization was high in quality: distinguished for tolerance, intellectual honesty, justice, common sense, cleanliness and efficiency. Men everywhere throughout the Empire were proud to be Roman citizens. They found more freedom and well-being within the ordered civilization of the Empire than they had ever found outside its borders. Thus the Empire was bound together by a high civilization as well as by Roman law and military power. And by the use of power in the service of a high civilization the Romans held together in a single peace group, from the reign of Caesar Augustus which began in 27 B.C. to the death of Marcus Aurelius in 180 A.D., the peoples who inhabited the present boundaries of Italy, France, England, Belgium, the Netherlands, Switzerland, the portion of Germany lying west of the Rhine and the Danube, the portions of Austria and Hungary lying west of the Danube, Yugoslavia, Albania, Greece, Bulgaria, Rumania (for some of the period), Turkey, Syria, the Lebanon, Palestine, Egypt, all North Africa, all the islands of the Mediterranean, Spain and Portugal. Within that vast area, peace was maintained for two centuries, while the legions, directed from Rome, stood guard on the eastern frontier of the Empire against the barbarians sweeping westward from the regions which now compose Germany, Poland, Czechoslovakia, Russia, Iraq and Iran.

The death of Marcus Aurelius in 180 A.D. was followed by a century of war and disorder. The Roman peace was never fully restored, and finally the barbarians overwhelmed the Empire. But the two centuries of the Roman peace remained in the minds of men as a lost Golden Age. Power exercised by a nation of high civilization had brought to the western world its only long period of peace, and, thereafter, the thought was never wholly absent from men's minds that a single highly civilized nation might gather about it other nations of the same cultural tradition in a great peace group.

During the two centuries of the Roman peace, the Empire began to be permeated by the teachings of Christ. But it was not until 313, when the Empire was in disorder, that the Emperor Constantine the Great accorded toleration to the Christian religion. Later he made Christianity the official religion of the Empire, and his chief claim to greatness is that he enlisted the civilizing force of Christianity in the service of the Empire.

The Athenians had taught that righteousness consisted in serving one's fellow citizens and one's country. Christ, embracing in His love all mankind, taught that the fatherhood of God and the brotherhood of man extended beyond any city or state or nation to all men everywhere, and that man could render his duty to God only by rendering his duty to men of all races. Throughout the dark ages of the barbarian invasions, the Church held together in a spiritual unity the lands which once had been given peace by the Empire. Such unity as existed in the world of western civilization was not a political unity but a unity of Christendom—a unity of moral standards and eternal hopes.

In spite of the efforts of efficient Roman Emperors like Diocletian and Constantine, the brief attempt of Charlemagne to unite some of the shattered remnants of the Empire, and the unifying influence of the Church, the western world wallowed in war for more than sixteen hundred years. Throughout those tragic centuries many good and great men strove to bring order out of the chaos into which the Roman Empire had been plunged by the barbarian invasions. The lights which guided them were three: The memory of the Roman peace, the memory of the Athenian democracy, and the living presence of Christianity.

The Church converted the barbarians and preserved the civilizing traditions of Greece and Rome as well as the teachings of Christ, and from time to time bright islands appeared in the sea of human misery. The cathedrals were built. The idea of chivalry was born: the ideal of the knight "without fear and without reproach." The Renaissance gave a new birth to the arts of Greece and Rome. The Reformation released the fettered minds of men. And the British, American and French Revolutions brought to triumphant success the old Athenian idea of democracy. But the western world failed to achieve any period of peace even faintly com-

parable to the Roman peace until after the Battle of
Waterloo in 1815.

Fifth: In the ninety-nine years between the Battle of
Waterloo and the outbreak of the First World War in
1914, there were wars between nations, revolts of subject peoples, and civil wars—including our own—but
none involved the fate of the whole of western civilization, and vast improvement in the physical conditions of
life produced the illusion that "progress" would be con-
tinuous. The relative calm of the century was largely
due to the dominance of Great Britain in world affairs.
The power of the British fleet, the strength of British
industry and the skill of British diplomacy kept wars
within relatively narrow limits. And even in war men did
not altogether abandon civilized customs or forget that
on the morrow they would have to live in peace with
their enemies of today. The major conflicts of the period
—our Civil War and the Franco-Prussian War—were
fought with a high degree of respect for the customs of
western civilization.

There was no physical unity in the western world
comparable to the unity of the Roman Empire; but
there was a unity of civilization throughout most of
Europe and America. And there was still a moral unity
in Christendom. The Emperors of Germany and Austria, like the Tsar of Russia, the Kings of England and
Italy and the Presidents of France and the United
States, called themselves Christians; and, if they did not
live up to the teachings of Christ, were at least ashamed

when they did not. Nations were inclined to respect their pledged word and felt obliged to apologize if they did not. The day after Germany invaded Belgium and Luxembourg, the German Chancellor, von Bethmann-Hollweg, speaking on August 4, 1914, before the Reichstag said: "Our troops have occupied Luxembourg and have possibly already entered on Belgian soil. Gentlemen, that is a breach of international law. . . . We were forced to ignore the rightful protests of Luxembourg and Belgium. The injustice—I speak openly— the injustice we thereby commit we will try to make good as soon as our military aims have been attained." A comparison of this statement of the German Chancellor in 1914 with the propaganda lies which accompanied the aggressions of Mussolini, Hitler and Stalin, is a measure of the degree to which international standards of shame, if not of honor, in 1914 differed from the totalitarian standards of today. Similarly, the decay of international morality since 1914 is somewhat strikingly shown by the fact that when the *Lusitania*, a British steamer carrying munitions but also noncombatant voyagers, was sunk on May 7, 1915, by a German submarine without warning and without provision being made to save the lives of the noncombatants, a wave of genuine horror and indignation at the immorality of the act swept the United States; but in the Second World War few Americans or Europeans felt that anything immoral had been done when bombs were dropped on the noncombatant inhabitants of cities.

Throughout the period from 1815 to 1914 the British, with notable exceptions, exercised their power with a sense of fair play as well as British interests. Under their leadership the industrial revolution was placing more and more of the forces of nature at man's disposal and the standard of living of all the western world rose prodigiously. The success of the democratic revolutions in America, France, Great Britain and many lesser European countries, the spread of Christianity, and the calming influence of British sea power, made it seem before 1914 that the world was moving slowly but steadily into an era of peace based on old Greek and Roman customs, ever-expanding democracy, and ever-extending respect for Christian principles.

It is difficult to recapture for those who are not old enough to have known the world before 1914 the early morning atmosphere in which men lived in that age which is separated from today by so few years but by such mountainous and disastrous events. In the century of relative peace after 1815, human slavery had been abolished. Greece, Serbia, Bulgaria and Rumania had been liberated from the rule of the Turks. The Young Turks had begun to curb the power of the Sultans. Italy had been freed from foreign domination and united; and was progressing fast under a democratic monarchy. The German people had been united, and possessed a free press and a parliament—so that they had in their hands the instruments of democracy although they had not learned how to play on them. Even the absolute power of the Tsars of Russia was being nibbled by a weak parliament called the Duma. The Emperor of China had been deposed and the Chinese Republic proclaimed. The authority of the Emperor of Japan was still in theory absolute; but there was a Japanese parliament, and the chief advisers of the Emperor were not militarists but relatively enlightened business men.

Mutual trust was so great among civilized nations that passports were not required anywhere in the world except in four backward countries: Russia, Turkey, Bulgaria and Japan. Barriers to international trade were low, and currency restrictions did not exist. Five European nations, France, Belgium, Switzerland, Italy and Greece, indeed, had made their coined monies interchangeable.

There were still many ancient wrongs to be righted. Ireland was not free. Poland was still enslaved. And everywhere social justice had lagged behind legal and political equality. Not even in the United States had we achieved fulfillment of the "promise that in due time the weights would be lifted from the shoulders of all men, and that all should have an equal chance." But the trade unions and the international socialist movement, which not only believed in socialism but also in democracy and all the liberties embodied in our Bill of Rights, were strong yeast in the dough of capitalist complacence, and the small man everywhere was beginning to get a squarer deal.

Before the First World War men did not laugh at the last words of Longfellow's last poem:

> Out of the shadows of night;
> The world rolls into light;
> It is daybreak everywhere.

They believed that.

Sixth: The advance of liberty and democracy in western civilization during the century before the war of 1914 was based on the democratic doctrine that man is an end in himself, and the state a tool of man—a means, not an end. Throughout western civilization the conviction was general that the state existed for man, not man for the state; that the value of the state was exactly the value of its services to human beings—insofar as it served to develop man it was good, if it hindered the development of man it was evil—and that, since the state was a tool of man, man was responsible for the moral behavior of the state. This conception dominated political thought in Europe and America until the foundation of totalitarian states in Russia in 1917, in Italy in 1922, and in Germany in 1933. The totalitarian doctrine of all those states was the exact reverse of the democratic doctrine with regard to man and the state. The totalitarians taught that the state was man's master, not his tool; that the value of man was exactly as great as his services to the state; insofar as he assisted the totalitarian state to develop he was good, but if he hindered the development of the totalitarian state he was evil; that man was a means to an end, not an end in himself; that the state was superior to human morality. This idolatry of the state produced not merely the suppression of personal liberty and democracy in the areas controlled by the totalitarian dictatorships of the Soviet Union, Italy and Germany but also justification for complete immorality in international relations. Idolatry of the state created as a corollary the doctrine that a state is justified in using any and every means—including its pledged word given and broken, and war—for the achievement of a political objective.

The habit of employing good faith in international relations had never become world-wide custom. But many nations of western civilization adhered to it. Indeed, one reason why the United States was so loath to sign international agreements promising future action was that Americans took their international promises seriously. Lenin, Stalin, Mussolini, and Hitler, however, rejected good faith with contempt—all of them alike considered honor a thing for fools but not for them or their states. There is no record of any totalitarian state keeping any international agreement its dictator wished to break. The record of the Soviet Union in this respect is as bad as the record of Nazi Germany. (See Appendix I.) All the totalitarian regimes habitually used their pledged word given and broken as a weapon in international affairs.

Totalitarian Italy and totalitarian Germany no longer exist. But the totalitarian dictatorship of the

Soviet Union still flourishes. And the problem of organizing world peace is complicated vastly by the fact that the pledged word of the Soviet Union has been broken so often. A minimum of good faith between nations and a minimum of human decency is necessary as the basis for any agreement between nations. As Pope Pius XII wrote at Christmas, 1945, "The indispensable element in all peaceful living among nations—the very soul of juridical relations among them—is mutual trust based on the belief that each party will respect its plighted word." The Soviet Union has proved by its actions that it does not respect its plighted word. In consequence, any treaty or other international agreement designed to secure peace between the Soviet Union on the one hand and ourselves on the other would bind us while not binding the Soviet Union. From it the Soviet Union would acquire genuine security while we would acquire only an illusion of security.

President Roosevelt knew as well as any man that the Soviet Union was a predatory totalitarian state. On February 10, 1940, after the expulsion of the Soviet Union from the League of Nations for unprovoked aggression against Finland, he stated to the Youth Congress: "I, with many of you, hoped that Russia would work out its own problems, and that its government would eventually become a peace-loving, popular government with a free ballot, which would not interfere with the integrity of its neighbors. That hope is today either shattered or put away in storage against some better day. The Soviet Union, as everybody who has the courage to face the facts knows, is run by a dictatorship as absolute as any dictatorship in the world. It has allied itself with another dictatorship, and it has invaded a neighbor so infinitesimally small that it could do no conceivable possible harm to the Soviet Union, a neighbor which seeks only to live at peace as a democracy, and a liberal, forward-looking democracy at that." [1]

The essential fact of the Second World War was that the American, British and French democracies, for their self preservation, became the allies of a Communist totalitarian state against two fascist totalitarian states. That did not alter the fact that the Soviet Union was, and is, a Communist totalitarian state, equally hostile to fascism and to democracy.

Seventh: Promises to keep the peace are not the same thing as a long-established custom of keeping the peace. In the year 1928, by the Briand-Kellogg Pact, all the great powers, and all the small, promised to renounce war forever as an instrument of national policy. In 1931 Japan invaded Manchuria. In 1935 Italy invaded Ethiopia. In 1937 Japan invaded China. In 1938 Germany invaded Austria. In 1939 Germany invaded Czechoslovakia and Poland. In 1939 the Soviet Union invaded Poland and Finland. By that time the Briand-Kellogg Pact had been violated by all the totalitarian states, and the difference between promises and

---

[1] *The Public Papers and Addresses of Franklin D. Roosevelt,* 1940. p. 93.

long-established customs had been made clear to anyone who cared to think about world problems. World peace can not be established by the writing of agreements. However cleverly they may be drawn by technical experts, they will be broken by evil men. A promise may be the beginning of a custom. It is not a custom. There is no short cut to peace by way of collecting promises that will not be kept. The problem of peace is nothing less than the problem of creating a world-wide custom of all nations treating one another as members of a single peace group.

Eighth: Customs grow from actions often repeated. A world custom of brotherly dealing between nations can grow only from long repeated actions in accord with the principle expressed in the words "do unto others as you would they should do unto you." Aggressions destroy the growth of such a custom. Aggressors kill not only such peace as may exist, but hope of future peace, since they cut the growth of the custom of brotherly dealing. Governments which seek peace by mere negative avoidance of collisions with aggressors, only increase the certainty of ultimate world war—witness the consequences of the attempt to appease Hitler at Munich. We can not even begin to create a world-wide custom of all nations treating one another as members of a single peace group until we have stopped aggressions. We can not achieve peace unless, while we respect the rights of other nations, we insist that they respect ours, and those of the least of their neighbors.

The purpose of politics in a world threatened by a Soviet Imperialism, which some day will add the atomic bomb to its armament, must be both to stop aggressions, and to raise men and nations to the level of serving their neighbors as themselves. To stop Stalin is not enough. Those who would find world peace must seek an indispensable minimum of international morality.

War is a symptom, not the cause, of the moral disease of mankind. The cause is that men have not yet learned to base their relations on the truth that each man owes an infinite duty to do unto his fellow men of all races, nations and creeds as he would have them do unto him. Man's sense of the duty of each to all increases, in so far as the political system in which he lives encourages him to carry out freely this duty. We have learned in the past twenty-five centuries what system of society increases man's sense of duty to his fellows. It is the system of democracy: the system of men governing themselves, and freely according to their neighbors the rights and privileges they claim for themselves. The test by which all political systems may be judged is the question: Do they help man freely and of his own volition to serve his neighbor as himself? Democracy does.

We Americans, and all other peoples who live in freedom and admit no master but God, can act together now with sufficient unity, will and power to oblige others to treat us as we treat them. The most necessary and legitimate use of force is to hold the field to permit the growth of moral ideas. For nations in their international lives, as for individuals in their personal lives, the way to peace is in Christ's words: "Seek ye first the kingdom of God and his righteousness, and all these things shall be added unto you."

V

"When bad men combine, the good must associate; else they will fall one by one, an unpitied sacrifice in a contemptible struggle."

EDMUND BURKE: *Speech on the Conciliation of America.*

THE ONLY totalitarian imperialism that threatens war in the world today is the Soviet Union. The United States, Great Britain, France, China, and all the less powerful nations, want peace, and have not the slightest desire to extend their control over other nations either by war or the installation of puppet governments. No vital interest of the peoples of the Soviet Union, who already hold a sixth of the land of the earth and have scarcely begun to populate it, lies behind the thrusts of the Soviet Imperialism. But the Communist Creed demands the installation throughout the earth of Communist dictatorship, and the Soviet Government uses the peoples of the Soviet Union as tools to achieve that aim. The peoples of the Soviet Union are not the masters, but the victims of the privileged and persecuting caste of orthodox Communists that directs them and their country by ukase, secret police and firing squads. The Russian people themselves are somewhat less cruelly enslaved by the Soviet Government than the Poles, Estonians, Latvians, Lithuanians and the other peoples of Europe and Asia whom they have conquered. But they have no freedom of speech, press, or assembly, nor any other of the rights embodied in the constitutions of democratic states and enforced by the courts. They are serfs driven to inflict worse slavery on others. In natural human qualities they are among the most attractive and highly endowed of the races of mankind. The "broad Russian soul" contains vast possibilities of good as well as evil. Their qualities are perverted by their dictators, who control every thought they are allowed to hear or read, and drive them to prodigies of evil. They are capable of equal prodigies of good. In the year 1830 the Polish insurrectionists against the tyranny of the Tsars inscribed on their banners words addressed to the Russian people: "For Your Freedom and Ours." And it is in that spirit that the peoples of the democracies today should approach the peoples of the Soviet Union.

The hope of the United States and of all the democracies is the rapid establishment of a just peace on earth. Our desire is to achieve one world now. The aim of the Soviet Government is the conquest of the world for Communism, which entails a policy of two worlds now, a Communist world and a democratic world, followed by the conquest of the democratic world by the Communist world. The immediate creation of a world wide custom of all nations treating one another as members of a single peace group is rendered impossible by Soviet Imperialism. The establishment of such a custom requires standards of good faith, tolerance and human decency that the Soviet Government has never lived by, does not live by and has no intention of living by. Since the creation of such a custom, and its maintenance until it becomes well established, is the only sure basis for peace, we and the other democratic peoples who want peace can not give up our aim to create it. Even though we know that, because of Soviet Imperialism, we can not achieve one world now, we are obliged by every dictate of common sense, human decency and self preservation, to work together for the ultimate drawing of all nations, the Soviet Union included, into a single peace group. We can not get rid of the fact of Soviet Imperialism by wishing that the Soviet Union were a peace loving democracy, or by pretending that it is a peace loving democracy. We must strive to achieve peace in spite of Soviet Imperialism. Our task is double: to stop aggressions by the Soviet Union, and to turn the present uneasy armistice into lasting peace. What actions can we and the other democracies take now to achieve these objectives?

Let us first reject with absolute finality the idea that we should attack the Soviet Union. Thanks to the possession of the atomic bomb and an airforce of overwhelming strength, we are today far stronger than the Soviet Union and could destroy it; but to make war on the Soviet Union because we know that the Soviet Government intends at a later date to make war on us would be to lower ourselves to a moral level not far above that of the Communists. We should lose our objective by the methods we chose to achieve it. We should fall into the error of Lenin himself, who because he was convinced that the end he sought was righteous, used most foul methods in his effort to achieve it, and, like all others who live by the creed that the end justifies the means, created a Frankenstein-monster of evil means so powerful that it swallowed up truth, honor, and brotherly love; and his followers inherited a vested interest in maintaining the privileges of their persecuting caste, and the instruments of tyranny. Man becomes what he does. Man can not murder without becoming a murderer. Nations can not plan and launch wars without becoming enemies of humanity. When Cain killed Abel he did not help the human family to become a peace group. We can not create the custom of all nations treating one another as a peace group by blotting the Russian people off the earth with atomic bombs during the years when we have the bombs and they do not have the bombs. We can use only means that conform to the highest moral standards we have, otherwise we shall throw away in advance all chance to lift international morality to the plane made requisite by the existence of the atomic bomb.

This does not mean that we should hesitate to use the atomic bomb to stop new crimes of Soviet Imperialism. To execute a murderer is not an immoral act. And the more certain the Soviet Government is that we shall use the atomic bomb against it if it continues its career of aggression, the more likely the Soviet Government will be to refrain from aggressions—at least until it has the atomic bomb. At the present time we have only to be ready to use our power, and let the Soviet Government know that we are ready to use it, in order not to have to use it. The Soviet Government will refrain from starting any war if it knows that, when it commits an act of aggression, it will receive swift retribution in the form of atomic bombs. The Russians understand well the sequence of crime and punishment.

The chance that World War III may burst on mankind before the Soviet Union gets the atomic bomb, lies in the possibility that Stalin may think that Great Britain and the United States will permit him to commit further aggressions with impunity. For example, Stalin may order his troops to attack Turkey, relying on war weariness to prevent Great Britain from honoring her agreement to go to war in support of Turkey if Turkey should be attacked, and relying on indifference to prevent the United States from giving aid to Turkey and Great Britain. If, however, we should leave no doubt in Stalin's mind that we would not permit further aggressions by the Soviet Union to succeed, there would be no armed attack by the Soviet Union on Turkey or any other of its neighbors. We can prevent aggressions by the Soviet Union during the period in which we have the atomic bomb and the Soviet Union does not have the atomic bomb, by maintaining the superiority of our airforce, and by warning the Soviet Union in the politest manner—and meaning it—that new Soviet aggressions will be met by American action.

At some point we shall have to stop Soviet Imperialism or submit to Stalin's rule. We can not get off this planet. If we try to save ourselves from war by closing ourselves within the Western Hemisphere and letting the Soviet Union control the rest of the earth, the Soviet Union will build up such a preponderance of force against us that our destruction will be certain. We might survive for a time, if we armed North and South America to the teeth, as the Eastern Roman Empire survived behind the walls of Constantinople, when the barbarians overran the Western Roman Empire. But we should have to devote all our best energies to production for war and drilling for war, our democracy would disappear, and we would not survive long. There were no airplanes or rockets or atomic bombs in the days of the Byzantine Empire, and the walls of Constantinople were a greater barrier than the Atlantic and Pacific Oceans are today. Before many years we would go down before the massed forces of Europe, Asia and Africa.

It is in our national interest to stop further aggressions by Stalin while his forces are still far from our shores and we have in our hands the means to stop him —a far stronger airforce than the Soviet airforce, and the atomic bomb. It is in our national interest to maintain our Atlantic Doctrine and our Open Door Doctrine with the same determination as our Monroe Doctrine.

We can not entirely prevent the Soviet Government from attempting to conquer new areas by the use of fifth columns, agents, propaganda, and economic, political and diplomatic pressure; but we can counter Soviet attacks of this sort by intelligent use of our own economic, political and diplomatic power. We have great allies—truth and the ineradicable desire of man to be free. Wherever the Red Army has trod in Europe or Asia, from Vienna to Korea—raping, murdering and looting—men, women and children have seen enough of life under Communist dictatorship to want no more of it. They pray for deliverance. And they hate the Soviet Quislings of their satellite governments. In countries of Europe and Asia which have not yet been controlled by Communists, Soviet propaganda is still able to mask the gruesome face of the N.K.V.D., and Communist parties have grown rapidly. These Communist parties, like all others, are fifth columns of the Soviet Government, and through them Stalin may be able to capture from within, by Trojan Horse tactics, some European states that still have independent democratic governments. It is in our national interest to see to it that no more of the independent states of Europe fall under the control of Moscow. And it is, therefore, in our interest to use our own economic, political and diplomatic power to help the democratic non-Communist governments of Europe to preserve the independence of their states.

The strongest opposition to Communist control of Europe today is provided by Socialist parties that share the general views of the British Labor Party and the French Socialist Party with regard to economic questions. The gulf which separates them from the Communists is profound. The Socialists stand for democracy, the Communists for dictatorship; the Socialists stand for the preservation of the human liberties guaranteed in our Bill of Rights, the Communists for suppression of all those liberties; the Socialists stand for a gradual solution of economic and social problems by democratic means and free elections, the Communists for armed revolution, the liquidation of all political parties except the Communist Party and the solution of economic and social problems by ukase of the Communist dictator. The Socialists are loyal to their own nation and work for international brotherhood, the Communists are loyal to the Soviet Union, and work for Soviet conquest of the world. The Socialists believe in fair play and do not use foul methods. The Communists believe that the end justifies the means, and use any foul methods they consider useful. The Socialists believe in extending civil liberties, even to Communists. The Communists believe in the "liquidation," that is to say murder, of their opponents. It is natural, therefore, that the Socialists and Communists have never been able to cooperate long in any country. Occasionally they have worked together; but the Communists hate the Socialists more than they hate any other political party, because the Socialist program offers the workingman both social gains and the preservation of his freedom, and is, therefore, a great obstacle to Communist success.

On the continent of Europe, especially in France and

Italy, new Catholic parties have sprung up during the past few years, which stand for the liberties of the Bill of Rights and are almost as advanced as the Socialists in their economic programs. They are even more heartily opposed to the anti-religious Communists than the Socialists are; but they will not coalesce with the Socialists, because they desire the state to support Catholic schools out of taxation, as well as schools in which no particular religion is taught, and the Socialists oppose such state aid.

These two advanced parties, representing Catholic and non-Catholic democrats, under different names in different countries, are the pillars on which freedom stands in Europe today. They were, for example, under the name of the Socialist Party and the Popular Republican Movement, the solid part of the coalition that supported General de Gaulle's government in France—since the Communists entered the Government only for the purpose of wrecking it by Trojan Horse tactics—and they are the solid part of the coalition that today supports the Government of M. Gouin. It is contrary to the interests of the United States to do anything which weakens a democratic non-Communist Government of France, and it is in the interest of the United States to give economic aid to a democratic non-Communist Government of France. If economic conditions in France should become so chaotic that Stalin should be able to capture France by the strength of his fifth column, which is called the French Communist Party, but takes its orders from Moscow like all other Communist parties, our Atlantic Doctrine, in support of which we fought the Germans in both World Wars, would crash in irretrievable ruin. Stalin would control not only France, but also French North Africa and Dakar. Threatened by a Communist France and the Soviet Union, the weaker countries of Europe would fall speedily under Stalin's rule, and Great Britain would face the doom which she has warded off by four hundred years of battle to prevent an enemy from dominating Europe. France, ruled by Communists and directed from Moscow, would be no less dangerous to the United States than France ruled by Nazis and directed from Berlin.

We knew at the time of both World Wars that it was contrary to our vital interests to permit the west coasts of Europe and Africa and the water gates to the Atlantic to fall into the hands of a state which might become hostile to us; and, therefore, supported France and Great Britain against Germany. The danger that France may be captured by Stalin's fifth column now confronts us; but we have as yet shown no sign that we know that danger exists. France was so drained of every economic resource by the Germans during the five years of occupation, that she is in desperate need of economic aid. We can help to keep France free by giving her economic aid. Unless we give that aid, we must expect another fall of France, and the consequent fall of all Europe into the hands of Stalin. "England would be but a breakfast. . . . Put all Europe into his hands, and he might spare such a force, to be sent in British ships, as I would as leave not have to encounter." Those words were written of another dictator, who planned to conquer the whole continent of Europe, by Thomas Jefferson,[1] on January 1, 1814.

If we are to achieve freedom and peace on earth, we must not merely stop further advance of Soviet Imperialism, but put through positive, concrete, constructive plans for European and Asiatic freedom and peace.

President Roosevelt made many noble statements of principle during the six years of the Second World War. President Truman, in his Navy Day Speech of 1945 and in his message to the Congress of January 1946, restated those principles admirably. And Secretary Byrnes, in his speech of February 28, 1946, once more restated them clearly and well, saying, ". . . We have joined with our Allies in the United Nations to put an end to war. We have covenanted not to use force except in the defense of law as embodied in the purposes and principles of the Charter. We intend to live up to that covenant. But as a great power and as a permanent member of the Security Council we have a responsibility to use our influence to see that other powers live up to their covenant. And that responsibility we also intend to meet. Unless the great powers are prepared to act in the defense of law, the United Nations cannot prevent war. We must make it clear in advance that we do

---

[1] Letter to Thomas Leiper.

intend to act to prevent aggression, making it clear at the same time that we will not use force for any other purpose. . . . We must face the fact that to preserve the United Nations we cannot be indifferent—veto or no veto—to serious controversies between any of the great powers, because such controversies could affect the whole power relationship between all of the great powers. . . . We will not and we cannot stand aloof if force or the threat of force is used contrary to the purposes and principles of the Charter." [2]

But the Government of the United States has never yet proposed a detailed plan for European or Asiatic freedom and peace. And the actions of some of our representatives, confronting Stalin and Molotov at international conferences, have been so at variance with the principles we have proclaimed that even the most specious exegesis cannot reconcile their performances with our stated principles. They have subjected themselves to the indictment: "Your actions speak so loudly that I cannot hear your words." They have appeased Stalin until no one in Europe or Asia knows whether or not we have ourselves decided what our principles mean, and are determined to embody them in action. No one doubts our physical strength. No one doubts our moral decency or our benevolence. Everyone doubts our mental capacity. We are beginning to be regarded throughout the world as a giant with a head of clay, and the peoples who look to us for leadership are beginning to wonder

[2] *The New York Times,* March 1, 1946.

if we are intellectually capable of planning our work for freedom and peace, or working our plan.

No official of the American Government is justified in defending his failure to act in accord with the vital interests of the American people by the excuse that American public opinion is not yet ready to face the fact of Soviet Imperialism, unless he has done his utmost to give the facts with regard to the acts and aims of the Soviet Government to his fellow citizens. Those facts have been coming into our Departments of State, War and Navy for many years, and still come in every day. There is no reason why they cannot be made available by the White House and the Department of State to the representatives of the American press. The facts speak for themselves. Our Government would not have to issue one word of comment on the facts to make the people of the United States understand that the Soviet Union is not a peace-loving democracy but a predatory totalitarian tyranny which is striving to conquer the earth for Communist dictatorship. Given the facts, the American people would recognize instantly that Soviet Imperialism threatens not only peace and liberty in Europe and Asia but also their lives in the United States, and would demand action now to protect their vital interests. The representatives of the American press are either excluded completely from areas controlled by the Soviet Government or so hampered by restrictions that they have no real liberty and can neither gather facts freely nor report them frankly

For example, the fact that the secret police of the Soviet-controlled puppet Government of Poland were murdering non-Communist political leaders was revealed not by the American or British press but by the British Secretary of State for Foreign Affairs, Ernest Bevin, in the House of Commons on January 23, 1946. Eight days later the American Secretary of State confirmed the report and expressed the displeasure of the American Government, but without giving the facts in detail to the press. Until the Government of the United States has shared with the people of the United States facts which concern their most vital interest of self-preservation, it will have no right to complain that their ignorance of the facts prevents it from following a foreign policy strong enough to meet the thrusts of Soviet Imperialism. If our Government were to give the truth, the whole truth and nothing but the truth about Soviet Imperialism to the American people, it would find in the people more intelligence, courage and will than it has yet found in itself.

At the present time we are attempting to use the United Nations both to stop further Soviet aggressions and to start a custom of all nations treating one another as members of a single peace group. We know well that the U.N. under its present constitution has no power to stop wars which involve the interests of any one of the permanent members of its Security Council—the Soviet Union, Great Britain, France, China and the United States—or of any state supported by one of these Great

Powers, because each permanent member of the Security Council has an absolute veto on any action by the U.N. We recognize, therefore, that the U.N., because of this provision of its charter which prevents action against an aggressor Great Power or one of its satellites, is not in any sense of the word a security organization. We know also that great wars are started by Great Powers or by satellites encouraged and supported by them. The U. N. can take action against minor aggressor states which happen to be unsupported by any member of the Security Council. The U.N. is an organization to enforce peace between such minor states; but such states do not start great wars. The U.N. is not an organization to enforce peace between the Great Powers or their satellites who do start great wars. Its constitution leaves the question of war between the Great Powers exactly where it was before the U.N. was organized. The Soviet Union is a very great power, and the outstanding fact in world affairs is Soviet Imperialism.

With a view to abolishing the veto power of the permanent members of the Security Council in order to make the U.N. an organization to enforce peace between the Great Powers, the British Secretary of State for Foreign Affairs, Ernest Bevin, at the time of the meeting of the U.N. in London, in January, 1946, indicated that Great Britain would like to see this veto power abolished. Ambassador Gromyko, the Soviet representative, however, in his first speech before the U.N., ended all hope that the Soviet Union might give up its veto power on action by the U.N. Just as the Tsars of Russia by threats of war prevented the Polish Parliament in the eighteenth century from getting rid of the *Liberum Veto* which paralyzed it, so today the Soviet dictator insists on the preservation of his *Liberum Veto* in the U.N. The Soviet Government does not want any international organization to have the right or power to force it to keep the peace.

That does not mean that the U.N. is useless. It means merely that the U.N. will not become in the foreseeable future an international security organization. The U.N. can serve usefully as a forum for world opinion, as a center of contact for representatives of all the nations of the world, as a conference where conflicting opinions can be clarified and perhaps reconciled. It is in our national interest to support the U.N. in every possible way. We have nothing to hide, and we have much to gain from a full exposure of the facts of international affairs to world opinion. Moreover, it is not impossible to hope that at some future time the U.N. may achieve abolition of the veto power, and may have to deal with facts less refractory than the facts of today, and may become a constitutional convention for mankind.

Meanwhile, we should try to make the U.N. work effectively, without hypocrisy or fear, on all international problems with which it is competent to deal. And we must not permit the U.N. to commit moral suicide by refusing to deal with the problem of protecting a weak state from aggression by a Great Power. The experience of the League of Nations proved that such aggressions are to be expected not from democratic states but from totalitarian dictatorships. No democratic state gave the League of Nations any grave trouble; but all the totalitarian dictatorships confronted the League with cases of blatant aggression. Italy attacked Ethiopia; Japan attacked China; Germany attacked Austria, Czechoslovakia and Poland; and the Soviet Union attacked Finland and Poland. Of these aggressors only the Soviet Union remains a great power. The Soviet Government was careful to have articles 5 and 6 of Chapter 2 of the Charter of the United Nations so drawn that it cannot be expelled from the U.N., as it was expelled from the League of Nations in 1940 for its attack on Finland. And so long as the Soviet Union remains a permanent member of the Security Council of the U.N. it will have an absolute veto on any official action by the U.N. But the other members of the U.N. cannot sit by and let the Soviet Union swallow weaker nations without rendering the U.N. a contemptible corpse.

The prospect that this possibility may become reality has caused some Americans to advocate the immediate replacement of the U.N. by a "Federal Government of the World" based on democratic principles and the human liberties guaranteed in our Bill of Rights. If such a World Government could be established immediately and maintained, the problem of world peace would be on its way to solution; but unfortunately there is not the slightest possibility that such a government on a world scale can be established now. The Soviet Government would have to abandon not only the Communist Creed that calls for the conquest of the world for Communism but also its entire system of government by dictatorship. And the members of the Soviet Government from Stalin down would have to abandon their lives, since a freed Russian people would treat them as the freed Italians treated Mussolini. The Soviet Government might agree to the establishment of a World Union of Soviet Socialist Republics directed from Moscow, based on secret police and firing squads and the abolition of freedom of speech, press, assembly and elections, and the replacement of the right of habeas corpus by the right of habeas cadaver. Indeed, that is the political objective of the Soviet Government. But neither the Americans, nor the British, nor any other people that has lived in freedom under a democratic government will abandon without a fight the civil liberties acquired by the struggles of their forefathers throughout the past twenty-five hundred years.

A federation of the free peoples of the world who share the same basic democratic customs could be established. We should, for example, have comparatively little difficulty in forming a federal union with Canada or Eire or Australia or New Zealand, or even the United Kingdom, if we should wish and they should wish to form one; but a federal government cannot at one and the same time be both a democracy and a tyranny. A democracy is a "government of the people, by the people and for the people." A tyranny of the Soviet sort is a government of the people by the dictator for a privileged and persecuting caste of orthodox Communists. A common government can be built only on a community of principle. Only peoples who share the same basic customs can maintain a federal union. Carlyle was fond of saying that to Herbert Spencer the supreme tragedy of human life was a beautiful theory slain by a refractory fact. Those who advocate the scrapping of the U.N. and the immediate establishment of a Federal Government of the World face the tragedy created by the refractory fact that, as President Roosevelt said, "The Soviet Union, as everybody who has the courage to face the facts knows, is run by a dictatorship as absolute as any other dictatorship in the world." [3]

The world is directed not by words but by acts. Since a Federal Government of the World is not at present within the realm of practical statesmanship, and the U.N. is not capable of taking action against an aggressor because of the veto power held by the permanent members of its Council, we are obliged to seek other methods of organizing the democracies to act against aggressors. This problem may confront us in urgent form, in the immediate future, before we and the other democracies have agreed upon methods of solving it.

[3] *The Public Papers and Addresses of Franklin D. Roosevelt,* 1940, p. 93.

The Soviet Union may continue its advance against Iran, or attack Turkey or Iraq or some other state, and may use its veto power to prevent action by the U.N. We shall then be obliged to improvise action by the democracies to prevent the Soviet Union from carrying its aggression to a successful conclusion. We are the most powerful of nations; but we have neither enough wisdom nor intelligence nor will to carry by ourselves the entire load of preventing aggressions. We need like-minded associates ready to carry their fair share of the load.

The Soviet Union is on the attack; the democracies are in retreat, not because they are weaker than the Soviet Union—we ourselves are stronger—but because they have not clarified their thinking and unified their forces to oppose Soviet aggressions. The more democracies we can gather together to oppose Soviet aggressions—with force if necessary—the more certain we shall be that the Soviet Government will not dare to start new aggressions. Our Government should, therefore, immediately commence conversations with the other democracies of the world designed to ensure their united action to prevent Soviet aggressions, which are likely, or aggressions by any other power, which are unlikely.

We have already made an excellent start toward the creation of an Inter-American League for the defense of all American states against aggression by the adoption of the Act of Chapultepec, on March 3, 1945, at the

Inter-American Conference at Mexico City. This Inter-American League, properly developed, should be able to preserve peace within the Americas, and oppose with united force any aggression against the Western Hemisphere. Thus our own vital interest expressed in the Monroe Doctrine may be buttressed by the support of all the other American states.

We have, however, made no effort to create an Inter-European League for the defense of Europe against aggression. Such a league, carefully developed, might be able to preserve peace in Europe and oppose with united force any aggression against Europe. It might become a powerful buttress of our vital interest expressed in our Atlantic Doctrine.

The Charter of the United Nations, Chapter VIII, Article 52, specifically permits the creation of "regional arrangements or agencies for dealing with such matters relating to the maintenance of international peace and security as are appropriate for regional action." Like the Inter-American League, an Inter-European League or Federation would be legitimate under this provision of the Charter of the U.N. There is, therefore, no legal obstacle to the creation of such a league or federation. There are, however, great practical obstacles, the chief of which is the Soviet Government's desire to keep the remaining democratic states of Europe isolated and divided, so that it can swallow them one by one.

When the Soviet Union was dependent for its life on

Lend-Lease aid, President Roosevelt, as a *quid pro quo* for Lend-Lease aid, could have obtained a written guarantee from Stalin that the western limits of the Soviet Union should be those of August, 1939, and that the Soviet Government would assent to the creation of a European Federation. Prime Minister Churchill had often advocated the creation of a European League or Federation,[4] and the President was repeatedly urged to join the Prime Minister in making a bargain of this sort with Stalin. President Roosevelt refused to take this action, not because he was opposed to the idea of a European Federation, but because he was hoodwinked into the belief that it was unnecessary for him to obtain any promises from Stalin with regard to Europe, that Stalin had no desire to incorporate in the Soviet Union portions of Europe, or to control independent European states through Soviet puppet governments, and would cooperate with him fully in creating a world of liberty, democracy and peace.

Few errors more disastrous have ever been made by a President of the United States, and those citizens of the United States who bamboozled the President into acting as if Stalin were a cross between Abraham Lincoln and Woodrow Wilson deserve a high place on an American roll of dishonor. A Government of the United States facing reality and ready to act in accord with the vital

---

[4] See Churchill's article in *The Saturday Evening Post*, Feb. 15, 1930, advocating a United States of Europe, and his world broadcast, March 21, 1943, etc.

interests of the people of the United States would have begun in 1941 to declare as a peace aim the creation of a democratic European Federation and would have directed all its political and economic policies in Europe toward the achievement of that aim.

Our continued appeasement of Stalin has permitted him to reduce the area of democracy in Europe to narrow limits. The only states of Europe that still remain democratic and entirely independent are Sweden, Norway, Denmark, the Netherlands, Belgium, Luxembourg, France, Switzerland, Italy, Greece and Turkey. Soviet Fifth Columns are threatening the independence of France, Italy and Greece. The Soviet Union has annexed Estonia, Latvia, Lithuania, eastern Poland, eastern and northeastern Rumania, the eastern end of Czechoslovakia and portions of Finland and East Prussia. It has set up puppet governments, which it controls completely, in Poland, Rumania, Bulgaria, Yugoslavia and Albania. It is steadily crushing Hungary and Austria. Finland and Czechoslovakia tremble under the point of a Soviet sword of Damocles. The Soviet Union today controls even more of Europe than Mackinder envisaged when he summarized his study of "The Freedom of Nations" in his famous formula:

Who rules East Europe commands the Heartland:
Who rules the Heartland commands the World-Island:
Who rules the World-Island commands the World.[5]

[5] Sir Halford Mackinder, *Democratic Ideals and Reality*, Henry Holt, New York, 1942, p. 150.

Soviet control of this vast eastern and central European area constitutes a terrible military threat to Western Europe and to Great Britain, and ultimately to the United States. No peace is to be found in a division of Europe into a huge zone controlled by the Soviet Union pressing against a small rind of disconnected democracies clinging precariously to the coasts of the Atlantic. Wishful thinkers who imagine that the Scandinavian states, the Netherlands, Belgium, Luxembourg, France, Switzerland and Italy will stop Stalin from reaching the coasts of the Atlantic should ask themselves the question: "With what?" The military forces of the western European democracies are today infinitesimal compared to the Red Army, and their economic life would dwindle to death if they should be cut off permanently from the central and eastern European market by its inclusion within the Soviet Trade Monopoly. For their own self-preservation Great Britain and the United States are obliged not only to defend the western democracies of Europe from armed attack by the Soviet Union but also to help them to unite for military and economic defense. France, if she remains an independent democratic nation and does not fall under control of Moscow—conquered by the Trojan Horse tactics of her own Communists—can regain in the noblest manner her old position in the world by taking the lead in the formation of the European Federation.

A democratic federation of European states would be no threat to any nation. By their very nature democratic federations are incapable of planning and launching wars of aggression. If the remaining European democracies remain separated, they will be swallowed one by one by the Soviet Union. A major portion of Europe will be united in a democratic federation, or all Europe will be united under Soviet tyranny.

Even if the European democracies which remain independent today should be united, they would, for a time, need economic aid from the United States and Great Britain, and, in case of Soviet aggression, full military support to enable them to defend themselves successfully. It is in the interest of Great Britain and the United States and all the democratic states of Europe, and world peace, that the democratic area in Europe should be extended until it becomes large enough to defend itself against Soviet aggression. If the doors of the European Federation should be kept open to all European states which are not puppets and have democratic governments and enforce a full Bill of Rights, it would exercise an enormous attractive force on those states of central and eastern Europe which are now in the maw of the Soviet Union, but have not yet been digested. This attraction would be enhanced if we should help the western European democracies to build up, within the boundaries of the Federation, a much higher standard of living than that in the enslaved areas of Europe under Soviet control. If not only liberty, but also decent living conditions, are open to the peoples of central and eastern Europe and the Balkans, on condition that they reacquire independence and democracy and join the European Federation, the democratic area of Europe may become large enough to defend itself against Soviet aggression, even without military aid from the United States and Great Britain.

Austria, Hungary and Czechoslovakia all desire passionately to escape entirely from Soviet control; and we should not consider any other of the independent states of the Europe of 1937 hopelessly lost to Soviet Imperialism. We should not hesitate to help the democratic elements in the states which are now controlled by Soviet puppet governments to control those governments. The people of Poland are struggling, as they have always struggled, for their independence. The slaughter and enslavement of the Poles by the Soviet Government and its Polish Quislings approaches in sickening horror the butcheries of the Poles by the Nazis. From the first day of the war in 1939, the Poles fought against the Nazis with a patriotism unsurpassed in history. Their side won the war, but they achieved only new slaughters and fresh slavery. One of their allies was in reality no less their enemy than the avowed enemy against which they had struggled for years. The nations which were their friends saved them from their avowed enemy, Germany, but failed to save them from their avowed friend, the Soviet Union. The Government of the United States did not throw Poland onto the road in front of the Soviet tank; but our Government did not pick prostrate Poland off the road when every dictate of morality and every interest of the United States demanded that we act. In consequence, today, while Polish patriots are being slaughtered by the Soviet puppet government of Poland, we receive in America Polish Quislings as alleged representatives of the enslaved Polish people.

The story is the same through all the Balkan states. The old Communist agent, better known as the self-appointed Marshal Tito, is having no easy time in maintaining the Communist dictatorship which we have helped him to rivet on the people of Yugoslavia. Rumania is in ferment. We have now recognized the Soviet puppet government of Rumania, but the resistance of the democratic parties of Rumania has not yet been entirely wiped out. In an effort to maintain a last shred of consistency between our stated principles and our acts, our Government momentarily has refused to recognize the Soviet puppet government of Bulgaria. But our policy has nowhere been one of giving serious help to the surviving democrats of the Soviet puppet states. They still look to us to help them regain independence, democracy and liberty. We answer their appeals by new appeasements of Stalin. If we should announce our support of a democratic Federation of European states, and supplement our words by acts, we would retain the support of the millions of democrats who now exist in the European zone terrorized by the N.K.V.D., and would add millions to their numbers.

Our ultimate aim should be to free all the states of central and eastern Europe and the Balkans from Soviet domination; our immediate aim to free as many as possible. A policy toward Europe in accord with the vital interests of the people of the United States may be stated in simple words: Act to create a Democratic Federation of European States, including as many countries as it may be possible to free from Soviet control.

Since the Soviet Government desires to swallow the European democracies one by one, it will use every form of threat and intrigue to prevent them from forming a defensive federation, and they will fear to act, unless Great Britain and ourselves agree in advance to protect them from Soviet aggression, while they are engaged in the consultations which will be necessary to create such a federation. This is an issue which our Government will have to meet, not only in Europe, but also in every other area close to the Soviet Union. Fear of invasion by the Red Army has the same paralyzing effect on many of the neighbors of the Soviet Union that the eye of a boa constrictor has on a rabbit. Unless the British and ourselves inform the Soviet Government politely that we will not permit further Soviet aggressions to pass unpunished, we shall be unable to carry out any constructive policy either in Europe, the Near East or the Far East.

One of the vital questions which demands immediate constructive action by the great democracies is the unsolved problem of drawing the German people along the road to democracy, so that someday they may be reintegrated in the body of western civiilzation. The atrocities inflicted by the Nazis throughout Europe have provoked a natural resentment so just and powerful that it is difficult for any man who has witnessed their crimes with his own eyes to avoid anti-Germanism, even though he knows that anti-Germanism is a no less vicious symptom of racism than anti-Semitism. For five years the Germans subjected the peoples of Poland, France, the Netherlands, Belgium, Greece, Norway, and the other countries they seized, to systematic starvation, and murdered Jews and political opponents with sadistic savagery, while they themselves lived high on the loot of Europe, better fed than they had ever been in their lives. In justice, the Germans merit not only the execution of the Nazi leaders, the Gestapo, and their criminal accomplices, but also five years of the same starvation rations they gave during five years to the Greeks and the Dutch; but justice is not enough in the ethic that we and the peoples of Europe must follow, if we are to lift the customs of the human race from the muck into which they have been thrust by the Nazis and the Communists. We cannot reeducate the German people by applying Nazi standards in our treatment of them, or merely by criticism and punishment of their former idols. We must allot to them not only justice, but also mercy and hope. There can be no reconciliation between the Germans and the democratic peoples of Europe, if we fail to bring forward concrete proposals for the reincorporation of the German people in the body of western civilization. The German people cannot be kept permanently in an economic and political ghetto, however much they may have merited such treatment by their treatment of the Jews and the democrats of Europe. They do not want Communism, but they want to live, and if the western democracies can offer them only chaos and starvation, they will prefer the existence in slavery offered them by the Soviet Union. If we do not admit the Germans as equal citizens of a free Europe, the Soviet Union will incorporate them as subjects of an enslaved Europe. The Communists have at least the negative virtue of not being racists. They accord to all the hundred and sixty-nine races and tribes of the Soviet Union equal and impartial bondage.

The First World War ended on November 11, 1918. There was world-wide complaint that more than seven months elapsed before the signing of the Treaty of Peace with Germany, at Versailles on June 28, 1919. More than twelve months have now elapsed since Germany's surrender on May 8, 1945, and not only has no peace been signed with her, but also there is no agreement among her conquerors as to the settlement to be imposed on her. Meanwhile, Stalin has acted. The Soviet Union has annexed the port of Koenigsberg and a portion of East Prussia; and has extended the frontier of her satellite Polish state to the Oder and Neisse rivers;

and has taken reparations in the form of loot and slaves from all Germany east of the Elbe. Moreover, the Soviet Government is now organizing economic life in the whole zone controlled by the Red Army on totalitarian lines, and is enrolling former Nazis in the Communist Party. The Soviet plan for Germany seems to be to break Germany's strength by deportations and looting, and to control a weakened German state as a satellite of the Soviet Union. Soviet agents are spreading Communist propaganda in the British, American and French zones of occupation, with the ultimate objective of installing Communist dictatorship throughout all Germany, and combining the forces of the Soviet Union and a rearmed Communist Germany for an assault on any state in the world that may remain democratic. The great democracies have brought forward no concerted plan to counter this drive of the Soviet Union, and their disagreements are increasing daily the probability that the Soviet Union ultimately will control all Germany.

A sane solution of the German problem involves first, the punishment of the Nazi leaders and their associated criminals; second, a reduction of Germany's war potential by transfer or control of certain industries; third, the dissolution of Prussia, which is not a state, but an agglomeration of states conquered by Brandenburg; fourth, the organization of such portions of Germany as it may be possible to keep out of the hands of the Communists into several democratic states, to be incorporated in a federation of the democratic states of Europe.

We should encourage admission to a European Federation of Democratic States, as separate entities, the states of western Germany, as soon as they have been organized as democracies with full Bills of Rights; and we should not despair of getting the portion of Germany between the Elbe and the Oder out of the hands of the Soviet Government, or of seeing it some day organized democratically, and admitted to a European Federation as a separate state or two states.

We should not attempt to fix the details of the Constitution of a European Federation. That is the right and task of the European democracies. But in return for our political and economic aid, we should insist that the Constitution of the Federation should ensure enforcement of a full Bill of Rights, and preclude all possibility of any one member of the Federation establishing a hegemony over the Federation. Winston Churchill, because he had the courage to let his constructive imagination rise to the demands of even the darkest hours, emerged as the noblest and most practical statesman of the Second World War. Our Government will emerge quickly from the befuddled perplexity with which it now regards the problem of Europe—of which the problem of Germany is a part—if it can find within itself the courage to act along the lines indicated in Churchill's world broadcast of March 21, 1943:

"One can imagine, that under a world institution embodying or representing the United Nations, and some day all nations, there should come into being a Council of Europe and a Council of Asia . . . it is upon the creation of a Council of Europe that the first practical task will be centered . . . It is my earnest hope . . . that we shall achieve the largest common measure of integrated life of Europe that is possible without destroying the individual characteristics and traditions of its many ancient and historic nations. All this will, I believe, be found to harmonize with the high permanent interests of Britain, the United States and Russia."

The present policies of the Soviet Government oblige our Government to start immediate conversations with the other democracies, designed to prepare united action to prevent aggressions. Since the present policies of the Soviet Government are merely logical products of the Communist Creed, they will be·continued in one form or another, so long as the men who control the Soviet Union aspire to conquer the world for Communism. A temporary agreement by the democracies, designed to meet a single emergency will, therefore, be inadequate. The democracies must remain united in a permanent league against aggression. This objective we might achieve by forming, within the framework of the U.N., a Defense League of Democratic States—designed to·endure until the Soviet Union shall have evolved into a democracy, and shall have abandoned its aim to conquer the world for Communist dictatorship. If and when such a moment comes, the time will be ripe for discussions of a federal organization of the world, and the Defense League of Democratic States will be unnecessary. Until that time, such a Defense League will be essential to stop further Soviet aggressions. It would be able to take the actions against aggressors which the U.N. cannot take, because of the veto power against all action which is in the hands of the permanent members of its Council. It would be a security organization, whereas the U.N. is not a security organization, and can become one only by various changes in its constitution—the first of which must be the abolition of the veto power—to which the Soviet Union will not agree.

Such a Defense League might include at the outset: the Inter-American League, the British Commonwealth, China—and the European Federation, if and when the European democracies succeed in creating it. Until a European Federation is created, the democratic states of Europe should be included as separate states, in the conversations designed to prepare immediate united action by the democracies in case of further Soviet aggression. At a later date, if and when we succeed in establishing democracy in Japan, and that democracy maintains itself, it will be time enough to consider the question of admitting a democratic Japan to the Defense League of Democratic States.

From the world of democratic brotherhood, which we must ultimately create if the present uneasy armistice is to be transformed into lasting peace, no people can be excluded. Racism is as foul a doctrine when applied to yellow or brown or black peoples as when applied to Jews or Germans. There are peoples which, because of historical accidents, are at the moment unable to govern themselves; there is no people which is incapable of learning to govern itself. One third of the human race lives today under some form of tutelage by the democratic states. We ourselves control the Philippines and Puerto Rico, and various smaller areas. Under our administration the Filipinos have developed rapidly toward democracy and independence, and we are not indulging in self-flattery when we claim that our behavior in the Philippines has been a model that should be followed, wherever possible, by the other democratic states. We must recognize, however, that we have been less successful in Puerto Rico, and that the problems which confronted us in the Philippines were small, compared to the problems that confront the British on the shores of the Indian Ocean, and in parts of the Near East and Africa, or the Dutch in Indonesia, or the French in Indo-China and North Africa. Nevertheless, we are correct in our view that the instructions which President McKinley gave to the Taft Philippine Commission on April 7, 1900, contained the right basis for approach to all dependent peoples: ". . . The Commission should bear in mind that the government which they are establishing is designed not for our satisfaction or for the expression of our theoretical views, but for the happiness, peace, and prosperity of the people of the Philippine Islands." The loyalty to the United States displayed by the Filipinos throughout the Second World War was striking proof that the policy of preparing a dependent people as rapidly as possible for independence is right. We, no less than the other democratic states which today hold in tutelage much larger populations, are vitally interested in the ultimate association of those dependent peoples with us and the other democracies, as members of a Defense League of Democratic States. It is as true of nations as of men that he who would have a friend must show himself friendly. Such influence as we now possess over our fellow democracies should be used to press them to adopt as a principle of action the promise that President Wilson made through Governor Harrison to the Filipinos in 1913: "every step we take will be taken with a view to the ultimate independence of the islands, and as a preparation for that independence."

We have a community of interest with all the peoples of the world—including the peoples of the Soviet Union —our mutual interest in freedom and peace. We have a community of interest with all democratic governments. We have no community of interest with the Soviet Government, which kills freedom and commits aggression whenever and wherever it can with impunity. If we build up a defense league of the free peoples of the world, the preponderance of force against the Soviet Union will be such that the Soviet Government will not dare to attempt further aggressions. The actions of the Soviet Government are still controlled by Lenin's advice: "The question whether it is possible to undertake at once a revolutionary war, must be answered solely from the point of view of actual conditions and the interest of the Socialist Revolution which has already begun." [6]

We should, in all our dealings, treat the Soviet Government with the most scrupulous fairness, frankness and reciprocity, respecting its rights under international agreements, and insisting that it respect ours and those of the other democracies. We should accord to the Soviet Union those rights and privileges it accords to us, and refuse it, if we choose, rights and privileges which it denies us. There is no reciprocity today in the relations of the American and Soviet Governments. We permit Soviet diplomatic and consular officials to travel without restriction throughout the United States and to talk with anyone they choose. The Soviet Government forbids American diplomatic and consular officials to travel in the Soviet Union, or in other countries it controls, except by special permission. Such permission is frequently refused and, if given, is usually accorded only after long delays. President Roosevelt was so outraged by this lack of reciprocity that in April, 1941, he forbade Ambassador Oumansky and all other members of the Soviet Embassy to leave Washington without special permission, until such time as the members of the American Embassy in Moscow should be permitted to travel freely in the Soviet Union. After Germany attacked the Soviet Union, this ban on travel by members of the Soviet Embassy in Washington was lifted. The ban on unrestricted travel by members of the American

[6] Lenin, *Twenty-One Theses*, Jan. 20, 1918, Thesis 12.

Embassy in Moscow never has been lifted. Moreover, the American Ambassador in Moscow is followed day and night by four agents of the N.K.V.D., and the American Consul in Vladivostok is not even permitted to discuss business with the local authorities, but only with a representative of the Soviet Foreign Office.

We permit a branch of the Communist Party to function in the United States. The Soviet Government will not permit branches of the Democratic or Republican or Socialist parties to function in Moscow. We permit the *Daily Worker* and other Communist publications, whose policies are fixed by the "Party Line" laid down in Moscow, to spread their views in the United States. The Soviet Government does not permit any newspapers of any kind in the Soviet Union, except those it controls. We permit Soviet propagandists to use our radio and our motion pictures to spread whatever views they may wish of the Soviet Union and its aims. The Soviet Government does not permit anyone but its own agents to use the Soviet radio or screen. We permit the Soviet Government to broadcast to the United-States without interference daily radio programs in English. We do not broadcast to the Soviet Union a single program in Russian, or any of the other languages and dialects of the peoples of the Soviet Union, and if we should attempt to do so, the Soviet Government would doubtless employ the same drastic methods to prevent its subjects from listening to our broadcasts, that it employs to prevent them from listening to British broadcasts. Nevertheless we know that throughout the Soviet Union, at peril of their lives, there are those who do listen with home-made sets to the broadcasts from outside the wall of silence with which the Soviet Government attempts to cut them off from the world of western civilization. Even though they may be few, we should make the effort to give them the facts. For we shall not be able to establish world peace until we have convinced the peoples of the Soviet Union of the truth that we stand for their freedom as well as for ours, and that the day they establish democracy, enforce a Bill of Rights and drop Soviet Imperialism, we shall welcome them as brothers in a world federation of democratic states. We can, if we try hard enough, let the peoples of the Soviet Union know the truth, and in time the truth may set them free.

The Soviet Government today is strong and firmly entrenched. But in the light of history it is weak, beyond the weakness of any democratic government, since it has set itself against the surge of all mankind toward freedom and democracy. By abolishing the human liberties for which men have fought for twenty-five hundred years, it has made itself as reactionary as the regime of its spiritual parents, the Tartar Khans of the Golden Horde. Like the Tartar Khans, Stalin has had great physical successes, but they have been purchased by moral degradation. And Stalin, too, like the Tartar Khans, will pass. History runs at constantly accelerated pace. The Soviet Regime in Russia has repeated in less than three decades much of the history of Tsarist Russia in the three centuries which separated Ivan the Terrible, the first Tsar, from Nicholas II, the last. Stalin, during the first ten years of his omnipotence, relived the era of Peter the Great. Before Hitler attacked in 1941, Stalin was enjoying the fruits of power in the grand manner of Catherine the Great. He is today in a situation similar to that of Alexander I at the close of the Napoleonic era. Many of his soldiers and officers have seen something of Europe; and, like the soldiers and officers of Alexander I, have realized that life outside Russia is far more worth living than life inside Russia. It was that observation which started the revolutionary waves that at last swept away the Tsars. The Russian people are a mighty people; and the words which Benjamin Constant wrote in 1813 remain true of Stalin: "When men who direct the destinies of the world deceive themselves with regard to what they can accomplish, it is a great misfortune. . . . Their obstinacy or, if one wishes, their genius, crowns their efforts with ephemeral success; but since they are in conflict with the habits, the interests and the whole moral existence of their contemporaries, these forces of resistance react against them: and after a time, very long for their victims, very short in the light of history, nothing remains of their enterprises but the crimes they have committed and the sufferings they have caused." [7]

How far Soviet Imperialism will spread before it is halted, and how long the Soviet Government will con-

[7] Benjamin Constant, *Of The Spirit of Conquest.*

tinue to oppress the Russian people and its other victims, depends in large measure on the ability of the
Government of the United States to conceive and carry
out in action a long-term foreign policy toward areas
remote from the Western Hemisphere. In the past, our
actions in the field of foreign affairs have often been
mere convulsive reactions to domestic political expedi-
ency; devices to gather votes, not integral parts of a well
considered plan to forward the vital interests of the
people of the United States—the chief of which is the
creation of a world of freedom and peace. It was ex-
pedient from the point of view of domestic politics for
our Government to pretend that the Soviet juggernaut
was an amiable tank that would stop if the officials of
our Department of State stood in the road and wagged
their tails at it. The pretense was not in the interests of
the American people or of world peace; but it was popular. If our Government now recognizes that its policy of
appeasing Stalin has placed our country in danger, and
desires to follow a foreign policy in accord with the vital
interests of the people of the United States, it might
adopt the following program for action now:

1. Support the U.N. as strongly as possible, while
recognizing that the U.N. is not a security organization
because the Soviet Union and the other permanent members of the Council, by exercise of their veto power, can
prevent any action by the U.N.

2. Give the people of the United States the facts which
reach our Government with regard to events in all areas

in which the freedom of the American press is in any way restricted.

3. Cease in all official communications and utterances to describe the Soviet Union as a "peace loving democracy," and treat it for what it is in fact, a totalitarian dictatorship, whose aim is to conquer the world for Communism.

4. Furnish to the Congress of the United States the facts which prove that Soviet Imperialism can be prevented from extending its control over Europe, the Far East and the Near East, only if we are ready to join the other democracies in action now to prevent fresh Soviet aggressions—and that Stalin does not dare risk war with us.

5. Maintain the superiority of our airforce, and increase production of the atomic bomb.

6. So long as the Soviet Government adheres to the Communist Creed of world conquest, do not give the Soviet Union the atomic bomb, or any economic or financial assistance that may enable it to hasten the day when it is able to manufacture the atomic bomb.

7. Assist the democracies economically and financially.

8. Develop and strengthen the Inter-American League, in accordance with the terms of the Act of Chapultepec.

9. Start conversations designed to lead to the creation of a European Federation of Democratic States, open to all States which are not puppets, and have democratic governments and enforce a Bill of Rights.

10. Start conversations with the other democracies of the world, designed to prepare within the framework of the U.N., united and immediate action in case of further Soviet aggressions; and to produce eventually within the U.N., a Defense League of Democratic States, to include the Inter-

American League, the British Empire, China and the European Federation.

11. Maintain steady and active opposition to the efforts of Soviet Imperialism to swallow Manchuria, North Korea, North China, Iran, Turkey and those states of Eastern and Central Europe and the Balkans which it now controls.

12. Treat the Soviet Union with the most scrupulous fairness, frankness and reciprocity, respecting its rights under international agreements, and insisting that it respect ours and those of the other democracies.

13. Give the peoples of the Soviet Union daily, in their own languages, the facts of world affairs, stressing the truth that we stand for their freedom, no less than for our own.

14. Act, and use our influence with the other democracies, to hasten the process of raising the dependent peoples we and they now control, to democracy and independence and association with a Defense League of Democratic States.

Is that all we can do now to hasten the day when man's control over the forces of his own nature will become sufficient to enable him to use his increasing control over the forces of inanimate nature for the creation of a better life, rather than the destruction of the human race? No. Far more moral advances of mankind have been made under the guidance of religious leaders than under the leadership of statesmen. Morality is individual before it is collective. In the task of lifting mankind to the moral level made vital by the atomic bomb, religion and statesmanship can labor shoulder to shoulder.

We, as individuals and as a nation, can ask God to make us the instruments of His justice and peace, and try to be worthy instruments. Our religious leaders can try to awaken the conscience, not only of America, but of all the world; and boldly work together with men of all faiths who know what things are true, honest, lovely and of good report. International morality has decayed for more than thirty years. That decay can be stopped by the will of each of us and all of us working together. International morality can be made to grow again by the acts of men of good will in the service of God.

Let us try to imagine how we shall feel when we learn, at some time during the next decade, that the Soviet Government is manufacturing the atomic bomb. We shall then wish desperately that we had a Federal Government of the World. Questions of national sovereignty will seem relatively unimportant, compared with our desire to avoid destruction. We shall begin to discuss furiously whether or not we should attempt to set up a World Government; and give it exclusive authority to manufacture and hold atomic and other new weapons of mass destruction; authority to inspect every inch of every country to make certain that there is no secret stock or manufacture of such weapons; authority to create a world police force armed with atomic weapons, and, therefore, more powerful than the armed forces of any nation; authority to enforce a world Bill of Rights. We shall wish to create a World Federal Government having much the same authority over national governments that the Federal Government of the United States has over our "sovereign states."

If we try hard enough, we shall be able to create a Federal Government of Democratic States which share our basic customs. But we shall not be able to create a World Federal Government so long as the Soviet Union remains a totalitarian dictatorship, controlled by men who of their own volition, by their own will, deliberately and consciously, have chosen to declare themselves the enemies of all peoples who live in freedom. Those men will not recoil from using the atomic bomb for reasons of humanity. If they had it now, and we did not have it, they would be using it now to impose their dictatorship on all the world. They will recoil from using it only for fear of overwhelming retaliation. There will be no true peace on earth, but only an armistice, so long as that privileged and persecuting caste controls the peoples of the Soviet Union. We can mobilize against those men today every moral force on earth. Our Government today has only to say "Stop" to them—and mean it— and they will stop their aggressions, in fear. We can build up such moral and physical force against them by uniting the democracies of the world that, when they succeed in manufacturing the atomic bomb, they will not dare to use it, because they will fear to use it. But until the peoples of the Soviet Union control their own government and live like ourselves in freedom and democracy, they will not be permitted by their masters to live with us in peace as fellow citizens of a united world.

We Americans are the children of men of all races and creeds, who came to this continent because they would not submit to any privileged and persecuting orthodoxy. And we will not submit now. We know that we can get peace only by the extension throughout the earth of the area of democracy, freedom and human decency. If our Government, in the name of seeking peace, continues to let that area be conquered, it will prepare for us not peace, but a desperate war against overwhelming attacking forces of Communist-driven slaves. If we stand firm now against the forces of evil, and strive to extend the area of God's righteousness, even peace may be added unto us. We shall find no peace in appeasement of Stalin. We may find peace if we have the courage to stop the aggressions of the Soviet Government now, and the good will to hold out, again and again, a hand of friendship to the Russian people, saying: "March with us— for your freedom and ours."

Four hundred years before the birth of Christ, Euripides wrote lines which are still true:

> There be many shapes of mystery;
> And many things God makes to be,
> Past hope or fear.
> And the end men looked for cometh not,
> And a path is there where no man thought,
> So hath it fallen here.

There is a Path to Peace.

APPENDIX I

Charges and particulars of violations by the Soviet Government of international treaties, agreements, and assurances, collated with the charges and particulars of similar violations caused by the defendants at the trial of the major German War Criminals (Appendix C of the Indictment at Nuremberg, issued by the U. S. War Department, October 19, 1945).

SOVIET VIOLATIONS

Charge I

Violation of the Covenant of the League of Nations, signed on June 28, 1919, and adhered to by the Union of Soviet Socialist Republics, hereinafter referred to as the USSR, on September 18, 1934.

Particulars

(A) In that the USSR did, on or about August 23, 1939, in violation of Article 10 of the Covenant, under the guise of a Non-Aggression Treaty with Germany, take part in a joint conspiracy to deprive Poland, Estonia, Latvia and Lithuania of their sovereign independence and their territorial integrity, and Finland and Rumania of their territorial integrity—all these States being, with the USSR, co-members of the League of Nations.

(B) In that the USSR did, on or about September 28, 1939, in

GERMAN VIOLATIONS

Charge I

Violation of the convention for pacific settlement of international disputes signed at The Hague, 29 July 1899.

Particulars

In that Germany did, by force and arms, on the dates specified in Column 1, invade the territory of the sovereign specified in Column 2, respectively, without first having attempted to settle its disputes with said sovereigns by pacific means.

Column 1	Column 2
6 April 1941	Kingdom of Greece
6 April 1941	Kingdom of Yugoslavia

Charge II

Violation of the convention for the pacific settlement of interna-

219

violation of Article 10 of the Covenant, conclude an agreement with Germany to partition the territory of the Republic of Poland, member of the League of Nations.

(C) In that the USSR did, on or about November 30, 1939, without recourse to peaceful means of settling disputes between the members of the League of Nations, and in particular to the provisions of Article 12 of the Covenant, resort to war against Finland, and was in consequence expelled from the League of Nations on December 14, 1939, by a unanimous resolution of the Assembly and the Council of the League of Nations.

Charge II

Violation of the Treaty of Peace between Estonia and the Russian Socialist Federative Socialist Republic signed in Tartu, February 2, 1920.

Particulars

In that the USSR, which on July 6, 1923, assumed all international obligations of the RSFSR, did, on or about August 6, 1940, incorporate Estonia into the USSR, in violation of the provisions of Articles 2 and 3 of the Treaty of Tartu.

Charge III

Violation of the Treaty of Peace between Lithuania and the Russian SFSR, signed in Moscow, July 12, 1920.

Particulars

In that the USSR did, on or about August 3, 1940, incorpo-

tional disputes signed at The Hague, 18 October 1907.

Particulars

In that Germany did, on or about the dates specified in Column 1, by force of arms invade the territory of the sovereigns specified in Column 2, respectively, without having first attempted to settle its dispute with said sovereigns by pacific means.

Column 1	Column 2
1 Sept. 1938	Republic of Poland
9 April 1940	Kingdom of Norway
9 April 1940	Kingdom of Denmark
10 May 1940	Grand-Duchy of Luxembourg
10 May 1940	Kingdom of Belgium
10 May 1940	Kingdom of the Netherlands
22 June 1941	Union of Soviet Socialist Republics

Charge III

Violation of Hague Convention III relative to the opening of hostilities, signed 18 Oct. 1907.

Particulars

In that Germany did, on or about the dates specified in Column 1, commence hostilities against the countries specified in Column 2, respectively, without previous warning in the form of a reasoned declaration of war or an ultimatum with conditional declaration of war.

Column 1	Column 2
1 Sept. 1939	Republic of Poland
9 April 1940	Kingdom of Norway

rate Lithuania into the USSR, in violation of the provisions of Articles 2 and 3 of the Treaty of Moscow.

Charge IV

Violation of the Treaty of Peace between Latvia and the Russian SFSR signed in Riga, August 11, 1920.

Particulars

In that the USSR did, on or about August 5, 1940, incorporate Latvia into the USSR, in violation of the provisions of Articles 2 and 3 of the Treaty of Riga.

Charge V

Violation of the Treaty of Peace between Finland and the Russian SFSR, signed in Tartu, October 14, 1920.

Particulars

In that the USSR did, on or about March 12, 1940, incorporate the city and region of Viipuri and other territories into the USSR, in violation of the provisions of Articles 2 and 3 of the Treaty of Tartu.

Charge VI

Violation of the Treaty of Peace between Poland and the Russian SFSR, the Ukrainian SSR and the Byelorussian SSR, later united in the USSR, signed at Riga, March 18, 1921.

Particulars

(A) In that the USSR did, on or about November 1, 1939, incorporate Southeastern Poland into the Ukrainian SSR, in violation of the provisions of Articles 2, 3 and 5 of the Treaty of Riga.

Column 1	Column 2
9 April 1940	Kingdom of Denmark
10 May 1940	Kingdom of Belgium
10 May 1940	Kingdom of the Netherlands
10 May 1940	Grand Duchy of Luxembourg
22 June 1941	Union of Soviet Socialist Republics

Charge IV

Violation of the Hague Convention V respecting the rights and duties of neutral powers and persons in case of war on land, signed Oct. 18, 1907.

Particulars

In that Germany did, on or about the dates specified in Column 1, by force of arms of its military forces, cross into, invade and occupy the territories of the sovereigns specified in Column 2, respectively, then and thereby violating the neutrality of said sovereigns.

Column 1	Column 2
9 April 1940	Kingdom of Norway
9 April 1940	Kingdom of Denmark
10 May 1940	Grand Duchy of Luxembourg
10 May 1940	Kingdom of Belgium
10 May 1940	Kingdom of the Netherlands
22 June 1941	Union of Soviet Socialist Republics

Charge V

Violation of the treaty of peace between the Allied and asso-

(B) In that the USSR did, on or about November 2, 1939, incorporate Northeastern Poland into the Byelorussian SSR, in violation of Articles 2, 3, and 5 of the Treaty of Riga.

(C) In that the USSR did, on or about October 10, 1939, detach from Poland and incorporate in Lithuania the city and region of Wilno, in violation of Articles 3 and 5 of the Treaty of Riga.

(D) In that the USSR did, on or about August 3, 1940, incorporate the city and region of Wilno, together with the Republic of Lithuania, into the USSR, in violation of Articles 2, 3, and 5 of the Treaty of Riga.

Charge VII

Violation of the Treaty of Neutrality and Non-Aggression entered into between the USSR and Lithuania on September 28, 1926, and of the Protocols of May 6, 1931, and of April 4, 1934, prolonging the validity of such treaty until December 31, 1945.

Particulars

In that the USSR did, on or about June 15, 1940, with its military forces invade and occupy Lithuania, thereby violating its neutrality and territorial integrity and destroying its sovereign independence.

Charge VIII

Violation of the Treaty providing for renunciation of war as an instrument of national policy, signed at Paris, August 27, 1928, known as Kellogg-Briand Pact, to which the USSR acceded on August 27, 1928.

ciated powers and Germany, signed at Versailles, 28 June 1919, known as the Versailles Treaty.

Particulars

(A) In that Germany did, on and after 7 March 1936, maintain and assemble armed forces and maintain and construct military fortifications in the demilitarized zone of the Rhineland in violation of the provision of Articles 42 and 44 of the Treaty of Versailles.

(B) In that Germany did, on or about March 13, 1938, annex Austria into the German Reich in violation of the provisions of Article 80 of the Treaty of Versailles.

(C) In that Germany did, on or about 22 March 1939, incorporate the District of Memel into the German Reich in violation of the provisions of Article 99 of the Treaty of Versailles.

(D) In that Germany did, on or about 1 Sept. 1939, incorporate the Free City of Danzig into the German Reich in violation of the provisions of Article 100 of the Treaty of Versailles.

(E) In that Germany did, on or about 16 March 1939, incorporate the Provinces of Bohemia and Moravia, formerly part of Czechoslovakia, into the German Reich in violation of the provisions of Article 81 of the Treaty of Versailles.

(F) In that Germany did, at various times in March, 1935, and thereafter, repudiate various parts of Part V, Military, Naval and Air clauses of the Treaty of Versailles by creating an air

SOVIET VIOLATIONS—*Continued*

Particulars

In that the USSR did, on or about the dates specified in Column 1, with a military force, attack the sovereigns specified in Column 2, respectively, and resort to war against such sovereigns in violation of its solemn declaration condemning recourse to war for the solution of international controversies, its solemn renunciation of war as an instrument of national policy in its relations with such sovereigns and its solemn covenant that settlement or solution of all disputes or conflicts of whatever nature or origin arising between it and such sovereigns should never be sought except by pacific means.

Column 1	Column 2
Sept. 17, 1939	Poland
Nov. 30, 1939	Finland

Charge IX

Violation of the Protocol signed at Moscow, February 9, 1929, between the USSR and Estonia, Latvia, Poland and Rumania, for the immediate entry into force of the Treaty of Paris of August 27, 1928, regarding renunciation of war as an instrument of national policy, later adhered to by Lithuania.

Particulars

In that the USSR did, on or about September 17, 1939, with its military forces attack, invade and commit other acts of aggression against Poland.

Charge X

Violation of the Treaty of Non-Aggression and Amicable

GERMAN VIOLATIONS—*Continued*

force, by use of compulsory military service, by increasing the size of the army beyond treaty limits and by increasing the size of the navy beyond treaty limits.

Charge VI

Violation of the treaty between the United States and Germany restoring friendly relations, signed at Berlin, Aug. 25, 1921.

Particulars

That Germany did, at various times in March, 1935, and thereafter, repudiate various parts of Part V, Military, Naval and Air clauses of the treaty between the United States and Germany restoring friendly relations by creating an air force, by use of compulsory military service, by increasing the size of the army beyond treaty limits and by increasing the size of the navy beyond treaty limits.

Charge VII

Violation of the treaty of mutual guarantee between Germany, Belgium, France, Great Britain and Italy, done at Locarno, Oct. 16, 1925.

Particulars

(A) In that Germany, did, on or about March 7, 1936, unlawfully send armed forces into the Rhineland, demilitarized zone of Germany, in violation of Article I of the Treaty of Mutual Guarantee.

(B) In that Germany did, in or about March 1936, and thereafter unlawfully train armed forces in the Rhineland, demilitarized zone of Germany, in vio-

Soviet Violations—*Continued*

Settlement entered into between the USSR and Finland on January 21, 1932, and of the Protocol of April 7, 1934, prolonging the validity of such treaty until December 31, 1945.

Particulars

In that the USSR did, on or about November 30, 1939, with its military and naval forces attack, invade and commit other acts of aggression against Finland.

Charge XI

Violation of the Treaty of Non-Aggression entered into between the USSR and Latvia on February 5, 1932, and of the Protocol of April 4, 1934, prolonging the validity of such treaty until December 31, 1945.

Particulars

In that the USSR did, on or about June 16, 1940, with its military forces invade and occupy Latvia, thereby destroying its sovereign independence.

Charge XII

Violation of Convention of Conciliation entered into between the USSR and Finland on April 22, 1932.

Particulars

In that the USSR, notwithstanding its undertaking to submit for amicable settlement in a Conciliation Commission disputes of all kinds which might arise between it and Finland, which were not capable of settlement by diplomacy, did, on or about November 30, 1939, with a military force attack, invade and occupy

German Violations—*Continued*

lation of Article I of the Treaty of Mutual Guarantee.

(C) In that Germany did, on or about March 7, 1936, and thereafter, unlawfully construct and maintain fortifications in the Rhineland demilitarized zone of Germany in violation of the Treaty of Mutual Guarantee.

(D) In that Germany did, on or about May 10, 1940, unlawfully attack and invade Belgium, in violation of Article II of the Treaty of Mutual Guarantee.

(E) In that Germany did, on or about May 10, 1940, unlawfully attack and invade Belgium, without first having attempted to settle its dispute with Belgium by peaceful means, in violation of Article III of the Treaty of Mutual Guarantee.

Charge VIII

Violation of the Arbitration Treaty between Germany and Czechoslovakia, done at Locarno, Oct. 16, 1925.

Particulars

In that Germany did, on or about March 15, 1939, unlawfully by duress and threats of military might force Czechoslovakia to deliver the destiny of Czechoslovakia and its inhabitants into the hands of the Fuehrer and Reichschancellor of Germany, without having attempted to settle its dispute with Czechoslovakia by peaceful means.

Charge IX

Violation of the Arbitration Convention between Germany and Belgium, done at Locarno, Oct. 16, 1925.

parts of the Finnish territory, thereby violating the territorial integrity of Finland.

Charge XIII

Violation of Treaty of Non-Aggression and Amicable Settlement entered into between the USSR and Estonia on May 4, 1932, and of the Protocol of April 4, 1934, prolonging the validity of such treaty until December 31, 1945.

Particulars

In that the USSR did, on or about June 16, 1940, with military forces invade and occupy Estonia, thereby destroying its sovereign independence.

Charge XIV

Violation of Convention of Conciliation entered into between the USSR and Estonia on June 16, 1932.

Particulars

In that the USSR, notwithstanding its undertaking to submit for amicable settlement in a Conciliation Commission disputes of all kinds which might arise between it and Estonia, which were not capable of settlement by diplomacy, did, on or about June 16, 1940, with a military force invade and occupy Estonia, thereby violating its territorial integrity and destroying its sovereign independence.

Charge XV

Violation of Convention of Conciliation entered into between the USSR and Latvia on June 18, 1932.

Particulars

In that Germany did, on or about May 10, 1940, unlawfully attack and invade Belgium, without first having attempted to settle its dispute with Belgium by peaceful measures.

Charges X

Violation of the Arbitration Treaty between Germany and Poland, done at Locarno, Oct. 16, 1925.

Particulars

In that Germany did, on or about Sept. 1, 1939, unlawfully attack and invade Poland, without first having attempted to settle its dispute with Poland by peaceful means.

Charge XI

Violation of Convention of Arbitration and Conciliation entered into between Germany and the Netherlands on May 20, 1926.

Particulars

In that Germany, without warning, and notwithstanding its solemn covenant to settle by peaceful means all disputes of any nature whatever which might arise between it and the Netherlands which were not capable of settlement by diplomacy and which had not been referred by mutual agreement to the Permanent Court of International Justice, did, on or about May 10, 1940, with a military force, attack, invade and occupy the Netherlands, thereby violating its neutrality and territorial integrity and destroying its sovereign independence.

SOVIET VIOLATIONS—*Continued*

Particulars

In that the USSR, notwithstanding its undertaking to submit for amicable settlement in a Conciliation Commission disputes of all kinds which might arise between it and Latvia, which were not capable of settlement by diplomacy, did, on or about June 16, 1940, with a military force invade and occupy Latvia, thereby violating its territorial integrity and destroying its sovereign independence.

Charge XVI

Violation of Pact of Non-Aggression entered into between the USSR and Poland on July 25, 1932, and of the Protocol of May 5, 1934, prolonging the validity of such pact until December 31, 1945.

Particulars

In that the USSR did, on or about September 17, 1939, having previously come to an understanding on that subject with Germany and acting as its accomplice, with its military forces attack, invade and commit other acts of aggression against the Republic of Poland, thereby violating its territorial integrity and destroying its sovereign independence.

Charge XVII

Violation of the Convention for Conciliation entered into between the USSR and Poland on November 23, 1932.

Particulars

In that the USSR, notwithstanding its undertaking to sub-

GERMAN VIOLATIONS—*Continued*

Charge XII

Violation of convention of arbitration and conciliation entered into between Germany and Denmark on 2 June 1926.

Particulars

In that Germany, without warning, and notwithstanding its solemn covenant to settle by peaceful means all disputes of any nature whatever which might arise between it and Denmark which were not capable of settlement by diplomacy and which had not been referred by mutual agreement to the Permanent Court of International Justice, did, on or about 9 April 1940, with a military force, attack, invade and occupy Denmark, thereby violating its neutrality and territorial integrity and destroying its sovereign independence.

Charges XIII

Violation of treaty between Germany and other powers providing for renunciation of war as an instrument of national policy, signed at Paris 27 Aug. 1928, known as the Kellogg-Briand Pact.

Particulars

In that Germany did, on or about the dates specified in Column 1, with a military force, attack the sovereigns specified in Column 2, respectively, and resort to war against such sovereigns in violation of its solemn declaration condemning recourse to war for the solution of international controversies, its solemn renunciation of war as an instrument of national policy in its re-

SOVIET VIOLATIONS—*Continued*

mit for amicable settlement in a Conciliation Commission disputes which might arise between it and Poland, which were not capable of settlement by diplomacy, did, on or about September 17, 1939, with a military force attack, invade and occupy parts of Polish territory, thereby violating the territorial integrity of Poland and, in partnership with Germany, destroying its sovereign independence.

Charge XVIII

Violation of Convention for the Definition of Aggression, proposed by the USSR and entered into at London on July 3, 1933, between the USSR and Rumania, Estonia, Latvia, Poland, Turkey, Iran and Afghanistan, and on January 31, 1934, acceded to by Finland.

Particulars

In that the USSR did, on or about the dates specified in Column 1, with a military force invade and commit other acts of aggression against the sovereigns specified in Column 2, in violation of the provisions of the Convention of London, and in particular of the Annex to its Article 3, containing a list of circumstances excluded as justifying aggression against states immediately adjacent to the USSR.

Column 1	Column 2
Sept. 17, 1939	Poland
Nov. 30, 1939	Finland
June 16, 1940	Estonia
June 16, 1940	Latvia
June 27, 1940	Rumania

GERMAN VIOLATIONS—*Continued*

lations with such sovereigns and its solemn covenant that settlement of solution of all disputes or conflicts of whatever nature or origin arising between it and such sovereigns should never be sought except by pacific means.

Column 1	Column 2
1 Sept. 1939	Republic of Poland
9 April 1940	Kingdom of Norway
9 April 1940	Kingdom of Denmark
10 May 1940	Kingdom of Belgium
10 May 1940	Grand Duchy of Luxembourg
10 May 1940	Kingdom of the Netherlands
6 April 1941	Kingdom of Greece
6 April 1941	Kingdom of Yugoslavia
22 June 1941	Union of Soviet Socialist Republics
11 Dec. 1941	United States of America

Charge XIV

Violation of the treaty of arbitration and conciliation entered into between Germany and Luxembourg on 11 Sept. 1929.

Particulars

In that Germany, without warning, and notwithstanding its solemn covenant to settle by peaceful means all disputes which might arise between it and Luxembourg which were not capable of settlement by diplomacy did, on or about 10 May 1940, with a military force, attack, invade and occupy Luxembourg, thereby violating its neutrality and territorial integrity and destroying its sovereign independence.

SOVIET VIOLATIONS—*Continued*

Charge XIX

Violation of Notes exchanged between the USSR and Poland on September 10, 1934, and of a Joint Statement with Poland on November 26, 1938, confirming the inviolability of peaceful relations between the two states on the basis of all existing agreements.

Particulars

In that the USSR, on or about September 17, 1939, having achieved a previous understanding on that subject with Germany and acting as its accomplice, did with its military forces attack and invade Poland, and, on or about November 1 and 2, 1939, annex Eastern Poland to the USSR.

Charge XX

Violation of the Pact of Mutual Assistance between Estonia and the USSR, signed in Moscow on September 28, 1939.

Particulars

In that the USSR, notwithstanding the provisions of that Pact, which reinsured the independent statehood of Estonia and non-interference in her internal affairs, did, on or about June 16, 1940, with its military forces invade, occupy and absorb into the USSR the sovereign territory of Estonia.

Charge XXI

Violation of the Pact of Mutual Assistance between Latvia and the USSR, signed in Moscow on October 5, 1939.

GERMAN VIOLATIONS—*Continued*

Charge XV

Violation of the declaration of non-aggression entered into between Germany and Poland on 26 Jan. 1934.

Particulars

In that Germany, proceeding to the application of force for the purpose of reaching a decision, did, on or about 1 Sept. 1939, at various places along the German-Polish frontier employ military forces to attack, invade and commit other acts of aggression against Poland.

Charge XVI

Violation of German assurance given on 21 May 1935, that the inviolability and integrity of the Federal State of Austria would be recognized.

Particulars

In that Germany did, on or about 12 March 1938, at various points and places along the German-Austria frontier with a military force and in violation of its solemn declaration and assurance, invade and annex to Germany the territory of the Federal State of Austria.

Charge XVII

Violation of the Austro-German agreement of 11 July 1936.

Particulars

In that Germany, during the period from 12 Feb. 1938 to 13 March 1938 did, by duress and various aggressive acts, including the use of military force, cause the Federal State of Austria to yield up its sovereignty to the

SOVIET VIOLATIONS—*Continued*

Particulars

In that the USSR, notwithstanding the provisions of that Pact, which reinsured the independent statehood of Latvia and non-interference in her internal affairs, did, on or about June 16, 1940, with its military forces invade, occupy and absorb into the USSR the sovereign territory of Latvia.

Charge XXII

Violation of the Pact of Mutual Assistance between Lithuania and the USSR, signed in Moscow on October 10, 1939.

Particulars

In that the USSR, notwithstanding the provisions of that Pact, which reinsured the independent statehood of Lithuania and non-interference in her internal affairs, did, on or about June 15, 1940, with its military forces invade, occupy and absorb into the USSR the sovereign territory of Lithuania.

Charge XXIII

Violation of Soviet assurances given on March 28, 1939, October 31, 1939, and March 29, 1940, to respect complete independence of Estonia, Latvia and Lithuania, as well as their political, social and economic systems.

Particulars

In that the USSR did, on or about June 15 and 16, 1940, with military forces invade and occupy Estonia, Latvia and Lithuania, and on or about August 3, 5 and 6, 1940, incorporate Estonia, Latvia and Lithuania into

GERMAN VIOLATIONS—*Continued*

German agreement to recognize the full sovereignty of the Federal State of Austria.

Charge XVIII

Violation of German assurances given on 30 Jan. 1937, 28 April 1939, 26 Aug. 1939 and 6 Oct. 1939 to respect the neutrality and territorial inviolability of the Netherlands.

Particulars

In that Germany, without warning, and without recourse to peaceful means of settling any considered differences did, on or about 10 May 1940, with a military force and in violation of its solemn assurances, invade, occupy and attempt to subjugate the sovereign territory of the Netherlands.

Charge XIX

Violation of German assurances given on 30 Jan. 1937, 13 Oct. 1937, 28 April 1939, 26 Aug. 1939 and 6 Oct. 1939 to respect the neutrality and territorial inviolability of Belgium.

Particulars

In that Germany, without warning, did on or about 10 May 1940, with a military force and in violation of its solemn assurances and declarations, attack, invade and occupy the sovereign territory of Belgium.

Charge XX

Violation of assurances given on 11 March 1938 and 26 Sept. 1938 to Czechoslovakia.

Particulars

In that Germany, on or about 15 March 1939, did, under duress

Soviet Violations—*Continued*

the USSR, thereby destroying their independence, as well as their political, social and economic systems.

Charge XXIV

Violation of assurance given on June 9, 1934, by exchange of letters between Foreign Commissar Litvinov of the USSR and Titulesco, Rumanian Foreign Minister, that the USSR guaranteed full and entire respect of the sovereignty of Rumania.

Particulars

In that the USSR did, on or about June 26, 1940, under the threat of an ultimatum, with its military forces occupy and absorb into the USSR the provinces of Bessarabia and Northern Bukovina, thereby violating the sovereignty of Rumania.

Charge XXV

Violation of the Agreement entered into between the USSR and Poland on July 30, 1941, and of the Declaration of Friendship and Mutual Assistance, signed by Stalin and Prime Minister Sikorski at Moscow on December 4, 1941.

Particulars

In that the USSR, in order to justify the annexation of Polish territory to the USSR, did, on or about April 25, 1943, sever relations with the Polish Government and substitute for it a group of agents of the USSR, which it subsequently, on or about January 1, 1945, recognized as the Polish Government.

German Violations—*Continued*

and by the threat of force, violate the assurance given on 11 March 1938 to respect the territorial integrity of the Czechoslovak Republic and the assurance given on 26 Sept. 1938, that, if the so-called Sudeten territories were ceded to Germany, no further German territorial claims on Czechoslovakia would be made.

Charge XXI

Violation of the Munich Agreement and Annexes of 29 Sept. 1938.

Particulars

(A) In that Germany, on or about 15 March 1939, did, by duress and the threat of military intervention force the Republic of Czechoslovakia to deliver the destiny of the Czech people and country into the hands of the Fuehrer of the German Reich.

(B) In that Germany refused and failed to join in an international guarantee of the new boundaries of the Czechoslovak State as provided for in Annex No. 1 to the Munich Agreements.

Charge XXII

Violation of the solemn assurances of Germany given on 3 Sept. 1939, 28 April 1939 and 6 Oct. 1939 that they would not violate the independence or sovereignty of the Kingdom of Norway.

Particulars

In that Germany, without warning, did on or about 9 April 1940 with its military and naval forces attack, invade and commit other

Charge XXVI

Violation of the Anglo-Soviet-Iranian Treaty of January 29, 1942, which provided that the forces of the Allied powers should be withdrawn from Iranian territory not later than six months after all hostilities between the Allied powers and Germany and her associates had been suspended.

Particulars

In that, in spite of the elapse of more than six months since the suspension of all hostilities between the Allied powers and Germany and her associates, and in spite of the protests of the Iranian, British and American Governments, the Soviet Government continued to maintain Soviet troops on Iranian territory after the date stipulated.

Charge XXVII

Violation of the Declaration of December 1, 1943, regarding Iran, signed at Teheran by Marshal Stalin, Prime Minister Churchill and President Roosevelt, stating that the Governments of the Soviet Union, Great Britain and the United States were at one with the Government of Iran in their desire for the maintenance of the independence, sovereignty and territorial integrity of Iran.

Particulars

In that the Soviet Government did, on or about November 19, 1945, set up in the Iranian Province of Azerbaijan a government hostile to the Iranian Government, and that Soviet armed forces prevented by force the

acts of aggression against the Kingdom of Norway.

Charge XXIII

Violation of German assurances, given on 28 April 1939 and 26 August 1939, to respect the neutrality and territorial inviolability of Luxembourg.

Particulars

In that Germany, without warning, and without recourse to peaceful means of settling any considered difference, did, on or about 10 May 1940, with a military force and in violation of the solemn assurances invade, occupy and absorb into Germany the sovereign territory of Luxembourg.

Charge XXIV

Violation of the treaty of non-aggression between Germany and Denmark signed at Berlin 31 May 1939.

Particulars

In that Germany without prior warning did, on or about 9 April 1940, with its military forces attack, invade and commit other acts of aggression against the Kingdom of Denmark.

Charge XXV

Violation of treaty of non-aggression entered into between Germany and U.S.S.R. on 23 Aug. 1939.

Particulars

(A) In that Germany did, on or about 22 June 1941 employ military forces to attack and commit acts of aggression against the U.S.S.R.

Iranian Government from reestablishing its authority over this portion of its territory, thereby violating the sovereignty and territorial integrity of Iran.

Charge XXVIII

Violation of the basic principles of international law and morality.

Particulars

(A) In that the USSR, in order to justify in advance the proposed annexation of Eastern Poland into the USSR, did, on or about October 22, 1939, under military occupation, organize fraudulent one-ticket elections to the so-called "National Assemblies" of Western Ukraine and Western Byelorussia.

(B) In that the USSR, in order to justify its attack on Finland and the proposed annexation of Finnish territory, did, on or about December 2, 1939, recognize a Soviet-appointed "People's Government" of Finland, and concluded with that body agreements disposing of Finnish territory.

(C) In that the USSR, in order to justify in advance the proposed annexation of the Republics of Estonia, Latvia and Lithuania, did, on or about June 14 and 15, 1940, under military occupation, organize fraudulent one-ticket elections to the so-called "Parliaments" of Estonia, Latvia and Lithuania.

(B) In that Germany, without warning or recourse to a friendly exchange of views or arbitration, did, on or about 22 June 1941 employ military forces to attack and commit acts of aggression against the U.S.S.R.

Charge XXVI

Violation of German assurance given on 6 Oct. 1939 to respect the neutrality and territorial integrity of Yugoslavia.

Particulars

In that Germany, without prior warning, did, on or about 6 April 1941, with its military forces attack, invade and commit other acts of aggression against the Kingdom of Yugoslavia.

APPENDIX II

Some excerpts from the *Daily Worker* of New York, official organ of the American Communist Party, showing changes in the policies of the Party in accordance with changes in the foreign policy of the Soviet Union, during the period July 1, 1939, to September 2, 1945.

I

Period before the Soviet-Nazi pact was signed in Moscow by Molotov and Ribbentrop on August 23, 1939

July 1

Editorial. ". . . Concessions granted to fascism are accelerators of fascist war . . ."

August 11

Editorial. "For the sake of world peace every firm stand of Poland . . . should be supported . . ."

August 18

Editorial. ". . . talk of American 'isolation' while the bandit Hitler goes about his robberies in Poland becomes real assistance to the Nazis in the present drive, and is a guarantee that should Fascism succeed this time, the injury to American security will soon be felt. We should never forget that the fascist dictators have already begun the second imperialist war, and that they are striving to expand the present conflicts into a world war directed against the leading democracies: the United States, France, Great Britain and the Soviet Union . . ."

August 19

Editorial. Measures Yet Needed to Halt the Fascist War Threat. ". . . Only the firmest stand on the part of the Warsaw government, definitely rejecting all trace of Munich capitulation, can save Polish independence . . ."

August 23

Editorial. The Soviet Union and Non-Aggression. "The people of Poland, whose national independence is in imminent danger from the threats of fascist aggression and Chamberlain's appeasement schemes . . . realize the firm position of the Soviet Union in uncompromising support for their freedom and independence . . . this support will be continued and further strengthened . . ."

II

Period from August 23, 1939, when the Molotov-Ribbentrop Pact was signed, to September 17, 1939, when the Soviet Union attacked Poland.

August 24

Text of the Molotov-Ribbentrop Pact given under the headline " 'Non-Aggression Pact Weapon for Peace, Open to All Nations,' says Browder." (Earl R. Browder, Secretary, American Communist Party, 1930 to 1945.)
Browder. ". . . there is a great deal of newspaper comment to the effect that this represents a change of policy by the Soviet Union, that it is a blow against Poland, and so on. All that, of course, is nonsense . . ."

August 25

Editorial. A Smashing Blow at Munich Treachery and Aggression. ". . . By compelling Germany to sign a non-aggression pact, the Soviet Union not only tremendously limited the direction of the Nazi war aims, but thereby bolstered the possibilities for the peace of the world . . . As to what the situation would be in the event of aggression of Nazi Germany against any nation, the Soviet Union's policy is crystal clear, not only in words but by repeated action as in China and Spain . . ."

August 29

William Z. Foster (Present Secretary of American Communist Party), speaking in Chicago:
". . . Even in the unlikely event of war . . . Chamberlain and Daladier will continue their 'appeasement' policy, and will be prepared to make a settlement and to steer the war against the Soviet Union . . ."

September 1 (Germany invades Poland).

Questions and Answers on the Non-Aggression Pact. "Q. If Germany marches into Poland and Poland needs aid and requests it, won't the Soviet Union find a way to give such aid? A. . . . if Poland resists and fights for its independence . . . it can be said that . . . the Soviet Union's policy is to assist every nation that becomes a victim of aggression . . . whether the Soviet Union would send in its Red Army, is a different question altogether. Certainly it would not unless the Polish government asked for it . . ."

September 2

Statement by Browder. "All progressive mankind feels the most profound hatred for the warmakers and equal sympathy for the Polish people, who must pay with their blood for the criminal stupidity of their own government's policy, dictated by Chamberlain, rejecting the proffered help of the Soviet Union, which alone could have arrested the danger. . . . our country cannot become involved in the quarrels that lead to the present conflict; America must actively seek an opportunity for a decisive intervention for peace, to follow up and cooperate with the energetic peace efforts of the Soviet Union."

(September 3, Great Britain and France declare that a state of war exists between them and Germany.)

September 4

Editorial. What U. S. Must Do to Defend Its Peace. ". . . Briefly and immediately, the peace and security of the American nation demands—
1. That the United States take the initiative in working out well-considered action to halt the war and to achieve peace,
. . . 3. That America pursuing this peace policy, immediately find every possible ways and means to aid Poland in defending its national independence . . ."

September 11

Editorial. All Aid to the Heroic Polish People:
". . . no people who can struggle so courageously can be downed. With them, the battle has just begun . . . Now is the time when Britain and France should be giving Poland the greatest aid . . ."

September 12

Letter to President Roosevelt by Foster and Browder on war crisis, dated September 11, 1939:
". . . we wish to place on record our firm accord with the stand of the President of our country against American involvement in the war, or in the rivalries and antagonisms which have led much of Europe into chaos . . ."

September 16

Editorial. The Capitalist Press and Pravda's Editorial on Poland. ". . . this is an imperialist war in which all the wreckers of small nations, from Hitler to Chamberlain, are vying for the domination of the world.

"Mighty and unruffled the USSR stands as the main bulwark of world peace, the defender of small nations, and the champion of human rights and progress."

III

Period September 17, 1939, when the Soviet Union attacked Poland, to June 22, 1941, when Germany attacked the Soviet Union.

September 17

Headline: Molotov Tells Nations of World USSR Stays Neutral in War.

September 18

Editorial. For National Freedom and World Peace. ". . . the Polish people . . . were being stabbed in the back by the Chamberlain Munichmen . . .

. . . In this situation the Soviet Government sent in the Red Army, as an army of liberation . . .

. . . Truly the Soviet Union has scored another triumph for human freedom—destined for the brightest page of history. It is in accordance with her steadfast unshakable peace policy and with her policy of neutrality . . .

. . . Hers was an act in aid of the Polish people who were betrayed and attacked by every single power involved in the present imperialist war . . .

. . . The whole foul scheme was to use Poland as a base for anti-Soviet provocations . . . But the Red Army's march smashed this plot, dealing another blow to Chamberlain's world war plans.

The whole of progressive mankind will be overjoyed at the Soviet's action for human liberation at a time when Chamberlain treachery is working feverishly to extend fascist barbarism and imperialist slavery over even wider areas.

. . . In her own interest, America will greet the Soviet Union's action as a service to world peace and freedom."

Editorial: Where There Is No Censorship. ". . . The Soviet Union makes no secret treaties. It does not say one thing and practice another behind the scenes . . ."

September 19

Declaration of the National Committee, Communist Party, USA. "The war that has broken out in Europe is the Second Imperialist War . . . This war, therefore, cannot be supported by the workers. It is not a war against fascism . . . not a war with any of the character of a just war, not a war that workers can or should support. It is a war between rival imperialisms for world domination. The workers must be against this war . . .

The British-French warmongers and their apologists . . . cry out that . . . they make war to 'destroy Hitlerism.' This is a hypocritical lie, one of those great historical lies . . .

Poland was deliberately sacrificed by the British and French statesmen in order to provide the occasion for their predatory, robber, imperialist war . . .

. . . Communists in all the belligerent countries . . . will vote against war credits . . . this war will bring the people nothing but misery, burdens, destruction and death . . .

. . . we must keep two guiding thoughts in mind: first, allow no single measure to be taken for purposes of giving American help to either side of the imperialist conflict; second, find the most effective means of keeping out of the war . . . These two guiding thoughts are inseparable . . ."

October 10

Editorial: The People Can Halt the War Now.
". . . Peace has been established in Eastern Europe because the USSR has been able to smash the Munich schemes for an anti-Soviet war with the Nazis as the spearhead of the warmakers.
. . . the basis for lasting peace has been laid in this area.
. . . German imperialism . . . has been forced to propose peace . . ."

October 25

Foster's article: ". . . the struggle to defeat the repeal of the arms embargo is a vital part of the people's fight to keep America out of the imperialist war. . . . We must especially counteract . . . the false notions that Great Britain and France are making war to defend democracy and that American participation in the war is inevitable."

November 1

Editorial: Molotov's Speech Expressing Mankind's Fight for Peace.
". . . The Anglo-French imperialists want to contrive, extend and enlarge this imperialist war. That definitely puts the responsibility on them for continuing the slaughter . . .
. . . the lifting of the embargo . . . is helping the Anglo-French imperialists . . ."

(November 29, 1939, the Soviet Union attacks Finland.)

December 1

A. Lapin from Washington: Headline: "U. S. State Department Files Give Secret of FDR's Drive to Use Finland as War Base."

December 6

Foster: "The Communist Party opposes the Administration's plan to spend three billion dollars next year to strengthen the navy, army and air forces. The reason for this opposition is that the present government is following the policy of territorial aggrandizement which leads straight toward war, with all the attendant misery, poverty, enslavement, and death for the workers and other toilers."

(December 14, The League of Nations expels the Soviet Union for aggression against Finland.)

December 14

Foster: Questions and Answers.
"Q. Is not the advance of Soviet troops into Finland a violation of the Finnish people's right of self-determination?
A. It is not. On the contrary, the Red Army is cooperating with the toiling masses of the Finnish people to establish a self-determination and national independence that has been denied them under their reactionary government . . ."

December 15

Foster: Questions and Answers.
"Q. Why didn't the Soviet Government accept President Roosevelt's proposal to use his 'good offices' for bringing about a peaceful settlement of the Finnish-Soviet difficulty?
A. Because President Roosevelt's intervention increased, not lessened, the difficulties between the Soviet and White Guard Finnish Governments . . .
Q. Did not the USSR become an aggressor by sending its armed forces into Finland?
A. It did not. The stigma of aggression rests upon Finland and the British and French Governments, who are responsible for the present conflict . . ."

December 28

Foster: "The broad outlines of a constructive American policy may be indicated as follows:

a. Foreign affairs—Stop giving active assistance to one side, the Allies in the imperialist war, and adopt a policy of neutrality . . .

b. Armaments—No support in the present huge Government expenditures for expanding the naval, air and army forces . . . oppose the M-Plan of industrial mobilization . . .

. . . From all the foregoing it is obvious that the Roosevelt Government is not following a peace policy . . ."

1940

January 2

Foster: ". . . in order to get a German Government that will do its bidding against the USSR, Great Britain has announced its determination to overthrow Hitler . . ."

January 5

Foster: ". . . it is . . . absurd to designate as imperialism the liberation of the peoples of Eastern Poland and Finland with the help of Red Army from their capitalist oppressors. 'Red imperialism' is a contradiction in terms, a lying invention of enemies of the people . . ."

January 12

Reproduction of a sticker: "The Yanks Are NOT Coming, signed Mr. and Mrs. America."

February 6

Browder (radio address to women): "President Roosevelt . . . has introduced a starvation budget into Congress . . . The best contribution our country could make to bleeding Europe . . . by serving notice that America will send not a dollar, not a gun, not a boy, for the imperialist war. Let's tell Europe, once and for all, that this time the Yanks are not coming . . ."

February 27

Foster, a speech: ". . . The Roosevelt Government, acting as the agent of finance capital, is actually dragging the American people into the war . . . Not only is it the basic interest of the American people to stay out of war, but it is also vital that the United States be not allowed to throw its reactionary influence into the present developing world struggle . . ."

(March 12, Soviet-Finnish war ends.)

March 14

Editorial: Unite for Further Victories Over the War-Makers.
". . . The imperialistic war-mongers in Great Britain, France and
the United States had made a military base in Finland. They
dreamed of throwing into it a lighted fuse . . . against the workers
republic, the Soviet Union . . . Events have proven that what
threatened the Finnish people was the war policy of the Manner-
heims and Tanners . . . For the small nations, particularly for the
Scandinavian countries, the peace in Finland means that the imperialistic moves to convert these countries into battlefields, has
been balked. . . . the present war . . . is a war from which the
working people have nothing to gain and everything to lose . . .
President Roosevelt's policy of today is in the interests of the
financial oligarchy and is directed at involving the United States
into the conflict . . . it was London, Paris and Wall Street which
were responsible for the war in the first place . . ."

April 6

Editorial: 'April 6th' Shall Not Be Again. ". . . Thousands will
march in America's towns and cities. On their banners they will
proclaim 'The Yanks Are NOT Coming.' . . . Among the demands
are: No aid, in the forms of loans, credits or any other manner to
any of the belligerents . . . Opposition to the war-and-hunger
budget of the Roosevelt Administration. No support to the foreign
policy of the Roosevelt Government which has turned the United
States into an arsenal for the war-makers abroad, which shares the
responsibility for inciting war in Europe, in Scandinavia and in the
Baltic . . ."

(April 9, Germany invades Norway and Denmark.)

April 23

Editorial: Roosevelt Attempts to Trade on His Past. ". . . The
Roosevelt record of 1940 is a record of broken promises and
betrayals . . ."

April 25

Budenz: FDR Dons "Liberal" Mask to Hide War Schemes.
". . . The cold-hard reality before the workers is that the White
House is resorting to every device—in following its war program
—of destroying the labor unions of both AFL and CIO. . . .
[Roosevelt] has not at all abandoned the plot to lead the wolf-
attack . . . on the Soviet peoples . . ."

(May 10, Germany invades Belgium, the Netherlands and Luxemburg.)

May 11

Editorial: This Is Not Our War—Keep U. S. Out of It. ". . . The imperialist bandits in each country—the Anglo-French and Hitler bandits—a handful of the population—are turning the world into a madhouse of murder . . . President Roosevelt cannot escape the share of responsibility for the criminal spreading of the war. . . . Starve the war and feed America. Keep America out of this criminal war . . ."

May 20

Browder's 49th Birthday. National Committee of the Communist Party to Browder: ". . . you have emerged as the most potent and creative political thinker in America . . . the leader of our Party . . . the teacher of our people . . ."

May 21

Foster, speech in Philadelphia on May 17: ". . . If British-French-American imperialism should win the present war the results would be even more reactionary . . . The Allied cause is not a 'lesser evil' in comparison to Hitler's . . . Nor would the entry of the U. S. into the war democratize it and make it a real fight for freedom . . . Its real war aims would be to grab off all possible territories for itself . . . to transform the imperialist war into a general war against the Soviet Union . . . In short, American imperialism in the war would be bound to be a strong and militant enemy of everything democratic and progressive . . ."

June 7

Foster. Questions and Answers. "Question: Why do Communists oppose President Roosevelt's program of national defense? Answer: . . . the Communist Party of the USA is against President Roosevelt's 5-billion dollar, 50,000 airplane plan because it is not a true national defense program. Nor is there anything of peace and democracy in it. On the contrary, it is an aggressing war program of Wall Street imperialists, whose wishes the present Administration is faithfully carrying out . . ."

(June 14, the Germans capture Paris.)

June 14

Foster. Questions and Answers. "Question: Should not the USSR, as a socialist country, support the Allies? Answer: . . . If the

British, French, and American imperialists were to win this war . . . they would speed straight for fascism . . . the only way it [the capitalist system] can be held together even temporarily in the face of the discontented and rebellious masses, will be through Fascist terrorism . . . support of the Allied imperialists . . . can only lead to the deepest enslavement of humanity . . ."

(June 15, Soviet troops occupy the Baltic States.)

June 19

Headline: Roosevelt Gets Ready to Attack South America.

(June 28, Soviet troops occupy Bessarabia and Northern Bukovina.)

July 3

Foster. Questions and Answers. "Question: Please explain the policy of the United States towards Japan . . . . Answer: . . . Roosevelt . . . fears a strong democratic China, and he would like to use Japan against the Socialist Soviet Union, in order to further American imperialist interests . . . [he] preferred to help Japan against both China and USSR . . ."

July 10

Foster. Questions and Answers. "Question: Would the entry of the United States into the war give the war a democratic character? Answer: It would not . . . It is for reactionary, imperialist objectives that the main sections of American big capitalism would join the war, not to crusade for human liberty . . . The United States did its full bit in checking the spread of European democracy and in laying the basis for the present war. Should the United States enter this war, its influence would be even more reactionary . . . The United States . . . true to its role as a great imperialist state . . . would follow no other cause than to support fascist-minded reaction . . . It is no less to the interest of the oppressed peoples of the countries involved in the war that they, in their fight for freedom, be not forced to confront the additional reactionary strength of our powerful imperialist government . . ."

July 19

Foster. Questions and Answers. "Question: Is . . . Churchill also an appeaser, or will he fight resolutely against Hitler and Hitlerism? Answer: Churchill . . . is an inveterate enemy of democracy in Great Britain and throughout the world . . . Should Churchill become convinced that the war against Hitler threatens to result in a decisive growth of people's democracy or Socialism, either in England or on the Continent, we may be sure he will . . . blossom forth as a full-fledged appeaser of Hitler . . . to the ruin of the British people's welfare, and even to the destruction of their national independence. Therefore, Churchill cannot be depended upon to fight Hitlerism, either at home or abroad . . ."

July 25

Foster [on Bessarabia]: ". . . In some cases Socialism is coming by the independent action of the masses in a given country, in others by decisive help from without . . . The occupation of Poland, Bessarabia and the Baltic countries by the USSR is part of this whole development . . ."

September 9

Browder's speech at Los Angeles: ". . . President's sensational coup of September 3 . . . In its cunning trickery, in its cynical betrayals . . . the Roosevelt coup d'etat is in the historical tradition of Louis Napoleon; in its social significance for today, it is a flagrant adaptation of the technique of Adolf Hitler; in its consequences for the American people it is a catastrophe . . . Roosevelt is leading the march . . . Willkie is his first assistant in the conspiracy against the well-being and very lives of the common people . . . only the Communist Party exposes and combats this gigantic imperialist counter-revolution . . ."

October 8

Foster's address at Boston: ". . . That the American war-mongers are exaggerating the danger of fascist attack upon the United States is clear . . . Japan is . . . in no shape to make effective war against this country . . ."

(October 27, Italy invades Greece.)

October 29

Editorial: Greece—the Latest Imperialist Victim. "London and Rome . . . both wolves pose as the noble friend of the lamb which is their victim . . ."

November 4

Final 1940 Election Address by Browder: ". . . I am not predicting a Japanese seizure of the Philippines. But I am calling your attention to the fact that the United States Navy is at this very moment all set to seize the French West Indies . . . United States seizure of Martinique will be as definite a war-initiative on the part of our government as would be the seizure of Manila on the part of the Japanese government . . . No, we Communists are not agents of Stalin . . . The Soviet Union has maintained peace with its neighbors . . . has made its defenses impregnable . . . The Communist Party would save America from catastrophe, by emulating the policy of Stalin . . ."

December 29

Browder. What Happened in the Year 1940. ". . . The most important net result of the year, on a world scale, has been the shift in the relation of forces as between the capitalist world . . . and the USSR . . . This is irrefutably established by the addition of six new Soviet republics comprising some twenty-three million inhabitants to the Soviet Union . . . The capitalist world has a net loss which includes further the gigantic destruction of its war . . ."

1941

January 5

Sunday Worker. Article by Milton Howard: U. S. Fast Becoming Military Base. ". . . The outlook for a handful of Wall Street aviation capitalists . . . is rosy; but what can the American farmer expect . . . Disasters, foreclosures, insecurity . . . As America is steered into 'war economy' for 1941, the American people face the biggest threat to their welfare in generations . . ."

January 14

Browder. Speech at Madison Square Garden: What is the Way Out of the Imperialist War? ". . . The Russian Revolution in 1917 under the leadership of Lenin and Stalin brought the end of the last world war. The present imperialist war will be brought to an end by a similar revolution in one or more major countries of Europe. It cannot be ended by present rulers, but only by their overthrow . . . the USSR . . . is a democracy infinitely higher than anything ever dreamed of before . . . it is a living example of the path out of the imperialist war . . ."

January 16

Editorial: Morgan-Rockefeller Banks Hail FDR's War Bill—Defeat It!—The Nation's Welfare is at Stake. ". . . The so-called 'lease-lend' bill provides for dictatorial powers which will permit President Roosevelt to transform America's present non-fighting belligerence into complete military participation in the war . . . The dictator bill now stands before the American people as the pet plan of the most reactionary, powerful banking interests in the

United States . . . the American people must stop this war dictatorship plan as a menace to their liberty at home and their security abroad . . . it is our right and duty to speak out against this dictatorial measure . . ."

January 17

Headline: War Powers Bill Means Fascist State.
Editorial: Get Out and Stay Out of the War. "What kind of bill is this 'lease-lend' war-powers Bill that Roosevelt is trying to pass through gag rule and terrorism of opposition? It appears that the Bill cannot stand up under calm investigation or reason. It requires hysteria and intimidation . . ."

January 23

Statement of the National Committee of the Communist Party: Defeat FDR's War-Powers Bill. Get Out and Stay Out of the War. ". . . Here are the facts . . . This Bill . . . would give the President *unlimited* authority to enter into foreign entanglements and secret alliances . . . This Bill would cancel the Bill of Rights and the Constitution . . . This Bill would saddle an unbearable burden of new taxes on the backs of America's workers, farmers, professionals and small business people . . .
People of America! Now is the time to make your voices heard! Now is the time to call a halt to the criminal plot . . . directed against you and your sons . . . Roosevelt, like Wilson before him, has deceived and betrayed you . . . Working people, do not be deceived again . . . the European conflict is a war between two gangs of thieves . . . in such a war all honest men can but hope and strive for the mutual destruction of both thieving outfits to the mutual benefit of their former victims—the people . . . Fellow Americans! . . . the way to aid the British people, and the German people . . . is by refusing any aid to either side in this imperialist war . . . Our most menacing enemy is not in Europe; it is the war-mad imperialism right here at home . . . No! it must not be! The workers and farmers, the people of America, have nothing to gain from war . . . Defeat the war-powers bill!"

February 13

Editorial: Mr. Willkie Reveals the Secret War Aim. ". . . This secret aim is for a joint British-American war against the Soviet Union at the earliest possible date . . ."

February 26

Browder's address at Mecca Temple. ". . . If my passport offense rates four years, what is the punishment that fits for the crime against the American people of Franklin D. Roosevelt? I think the punishment that will inevitably be inflicted for that crime, the supreme punishment will be written by history which will write down that name as the man who betrayed the peace and prosperity of the American people . . ."

March 18

Headline: 18,000 at Rally Roar "Free Browder."
Browder at the Rally: ". . . incredible as it seems, Roosevelt's central strategic conception was and remains essentially the same as that which led Chamberlain to Munich—namely, that the chief aim of the war is to force Hitler to march against the Soviet Union, with the threat of sustained war if he does not, and the promise of help and amnesty if he does . . . This is the great illusion. It is the too clever scheme which comes to wreck upon the rock of a simple fact. That fact is, that Hitler and the German high-command know it is less costly for them to fight all the rest of the world put together than to fight the Soviet Union . . ."

April 15

Editorial: The Soviet Union Wins a Victory for Peace. "In its neutrality pact with the Japanese Government, the Soviet Union registers once more the strength and consistency of its peace policy . . . The pact constitutes a major victory for Soviet peace diplomacy . . . Out of the present Soviet-Japanese pact the Chinese people will gain . . . The USSR gives to the American people a powerful example how to carry a policy of peace . . ."

April 29

Manifesto of the National Committee of the Communist Party. ". . . The imperialists have made the war; we, the people, must make the peace. *Get out and keep out of the imperialist war—No convoys, no AEF*—The Yanks are not coming—Dissolve the Anglo-American war alliance—For a people's peace with no indemnities and no annexations—Against the militarization of the United States under the false pretense of national defense . . ."

May 8

Editorial: Priming America for the Fatal Plunge. ". . . Every promise which Roosevelt made . . . to keep America out of war has been callously violated . . . After Stimson's speech . . . it is the brink of the precipice . . . When will President Roosevelt push that button of disaster? . . . The time for the great awakening . . . is here and now—the American people do have it in their immense organized power to compel a reversal of the war policy. . . . It is not 'defense,' not national welfare, not national safety, which is involved in the rush into the war by the Government. It is empire, conquest, profits . . . If the nation hesitates now in its duty, the Stimsons will take us into the Inferno."

June 15

Sunday Worker. Headline: British Press Hoping for War Upon USSR. ". . . any analysis of the political situation shows that an Anglo-German deal is the only possible basis for an eventual attack against the Soviet Union . . ."

June 20

Editorial: Wall St. Indulges in Wishful Thinking About the Soviet Union. ". . . The extravaganzas now being dressed up as 'news' of a crisis between Germany and the Soviet Union . . . have been resorted to time after time in the past . . . As happened so often in the past, the Soviet Union will be able to take care of itself in the midst of the capitalists sharks. When all is said and done, it will emerge from the present campaign of incitement against it, stronger than when that campaign was launched."

June 21

Editorial: The Telegram Spills the Beans. ". . . The Telegram editorial reveals what kind of war Washington and Wall Street want—an anti-Soviet war . . . How quickly they could swing around to support a Hitler attack against the neutral Soviet Union! The wisdom of Stalin . . . becomes a thousand-fold apparent . . ."

IV

Period June 22, 1941, when Germany attacked the Soviet Union, to December 7, 1941, when Japan attacked Pearl Harbor.

June 23

Statement of the Communist Party (signed by Foster and Minor). "The armed assault by German fascism and its satellites against the champion of peace, freedom and national independence—the land of Socialism. This military aggression by the fascist rulers is also an attack upon the people of Germany. It is an attack likewise upon the peoples of the United States and of the entire world. . . . the Soviet Government is now waging . . . a just struggle for the cause of the freedom of all nations and peoples . . . The Soviet Union adopted and pursued a consistent policy of neutrality toward both sides in the imperialist war, a policy based upon rendering aid to those nations that were waging a just struggle for national independence and liberty . . . It liberated the peoples of the Western Ukraine, Western White Russia, Bessarabia and the Baltic States . . . Thus it served the best interests of the

working class and peoples of the entire world . . . The American
people . . . will see in the cause of the Soviet Union the cause of
all advanced and progressive mankind. They should defeat every
attempt at a new Munich conspiracy . . . For full support and
cooperation with the Soviet Union in its struggle against Hitlerism!"

June 25

Editorial: For Full and Immediate Aid to the USSR. "The
most dangerous political speculation at this moment in the country
comes from a group of pro-fascists typified yesterday by the utter-
ance of Senator Truman of Missouri.
This reactionary proposes for the American people the policy
whereby 'if we see that Germany is winning we ought to help
Russia, and if Russia is winning, we ought to help Germany, and
that way let them kill as many as possible . . .'
We ought to help Hitler Germany! This is the essence of Senator
Truman's cynical calculation . . . Calculations such as these are
an obvious menace to the American people and the security of the
country. They are the original Munich calculations magnified ten-
fold . . . Such super-Munichs are aimed not only at the Soviet
Union; the bitter price will have to be paid by the degradation of
the English people . . . It is a mockery to propose such a policy in
the name of American interests . . ."

June 26

Editorial: Action is Needed, Mr. President. ". . . the American
people, eager to aid the Soviet Union destroy the Nazi menace,
cannot fail to note the half-hearted, even flippant manner in which
President Roosevelt approached the issue of aid to the Soviet
Union at his press conference . . . It becomes clearer every hour
that the defeat of the Hitler fascist regime by the Soviet Union is
vital to the interests of the American people . . . The people note
with disquiet the absence of definite commitments and proposals on
the part of the Government . . . immense resources of our country
. . . can be made available and placed . . . in the hands of the
Soviet forces . . ."

June 30

Manifesto of the National Committee of the Communist Party:
". . . The involvement of the Soviet Union in the war has changed
the character of the war . . . Hitler's attack upon the Soviet
Union imports a new and sinister aspect to the menace of Hitlerism for the American people, the British people and the people
of the world . . . In this struggle, the American people are by no
means neutral or unconcerned. They cannot but strive for the

defeat of Hitlerism. They cannot but adopt a policy that favors
and gives to the Soviet Union ALL SUPPORT . . . the American
people must throw in the full weight of their might and power to
defeat German fascism . . . The people of America are beginning
to realize that to defend the Soviet Union means to defend the
United States . . . Within the Roosevelt Administration itself
there are those who would conciliate and compromise with the
friends of Hitler and fascism . . .
The chief guarantee for the successful realization of this program
is the struggle for the United front of the working class and the
unity of the American people in a genuine people's front. Such a
united and people's front would be broad enough to embrace in
fraternal collaboration all honest opponents of Hitlerism, both
here and abroad . . . We, on our part, speaking in the name of
the Communist Party of the United States, pledge our all, to work
and struggle as a part of the American people for the realization
of this program . . .
. . . Defend America by giving full aid to the Soviet Union,
Great Britain and all nations who fight against Hitler! For full
and unlimited collaboration of the United States, Great Britain
and the Soviet Union to bring about the military defeat of fascism!
. . . Stop all government attacks on the Communist Party! Release Earl Browder! . . ."

July 1

Abridged text of the report of William Z. Foster, National Chairman of the Communist Party, delivered at the meeting of June 28:
"Our National Committee is indeed meeting at a historic moment.
After 23 years of plotting and scheming the capitalist reactionaries, captained by Hitler, have finally launched their armed attack
against the Soviet Union . . . Hitler's attack upon the Soviet
Union changes the character of the world war, and thereby makes
necessary changes in our Party's attitude toward that war. Previously the war had been a struggle between the rival imperialist
power groupings . . . We correctly did not take sides. Our slogan
was to 'get out and stay out of the war.' We opposed both imperialist camps . . . But now with Hitler's war against the Soviet
Union, the whole situation is basically altered . . . It is not only
that the life of the first Socialist country is at stake—the democracy and national independence of every country is jeopardized,
not least that of the United States . . . Our Party, therefore,
throws its full support in defense of the Soviet Union in its
struggle against Hitler . . . The great might of America must be
thrown against Hitler . . . aid to Britain must be increased . . .
The Hitler war against the USSR is thus both a bread and butter
question for the American people and a menace to all their liberties
. . . The way to defend America is by helping the USSR smash
Hitler . . ."

July 5

Editorial: Stalin's Pledge: Tomb of Fascism. ". . . The people of America have come to the realization that the German fascist domination of Europe and the Soviet Union endangers the very existence of the United States as an independent, democratic nation . . . America's mortal enemy, Hitlerism, can be thoroughly defeated . . . in the heroic Soviet peoples, now shedding their blood, America has a powerful and loyal ally. America has made pledges of full aid to the Soviet peoples . . . Our honor, our safety, demand that these pledges be kept and realized at once. . . . The power and strength of the United States thrown into the scales against Hitler, can become decisive in the world conflict to destroy German fascism. To accomplish this is our historic duty."

July 13

Sunday Worker. Article by Gil Green: The Nazi Aggression Against the Soviet Union and the Changed Character of the World War. ". . . Until June 22 the war was an imperialist war because the ruling classes waging it did so for imperialist objectives, for world power. The war was therefore an unjust war on both sides. Of course, there were just causes involved. The struggle of Yugoslavia and other small nations for their national independence were just causes, but these were not powerful enough to basically alter the dominant imperialist character of the struggle . . . The involvement of the Soviet Union introduces a just war of a big power . . . Therefore a mighty democratic, anti-imperialist and Socialist force has become involved in the struggle . . . (it) has therefore basically altered the dominant character of the war . . . we must recognize that now there is only one war . . . Every blow struck against this main enemy is a blow in the interests of the Soviet people, the people of Europe, and the peoples of the world. The war against Hitler fascism has therefore become a just war on the part of all those who wage it . . . But this struggle cannot be left to the Soviet and British people alone . . ."

July 15

Editorial: United States Aid to the British-Soviet Pact. ". . . The Pact embodies the changed character of the war, revealing it now as a war in which the main aim is the preservation of national independence against Nazi conquest . . . How vital in this moment become the pledges for all-out aid to Hitler's enemies, Britain and the Soviet Union. Hitler has feared like death the opening up of a vast western front against him while he invaded the USSR. Now this western front can be electrified into a smashing assault against the Nazi machine. American aid becomes the powerful lever for opening up the western front . . . America's opportunity is just here . . . No toying with a 'truce' on Hitler's western front!"

Editorial by James S. Allen: The Urgent Need for an Offensive from the West. "The Anglo-American combination certainly cannot afford to merely speculate upon a long Soviet-German war, while strengthening their own positions . . . A great offensive upon the Continent—this is the crying need of the moment."

July 17

Speech of Foster in San Francisco on July 16. ". . . The signing of the British-Soviet Mutual Assistance Pact is of gigantic significance . . . it is the historic duty of the American people to give the Soviet-British alliance the fullest support and to become a full fledged member of it at the earliest practical moment . . . Already this country, a declared enemy of Hitler, is virtually a war ally of Great Britain . . . But the full logic of the situation can be realized only when the United States openly supports the pact and becomes officially a part of it."

July 27

Foster at Los Angeles: ". . . The United States must throw everything necessary into the struggle—munitions, funds, and when needed, also men . . ."

August 5

Foster at San Francisco. ". . . The first great collision between Hitler and the Soviet peace policy . . . occurred just when Hitler had smashed the British and French armies . . . Great Britain was thrown into a panic . . . Why did not Hitler deal the fatal blow? Well, right at the most decisive moment, on June 28, 1940 . . . when Britain was in deepest demoralization, the Red Army suddenly marched into Bessarabia. This march was in line with the policy the USSR previously had been following . . . of strengthening its defense by incorporating into its ranks a number of small bordering countries—eastern Poland, Estonia, Latvia and Lithuania . . . Hitler was obviously deeply alarmed . . . so he withheld his crucial invasion blow against England and turned his attention for the next three months to the Balkans . . . it was the march of the Red Army into Bessarabia that caused Hitler to hold up his invasion . . ."

August 26

Editorial: Saving Iran from Hitler's Clutches. ". . . The present occupation of the country . . . is not for purposes of conquest. The entire course of relationship on the part of the Soviet Union with that country has been in the interests of Iranian independence."

September 10

Editorial: America Must Give Its Answer. "The actions of Hitler on the high seas must not go unchallenged. They require the type of answer that will make it clear that the United States intends to fulfill its obligations and do its share to defeat Hitler . . . America is in this war—that fact has been decided by Hitler himself . . . The safety of the country. requires the military destruction of Hitlerism."

September 11

Editorial: More and Speedier. ". . it is certainly true that the Soviet Union is not getting sufficient help . . . Every day of delay in opening the western front against Hitler is an advantage to the Nazis . . ."

September 12

Editorial: On the Central Front. ". . . now is the time to strike from the West. It is not only possible but necessary to deal Hitler a crushing blow now . . ."

September 13

Editorial: None Too Soon. ". . . The United States is in the most extreme danger that it has faced since the battle of Gettysburg. We are being attacked; a gigantic power is making war upon us . . ."

September 18

Editorial: Herbert Hoover—America's Petain. ". . . Hooverism is the advance-guard of the Nazi invasion . . ."

September 21

Sunday Worker, Editorial: America's Immediate Duty to Itself. ". . . The Nazis have long since attacked America . . . It has long since been a question of 'going to war.' America has been at war for a long time. . . . To 'wait for Hitler to attack us' is to give America's most ruthless enemy the maximum advantages, and guarantee him the victory. It is the counsel of treason . . . The safety of the United States demands a two-fisted war against Hitler, east and west. Millions in France and Norway await the armies of invasion . . . Let the United States, inspired and aided by the Red Army's resistance, take its rightful place in the battle."

October 2

Editorial: Delay Increases United States' Peril. ". . . The decisive need of the hour is a two-front war, the immediate opening up of Western hostilities . . . A million allied troops landed on the Continent today would set Europe on fire . . . our country, in its own national interest, must undertake equal responsibility for the military annihilation of Hitler."

October 9

Editorial: Hitler's Western Front is Weak—Strike Now! ". . . The United States and Britain now jointly stand face to face with an open western coast, where they can deal Hitler a death-blow while he is engaged by the Red Army in the east . . . This is the golden opportunity . . . The time is here and now . . ."

October 10

Editorial: What Are You Doing to Save America? ". . . Stop all delay and hesitations in putting into effect the President's 'shoot first' policy. Open up a western front as the joint military undertaking of America and Britain . . ."

October 16

Editorial: Moscow is in Danger. ". . . It is another way of saying that New York is in danger . . . Never was the peril to our own America as grave as now . . . the duties of our Government are clear and unmistakeable—First, let it join hands with Britain to open new fronts against Hitler . . . second, repeal the unreal Neutrality Act . . ."

October 17

Editorial: America's Duty in the Far East. ". . . our country is in the center of a gigantic pincer drive, with one arm stemming from Berlin through Moscow and the other taking shape from Tokio through Siberia. . . . In self-defence the United States and Britain must undertake to guarantee the Far Eastern territory of the Soviet Union. Japan should be told that if it makes one aggressive move upon Siberia or the Soviet's Maritime Provinces, this government would regard it as a hostile act. The American navy is in a position to back up such an announcement with deeds . . ."

October 30

Foster: Questions and Answers. Q. What is the attitude of the Communist Party towards a declaration of war by the United States against Nazi Germany? A. From the outset of Hitler's attack upon the USSR, on June 22, and the consequent transformation of the imperialist war into a people's war . . . the Communist Party is fully in favor of the United States' full participation in the war, for a declaration of war against Nazi Germany.

Q. Did the USSR make a mistake in signing the non-aggression pact with Nazi Germany? A. It did not . . . had the USSR gotten into the war against Germany two years ago it would not only have had to fight Nazi Germany, but it would have confronted as well the opposition of the United States, Great Britain and France . . . They considered the USSR as their main enemy and would have gone far to encompass its downfall. The Beck Government of Poland, then a close collaborator with Nazi Germany, might even have forced that country to take up arms against the USSR . . ."

November 19

Foster: Questions and Answers. "Q. How is it to be explained that the Daily Worker is now greatly emphasizing the danger of invasion of the United States by Hitler's forces, whereas before the Nazis attacked the USSR, it did not stress this danger? A. Until Hitler attacked the USSR this country was in no imminent danger of actual invasion . . . should Hitler succeed in basically weakening the Soviet Union the United States would be right in the line of fire . . ."

November 25

Foster: Questions and Answers. "Q. What is the Communist attitude toward universal military conscription? A. Universal military service is the democratic form of the American national armed forces. The Communist Party favors it. The reason why the Communists worked against the passage of the Universal Selective Service Act . . . was because this measure was part of the general military preparations for American participation in the imperialist war, to which the Communist Party was opposed."

V

Period December 7, 1941, when Japan attacked Pearl Harbor to the Conclusion of the Teheran Conference December 1, 1943.

December 8

National Committee of the Communist Party: "This unprovoked act of war . . . is directed also against the USSR . . . The Communist Party pledges its loyalty, its devoted labor and last drop of its blood in support of our country in this greatest of all the crises that ever threatened its existence.

1942

January 11

Sunday Worker. Article by Howard. ". . . Just wars become unjust; and unjust wars can become transformed by changed conditions into their opposite. This is the dialectic method of Marxism . . ."

January 13

Editorial: ". . . As to the Communist Party: its record is an open book in its consistent stand for American national defense against the Axis aggressors . . ."

January 15

Lapin from Washington: "Joseph E. Davies' 'Mission to Moscow' . . . is now required reading in official Washington, and is provoking plenty of serious thinking and re-evaluation of the role of the USSR, particularly about . . . the consistent anti-Hitler trend of Soviet foreign policy."

February 11

Foster's speech at Schenectady: Smash Hitler's Spring Offensive Now. ". . . our country and the United Nations as a whole, absolutely must militantly take the offensive . . . Great Britain is making a similar mistake, by keeping her huge, highly equipped army idle in her home island, waiting for Hitler to attack it . . . the creation of a new European front by Great Britain and the United States is imperative . . ."

February 25

Headline: Davies Addresses 20,000 at Chicago Russian Aid Rally. ". . . Lashing out at the 'weasel' attacks against the integrity of the Soviet Union, Mr. Davies declared, 'by the testimony of performance and in my opinion, the word of honor of the Soviet Government is as safe as the Bible.' '. . . The Soviet Union,' he pointed out, 'stands staunchly for international morality.' It stood by Ethiopia, gave money, munitions and 'real help' to China, wanted to come to the aid of Czechoslovakia, but was 'ignored, scorned, insulted, excluded' by its own allies . . ."

February 28

Headline: Cliveden Set Serves Hitler's Game—Davies. ". . . From personal experience and observation in the Soviet Union, Davies said he was convinced that the Russians would never violate a treaty or promise of any kind. 'The record of the Soviet Union,' he said, 'is one of complete observance of its agreements.' 'If I were lost in the wilderness and badly injured, I would as soon have Stalin, Litvinoff or Voroshilov for my companion as any other man in the world, because I would know that they would stand by me and see me through safely if it were in their power to do so,' Davies said. '. . . the Russians like ourselves . . . have no territorial ambitions . . .' "

April 1

Editorial: Hitler is Weak on Europe's Coast. ". . . what is the 'earliest date' of which General Marshall speaks? It is obviously the immediate present. The combined British and American forces are formidable . . . the time to strike Hitler on a second front is here and now."

April 16

Article by Foster: For a Western Front—The Means are at Hand. ". . . there are some three millions of fully-trained and highly armed soldiers now idling on the defensive in Britain . . . what is imperative for victory is a major Anglo-American offensive, the establishment of a great Western Front. To postpone such offensive action until 1943 would be to invite irretrievable military disaster to our country, as well as the rest of the world . . . it is not only military ineptitude, but sheer cowardice to assert that a western front is impossible this year. It can and it must be achieved."

May 2

Editorial: Stalin's Order of the Day—The Inspiration to Crush Hitler in 1942. ". . . Every material possibility for an immediate world-wide counter-drive against Hitler from all directions, and especially in a Western Front in Europe, is completely available . . . Failure to act means endless war for survival, torment and incredibly greater losses than would be needed to win now . . . Stalin's reiterated pledge against seizure of foreign lands also knocks to pieces propaganda . . . about the Soviet Union's 'conquest of Europe' . . ."

May 8

Headline: Red Army Defends United States, says Davies. ". . . It is neither good Christianity, good sense nor even good sportsmanship, to impugn the good faith, honor or integrity of the promises of the Soviet Government. They have given their word as to what their promises are. . . . The Red Armies are standing at the ramparts of civilization . . . In the name of high mindedness, patriotism and fineness, which I know is to be found in American businessmen, I am sure you will put your shoulder to this wheel. It is good business. It is fine humanitarianism . . ."

May 9

Headline: Second Front Will Lick Hitler Now, Davies Says in Magazine Article. ". . . The Nazis have shown by deeds as well as words that their purpose is to dominate the world. Stalin has never aimed at such domination . . . In the event of an Allied victory, Stalin would not be the master of Europe, nor would he, in my opinion, seek mastery. His objectives, publicly stated, are these: 1. to put an end to the Hitler menace and liberate the Hitler-subjugated countries, 2. to ensure to those countries governments of their own choice. In any post-war world, Russia and the United States (and England and China) could get along because of a mutual fairness, tolerance and an inclination to live and let live. Russia and the United States, furthermore, supplement each other economically."

May 27

Editorial: The Attitude of the Frightened Rabbit. ". . . the reluctance to open a Western Front . . . still strangely persists . . . The 'argument' of Pearson and Allen that 'Hitler couldn't invade England' . . . is a sheer fallacy. It forgets that Hitler couldn't invade England, not because of any shipping difficulties at all, but because the Red Army was constantly moving up behind his heels as he advanced through France toward England. It was the Red Army which saved Britain . . ."

June 17

Article by James S. Allen, Foreign Editor, *Daily Worker*: The Soviet Union and the Atlantic Charter. ". . . These Balticists and Dunkirkists are misrepresenting . . . the basic and consistent position of the Soviet Union . . . The USSR embodies the principle of the right of self-determination in practice . . . Today, although their countries are overrun, citizens of the Baltic Soviet countries are fighting shoulder to shoulder with the other peoples of the Soviet Union to drive the occupationists out of the Soviet land, which is now their land . . . Many of the commentators . . . have spun all kind of fancy theories . . . none of them seem to understand the simple truth as far as the Baltic countries are concerned: they were Soviet territory when the Nazis started their invasion and they will remain Soviet territory when Hitler is defeated; it was not a question open for discussion."

June 22

Editorial: June 22, 1941—Our Duty Today. ". . . So long as the Red Army stood behind him, Hitler knew . . . that he could not invade Britain . . . Let us commemorate this day with renewed efforts for the Second Front, for complete unity behind the Roosevelt-Molotov Pacts . . . In ever firmer alliance with the Soviet Union does the progressive future of America rest . . ."

July 9

Editorial: The Peril of Delay. ". . . Mortal peril lies to our country . . . in every moment's delay of a full-blown offensive against Hitler in Western Europe . . . The favorable weather conditions for a decisive Allied invasion of the Continent are slipping fast . . ."

July 31

Editorial: A Grim Warning to America and Britain. ". . . The whole country must be mobilized to smash the unprecedented danger facing our nation. A veritable avalanche of voices . . . must be raised for the establishment of the Second Front now— without another moment of delay !"

(August 7, American forces attack at Guadalcanal.)

August 7

Headline: Soviets Still Fight Alone, Hold at Stalingrad.
Editorial: Mrs. Roosevelt's Letter. ". . . Mrs. Roosevelt dragged the issue of Communism into the election campaign . . . The Communist Party of the United States is not, and never has been, controlled by Russia, as Mrs. Roosevelt charges . . ."

August 30

Sunday Worker. Editorial by Allen: Three Years of War in Europe. ". . . The line of Munichite appeasement prevailed as the dominant policy from 1938 to June 1941 . . . In a few weeks . . . Western Poland was under the Nazi· heel, while England and France did not move a finger . . . Only the Soviet Union acted, at first in Eastern Poland, later in Finland and the Baltic countries, and her determined stand halted Hitler's eastward plunge . . . the action of the Soviet Union in marching into Bessarabia and Bukovina . . . had caused Hitler to postpone his invasion of England . . . With the entry of the Soviet Union in the war . . . the war was transformed into a people's war of liberation against Nazi tyranny . . ."

September 13

Sunday Worker. Foster: Our National Humiliation. ". . . It can be confidently said that had the Red Army, under the given circumstances, faced the task of getting across the English Channel, it would have accomplished it many months ago . . ."

(November 7, the American and British armies invade North Africa.)

December 22

Editorial: Our Great Opportunity. ". . . We cannot and must not permit this winter to slip by without a second front as we did last year . . . We must meet the enemy in battle . . . Victory is within our grasp. The war can be decided this winter."

1943

(January 24, at the Casablanca Conference, Roosevelt and Churchill announce the war will continue until the "unconditional surrender" of Germany, Italy and Japan.)

January 30

Editorial: The Approaching Doom. ". . . We stand in what can become the final phase of the war . . . Strengthen national unity around the Commander-in-Chief . . ."

February 14

Sunday Worker. Foster: Soviet Democracy. ". . . It is safe to forecast . . . that when the Axis is defeated, when the world builds reasonable safeguards against the recurrence of war and, thus, when it will be possible to relax the present Soviet discipline, democracy in the USSR will flourish in a manner that will amaze the world . . . The assertion . . . that Stalin is an autocrat and dictator over the Soviet people, is a lie . . . Americans should beware of the slanderers of the Soviet Union, those who shout about 'Red imperialism,' they are the . . . friends or the dupes of Hitler propaganda . . ."

February 15

Allen: The Anti-Soviet Offensive. ". . . an extremely brazen piece by an American writer in the *Washington Star* fantastically charging that the Soviet Union intends to take over practically all of Europe and parts of Asia . . . Krock . . . speculates . . . a victorious Russia, master of Europe, may need more than the sermons of Henry Wallace . . . Fortunately, more farsighted . . . Walter Lippmann . . . has been arguing rather consistently against those 'frightened of victory' . . ."

February 16

Editorial: Speed, Speed, Speed . . . "The main problem, Mr. *Times* [N.Y.], is not to warn the Soviet Union about its obligations to respect the self-determination of the European peoples . . . but to assure the speedy liberation of the peoples by opening the Western Front without further delay . . ."

February 24

Editorial: Stalin's Call. "When Munichites and appeasers in high places encourage Finland, Polish and other emigre circles to press their reactionary and anti-Soviet demands, they are endangering the security of our nation . . ."

March 7

Browder: Defeatist Attack on Soviet Alliance Menaces Victory. ". . . Fear of victory is creating confusion and chaos in our war effort . . . the fear of sharing victory with the Soviet Union is an example of a phobia, an unreasoning fear . . . a form of insanity . . . At present the Government is of two minds; the President advances one policy, Congress and a part of the President's Cabinet an opposite policy . . . The Soviet Union is only an advanced expression of the genius for self-government . . . its inner organizations prevent the rise of any aggressive forces within it, directed against the rest of the world . . ."

March 10

Editorial: Standley's Provocation. "Admiral Standley's statement in Moscow came as a shock to the peoples of America and all the United Nations . . . All patriotic Americans will be ashamed at the disgusting lack of modesty shown by Standley . . . Clearly, Ambassador Standley does not represent the views of the American people and the policies of our Government . . . American patriots! . . . Now is the time to speak out, now is the time to act. It is time to call a halt to all Anti-Soviet . . . intrigues . . . Above all it is imperative to secure the opening of the second front in Europe now."

(April 25, the Soviet Government breaks relations with the Polish Government.)

April 27

Editorial: A Blow Against Hitler and His Polish Intriguers: ". . . the Soviet Union's note, breaking off relations with the Polish fascist regime, performs a service to the cause of the United Nations . . . In becoming a tool of Berlin, the Polish regime becomes an enemy no less of the United States and of Britain than of the Soviet Union and of the heroic Polish people . . . Having surrendered Poland to Germany, this regime now resumes its struggle to prevent the liberation of the Polish people . . . Such is the real situation. On it, America must act. The continuance of American relations with the pro-Hitler Polish regime-in-exile is now incompatible with American national security . . ."

May 1

Communist Manifesto For May Day. . . . On this May Day, the working class from Communists to Conservatives, renews its pledge of support and loyalty to the Commander-in-Chief, President Roosevelt, pledging all its energy and devotion for the fulfilment of our nation's most immediate, most urgent need—the Second Front invasion of Europe . . ."

May 3

Gold: "Mission to Moscow," The "Uncle Tom's Cabin" of the Present Era. ". . . a quiet, reasonable, sensible objective portrait . . . one realizes that nearly everything said about Russia was a lie."

May 7

Headline: Stalin Reaffirms Soviet Union's Hope to See a Strong and Independent Poland.
Editorial: Stalin and Poland. ". . . For the Labor movement and the nation the issue is clear. Nothing must be allowed to mar the relations between our own country and our powerful ally . . ."

May 24

Editorial: The Historic Act of the Comintern. "The proposal to dissolve the Comintern is . . . made to the interest of . . . promoting the fighting alliance of the anti-Hitler coalition . . . it should be clear that the fraternal relation of the Communist Party of the USA . . . to the Comintern never was an obstacle to the American-Soviet relations."

Browder's statement: "The proposal of dissolution of the Comintern . . . does not affect organizationally the status of the Communist Party of the United States, because since 1940 the C. P. of the U. S. has maintained no affiliation outside the borders of our country. It is my opinion, however, that the C. P. of the U. S. will express its agreement with the proposal and its motivation."

May 29

Headline: A Warm Welcome in Moscow (a photo of Stalin with Joseph E. Davies).
Editorial: The Grand Alliance. ". . . Mr. Davies' comment . . .

indicates that some of the important obstacles to closer United States-Soviet understanding have been removed."

May 31

Headline: Proof of Republican Anti-War Plot. "Mission to Moscow" Denounced as Phony Propaganda. Drive on "Mission" Aimed at FDR. ". . . what is in effect a 'save Hitler' conspiracy among the anti-Willkie republicans, anti-Roosevelt democrats, Trotzkyites, Christian Fronters and other fifth columnists disclosed itself more brazenly than ever . . . patriotic American people will have to get together back of the President for unity . . ."

June 12

Editorial: Hoover vs. the Nation. "The country knows Hoover well by now as a leading defeatist . . . a sworn foe of labor and the American people . . ."

June 20

Editorial: Two Years After. ". . . The radical change in the thinking of the public about the Soviet Union is the biggest 'revolution' brought about by the war within our own country . . ."

July 14

Excerpts from Browder's broadcast. ". . . the Communists have long agreed with the Soviet leaders on the answers to most of the main world questions of the day. That is . . . natural . . . inevitable . . . No, the Communists will never accept dictation from any source now or in the future . . ."

July 23

Editorial: Catholics and Rome. ". . . American Catholics, as true to their country, have no choice but to call for more bombings of Rome . . . They can let such views be known to the Commander-in-Chief . . ."

August 6

Editorial: A Great Day. ". . . the collapse in Sicily, the debacle of Mussolini, the impasse of the Italian king and his marshal . . . all these stem from the new and growing power of the Red army on the Eastern front . . ."

August 18

Editorial: Byrnes' Speech. ". . . Nowhere in his speech does Byrnes take account of the golden opportunity for striking the fatal blow at Hitler Germany which is presented by the Soviet victories . . . instead we are presented with a lot of mythical statistics to prove that we have a long and hard war ahead of us . . ."

September 1

Editorial: The State Department. ". . . The people expect that Hull . . . will . . . clean out the cesspool of anti-Soviet and anti-democratic intriguers . . ."

September 4

Editorial: Invasion of Italy. ". . . The American people welcome the Anglo-American offensive in Italy . . . But what the American people demand above all else is that simultaneously we now strike from England . . . in Western Europe . . ."

September 6

Allen: Harry Hopkins' Timetable. ". . . He concentrates attention upon a pure speculation, completely unfounded, that 'we may lose Russia.' He cannot mean that we will lose her as an ally through the defeat of the Red Army . . . It is hard to believe that such a high-placed adviser should suffer from the paralysis of indecision . . . it does seem to me that our Commander-in-Chief might need new advisers . . ."

October 9

Foster: Soviet Democracy: A War Factor. ". . . it is the most profoundly democratic of all states . . ."

October 15

Lapin: Copperhead Offensive. ". . . fantastic notion that it is possible to equate the puny, limited war effort of Great Britain and the United States with the achievements and the sacrifices of the Russians who have carried practically the whole brunt of the war . . ."

October 25

Allen: The Historic Fact. "It is inevitable, inescapable, totally natural that the Soviet Union is viewed by the peoples of Europe as their liberator. The Soviet Union is mainly, some people would say almost entirely, responsible for the coming liberation of Europe . . . No policies drawn up in the chancelories, no relations now evolving have any prospect of permanent success unless the historic fact of our times is known and accounted for."

October 30

Foster: United States Policy at Moscow Parley. ". . . our delegation should give the USSR a definite date, and an early one at that, for . . . the second front . . . We must concede that country its legitimate borders . . . it is to be hoped that our delegation is setting its face like flint against the brazen attempt of American defeatists to force the USSR into the war against Japan."

November 7

Sunday Worker. Browder: ". . . The Soviet Power is a natural friend and ally of the United States, and perhaps the only one which gives to us more than it expects from us . . ."

VI

Period from December 2, 1943, when Roosevelt, Churchill and Stalin concluded the Teheran Conference, to February 11, 1945, when they concluded their Conference at Yalta.

December 7

Editorial: The Historic Teheran Meeting. "Like no other event that men and women of our generation can remember, the meeting of our President with Marshal Stalin and Premier Churchill overwhelms the imagination . . . the handclasp of our leaders is a pledge that out of this war comes a new dawn for all humankind."

December 8

Editorial: The Iran Guarantee. ". . . It means that the countries whose armed forces helped . . . in Persia . . . reject every conception of 'spheres of influence' . . . The Soviet Union of course . . . broke completely with the imperialist policies of the Czar . . . In brief, all these speculators who glibly chatter about alleged Soviet aspirations for the Persian gulf or the Mosul oil-fields are thoroughly rebuked . . ."

December 12

Browder Answers Slanders of *Times* Against U. S. Communists. ". . . To suppose that we are 'stooges' of a vile nationalistic policy of a foreign country is, in this case, to presuppose that the Soviet Union had such an 'isolationist' policy—which all of current history disproves . . . The Communist Party was never pacifist, and it never opposed but always favored universal military training and service, which we consider not militaristic, but democratic. We opposed the Wadsworth bill because it was inseparable from a policy of entrance into a Chamberlain war into which we were drifting . . ."

December 13

Starobin: Mowrer Out of Step on Teheran. ". . . what is this clap-trap about the small nations? . . . it is high time for a man whose career is in the liberal tradition to be a little bit less arrogant . . ."

December 14

Editorial: GOP After Teheran. ". . . men of Bricker's stamp—like Landon, Hoover and Dewey—cannot possibly be entrusted with the nation's foreign policy . . . As Earl Browder put it in Bridge-port . . . the demand will go up even stronger, now that we have heard the Republican maharajahs, for President Roosevelt to accept the heavy burden of national leadership in the next critical years . . ."

December 18

Editorial: The President Returns. ". . . on the eve of decisive battles it is in unity behind the Commander-in-Chief that the way forward lies . . ."

December 19

Sunday Worker. Soviet-Czech Pact Projects East-European Se-curity. ". . . this treaty is a death-knell of any idea of a 'cordon sanitaire' against Russia, or a confederation of dissimilar states in eastern Europe that might become the pawn of reactionary, fascist influence . . . The great Soviet Power will not, as it never has, interfere in their internal affairs . . . the Teheran conference is of a universal order; the Soviet-Czechoslovak agreement em-braces primarily central and eastern Europe. There is no contra-diction between them."
Editorial: Eastern Europe. ". . . (the treaty) drives another nail in the coffin of reactionary confederations that could be directed against the USSR. It signifies the new position of the USSR in Europe and in the world, already acknowledged by the Moscow conferences and at Teheran."

December 29

Editorial: The Dimitroff Tribute. ". . . It is time to recognize that what's good in Yugoslavia is certainly good—and needed—in the United States . . ."
Allen: Impressions of Teheran. ". . . The new approach is becom-ing most immediately apparent with respect to European problems. . . . We have the dramatic turn in the Anglo-American policy towards . . . Marshal Tito . . . We will see equally dramatic changes with respect to Poland, Finland and the Baltic. In Italy and Spain it may take more time and more struggle . . ."

1944

January 1

Editorial: Hail the Year of Victory. "The year of 1943 goes down in history as the year of the Great Change. The year 1944 will be the year of the Great Decision . . . Teheran ended the nerve-wrecking uncertainties of millions . . . The leader of our national unity, President Roosevelt, who commands the support and respect of all healthy and forward-looking people, must carry the banner of our national destiny in the elections of 1944 . . . There can be no greater cause for labor and the nation than the historic cause declared at Teheran . . ."

January 7

Editorial: Bar Mikolajczyk. ". . . The time has come to end this farce. Every honest patriot must want to know why the Polish Premier Mikolajczyk should be permitted to come to this country to arouse anti-Soviet prejudice and rally the defeatists and pro-fascists . . ."

January 10

Headline: Communist Party Adopts Unity Program for 1944, Post War, Proposes Change of Name. ". . . The proposal is that the name shall no longer contain the word 'party' . . . Of the 28 members of the National Committee present all voted in favor of Mr. Browder's proposal. Two hundred additional leaders . . . approved the proposals unanimously . . ."

Statement to the Press (excerpts): ". . . The Moscow, Teheran and Cairo agreements give a program to banish the specter of civil wars and war between nations for several generations . . . Not only a prolonged world-peace without precedent in history, but also a flourishing of economic relationships . . . is the prospect open for the world . . . It is equally evident that the political issues of this time will be decided within the form of the two-party system traditional in our country. In this framework can be fought out and won the necessary struggle of the American people to safeguard our country's victory . . ."

Foster in CBS Broadcast Says Teheran Guide to Post-War. ". . . It (Teheran) is the most decisive turning point in all modern history . . . it assures us of an orderly peaceful world after the victory . . . there is no issue—'free enterprise,' or the change in the capitalist system—before the people of this country . . . we must remove all unreal issues . . ."

January 11

Headline: Browder Urges Unity for Victory, Post-War Order. 20,000 Hear of C. P. Plan for New Name. (Excerpts.) ". . . [at

Teheran] Capitalism and socialism have begun to find the way to peaceful co-existence and collaboration in the same world . . . National unity in the United States . . . must be a compromise between classes, groups and tendencies . . . It is my considered judgment that the American people are so ill-prepared, subjectively, for any deep-going change in the direction of socialism that post-war plans with such an aim would not unite the nation, but would further divide it . . . they would help the anti-Teheran forces to come to power in the United States . . . Marxists will not help the reactionaries by opposing the slogan of 'Free enterprise' with any form of counter-slogan . . ."

January 13

Browder (excerpts from his speech at the meeting of the National Committee of the C. P., January 9): ". . . we were not entirely unprepared in this Plenum for the decisions that we are making, unprecedented as these decisions are. True . . . we are departing from orthodoxy, because none of our textbooks foresaw or predicted a long period of peaceful relations in the world before the general advent of Socialism . . . But we know . . . without Teheran the catastrophe that would come upon us . . . would be all the more certain and complete . . ."

January 22

Editorial: Lenin and Tehran. "From a policy of encirclement to a policy of collaboration—that is the span from 1917 to 1944. And it must change the face of the whole world . . ."

January 23

Sunday Worker. Browder Answers Your Questions (interview with T. Moody, an Australian journalist). ". . . We have definitely taken a position that it is not on the order of the day for the post-war period for us to try to secure the establishment of socialism in the United States. Question: That means that even in the post-war period you will not raise the question of socialism? Answer: Not in any way to disturb the national unity. Q.: That is, for a long term of years? A.: Yes . . . if any country decides to establish a socialist system, it will be purely on the basis of its inner decision . . . it will not be the result of outside intervention . . . For us, Marxist theory is not a series of dogmas but a guide to action . . . Q.: The press accused you of merely changing your tactics, of boring from within. A.: That is an attempt to import European phrases into American political life . . . would not apply in England . . . Europe and Australia . . . Q.: Do you mean in effect a new lease of life for capitalism, a more democratic form? A.: It means a democratic capitalism with a rising standard of life, not a declining one . . ."

January 25

Editorial: The Fourth Term. ". . . Roosevelt is a national asset . . . The people want Tehran for America and for the world—and that means they want Roosevelt . . ."

February 9

Starobin: What's the *Times* Game on the USSR? ". . . there is every indication that when Mr. Hull returned from Moscow he knew that the status of the Baltic States was not an all-European problem . . . The only point at which the European Commission conceivably begins to operate as far as Poland is concerned would be the disposition of east Prussia . . . the *Times* wishes to run the Soviet Foreign Office. This is just preposterous."

February 10

Starobin: Between the Lines. ". . . The entire content of what American Communists are doing these days flows from a positive estimate of Tehran accord . . ."

February 22

Editorial: Hull Firm on Teheran. ". . . the State Department is no longer a great incubator of anti-Soviet rumors . . . the highest State Department officials see the obvious parallel between the Soviet attitude on Poland and the American position on Bolivia. I am absolutely convinced . . . that both the President and Secretary of State Hull . . . are completely sold on the policies of Tehran and are certain this Government can get along with the Soviet Union . . ."

February 29

Starobin: Progress All Along the Line. ". . . Mr. Hull's attitude is particularly praiseworthy . . . Things are going very much better. In terms of a table, you might get the following picture: Allied policy toward Poland: great progress in the right direction. Toward Yugoslavia: excellent . . . Toward Italy: not good at all, but subject to change . . . Toward Greece: very obscure . . ."

April 4

Editorial: Answering Three Lies. ". . . the second lie was the USSR would be 'bolshevizing' the smaller nations along its western border. Molotov makes it clear that . . . the Soviet Union . . . is not concerned with Rumania's social structure . . . makes no demands for territory at Rumania's expense . . ."

April 18

Editorial: MacArthur's Reply. ". . . he is only part of a vast defeatist conspiracy in which the leadership of the Republican Party is deeply involved . . . The world must be shown that the MacArthurs do not speak for America."

May 2

Editorial: What We Stand For. ". . . We stand for full support to the foreign policy of the Roosevelt Administration . . . as worked out in the Moscow and Teheran Conferences . . . We stand for national unity behind the Commander-in-Chief regardless of partisan considerations—a unity that requires that President Roosevelt continue in office another four years . . ."

May 11

Lapin: Polish Solution Soon. ". . . most of the 108 speeches in the House and Senate last week to commemorate the Polish Constitution of 1791 were attacks on the Soviet Union—and on the Roosevelt Administration . . . I submit that the very hysteria and frenzy of the supporters of the Polish government-in-exile betrays the real reason. They know that they are fighting a lost cause . . . the fact is that the Churchill and Roosevelt Government have not permitted the Polish issue to become a major cause of friction with the Soviet Union . . ."

May 21

Sunday Worker. Bob Digby: False Prophets of Hunger. The Hoover-Dewey Food Shortage Scare. ". . . had not Hoover had experience . . . in starving the peoples of democratic countries in Europe, especially the Soviet Union . . . It was Herbert Hoover who sounded the signal for the wave of 'scarcity' speeches . . ."

May 22

Browder: ". . . America and the world must choose between Teheran and Hitler . . . Every one who casts doubt upon Teheran . . . is working for Hitler . . ."

May 28

Editorial: Communist Convention. ". . . of vital concern to all America. After 25 years of existence the Communist Party was dissolved and the Communists have organized into a non-partisan Communist Political Association . . . It enthusiastically supported Mr. Roosevelt . . . the national unity which is required can only be attained in America at present on the basis of the capitalist 'free enterprise' system . . ."

(June 6, American, British and Canadian armies invade northern France.)

June 18

Sunday Worker. Browder: The War and the Elections. ". . . In 1944, it is clear that any nonpartisan approach to the elections can only result in the demand for continuance of the leadership of Franklin D. Roosevelt. There is no alternative candidate for President of the United States who does not base himself upon the questioning or even the rejection of the Teheran accord and all that flows from it. . . . There is no alternative . . ."

June 30

Editorial: The GOP Convention Ends. ". . . Defeated in battle, the Axis enemy . . . pins its hopes on a GOP victory . . . Those who realize what GOP stands for should also realize that it will stop at nothing to confuse and divide the people . . . The interests of all Americans . . . can be saved by a resounding repudiation of that party and the reelection of the President."

July 13

Editorial: The People Want Him. ". . . The anti-Wallace movement is essentially an anti-Roosevelt movement . . . because of this, and because of Wallace's policies and great services to the nation, he should be continued in office . . ."

July 23

Sunday Worker. Starobin: Poland's Road. ". . . the United Nations must finally acknowledge the illegality of the exiled government, and act accordingly . . ."

August 9

Headline: Soviets Doubt Pole Exile Gov't. Claims. ". . . informed Soviet circles discount or are highly skeptical of claims . . . that the Polish underground is engaged in heavy fighting inside Warsaw. Informed quarters said that was a part of a campaign by General Sosnkowski . . . to impress Anglo-Americans with fictitious strength of his followers . . ."

Headline: Pole Reactionaries Continue Anti-Soviet Campaign in London. ". . . it seems that the news of the rising was manufactured in London to strengthen . . . Mikolajczyk's position and show the world that the Red Army was not taking Warsaw alone . . ."

August 13

Sunday Worker. Headline: Polish Issue Clear—Democracy vs. Autocracy. ". . . the true reason for the breakdown of unity negotiations between the Polish Committee of National Liberation and the emigre premier Mikolajczyk . . . elections will take place immediately after Polish soil is cleared. At this, Mikolajczyk balked . . ."

(August 15, American and French armies invade southern France.)

August 21

Editorial: Success in France. ". . . Some people are amazed at our progress . . . our successes should surprise no one . . . The Nazi army of 1944 is not the army of 1941. It has met the great Red Army and been ground down by it . . ."

August 24

Headline: Patriots Free Paris.
Editorial: Paris Free. ". . . a lump rises in the throat of mankind and tears of relief and jubilation fill the eyes. It was that way with Moscow in November 1941, with Leningrad last winter . . . The backbone of German power was broken on the Soviet front, as the people of Paris well understand . . ."

(August 25, American and French forces liberate Paris.)

August 26

Starobin: Paris—the Lightning Flash. ". . . The fact is that the people liberated itself . . . What courage, what a sense of history for hundreds of thousands of virtually unarmed men and women to come out and challenge the enemy who had been there for four years . . . Paris remains 'Red Paris' . . . The action of FFI inside of Paris was as unexpected as it was exhilarating . . ."

August 30

Headline: Pole General Tells Truth of Warsaw Uprising. ". . . from a military point of view, General Rola-Zymierski continued, the attempt to capture the city by badly armed, numerically weak forces, without coordination with the Red Army, was an absolutely hopeless venture . . ."

September 10

Kournakoff: The Drama of Warsaw. ". . . The Red Army was not going to change its entire strategic plan . . . on short notice . . . dropping supplies into a city where street fighting is going on . . . is almost tantamount to dropping supplies to the enemy . . . the Russians do not need lessons in humanitarianism . . ."

September 29

Browder's speech in Madison Square Garden on September 28. Excerpts: ". . . [Dewey's election] would be an announcement to the whole world that America has turned her back upon the whole idea of a world peace organization, which can become a reality only by the establishment of the principle of collaboration between non-Communists and Communists, and the complete cessation of the old 'war between two worlds' of anti-Communism and Communism. . . . We do not want disaster for America, even though it results in socialism. If we did, we would support Dewey and Hoover . . . That is why American Communists, even as our great Communist forebears in 1860 and 1864 supported Abraham Lincoln, will in 1944 support Franklin D. Roosevelt . . ."

October 11

Editorial: Dewey and Dumbarton Oaks. ". . . Whether the great powers will ever face the possibility of voting against each other will never be a real issue provided anti-British or anti-Soviet hostility is eliminated in our own Government . . ."

October 24

Minor: "Poor Little" Who? ". . . Now for the first time in centuries, a great, powerful and really independent Poland, and a Finland of like character, are about to come into their own. These two peoples, of a great historic past and a present vitality which assures them a brilliant future—have not been really independent during the past 25 years . . . political brothel on the borders of Russia for their imperialist intrigues: first a Clemenceau, then a Chamberlain, then Hitler . . ."

October 29

Browder: Watch Out for Dewey's "Surprise." ". . . Candidate Dewey's campaign has so far been so meticulously according to the textbook of Herr Hitler . . ."

November 5

Sunday Worker. Editorial: Our Compact with History. "This election will define the moral health and the political maturity of

America. It is Roosevelt or chaos . . . It is Teheran or Munich. It is democracy or fascistic reaction . . ."

Browder: Dewey Reveals His Foreign Policy. ". . . His foreign policy is to . . . prepare to crush the Soviet Union by military force . . . All hope of victory and a durable peace rests squarely upon open and honest collaboration with the Communists. Without this there is no victory and there is no peace."

November 7

Headline: Iran Premier's Rejection of Soviet Oil Bid Has Questionable Background. ". . . Iran's sovereignty, independence and national dignity is in no way threatened by her powerful northern neighbor, whose watchword is equality for all nations . . ."

Editorial: The USSR at 27. ". . . The new Russia . . . shares with us a common respect for the human being, a common passion for the subordination of science to human welfare, a common desire to live at peace with a peaceful world . . . Americans . . . are thankful and respectful of this power . . ."

(November 7, President Roosevelt reelected.)

November 9

Browder: Vote Clears Way for Quick Victory. "The most arrogant, shameless and dangerous bid for power in our country by a group of irresponsible men . . . was broken . . . The whole United Nations is stronger and happier today . . . The Communists . . . did everything in their power to remove the issue of Communism from the election . . . they dissolved their own party . . . They gave everything they had, and ask for themselves nothing . . ."

November 12

Sunday Worker. Headline: See Hand of Foreign Oil Barons Behind Soviet-Iran Rift. ". . . the USSR does want a say in Iran's economic development, which would greatly accelerate the rise in living standards of her people . . ."

November 27

Editorial: For Universal Training. "We believe the great majority of Americans are convinced universal military training is essential today . . . such a step is inseparably connected with the kind of foreign policy the people voted for November 7 . . . we join in urging support for such a measure."

December 5

Editorial: Help Europe's Heroes to Help Us. "What happened in the squares of Athens on Sunday must alarm every American . . . The peoples of Europe have built a new legality out of bloodshed and heroism, just as our forefathers did in 1776. We should honor that new legality, help to stabilize it and not to undermine it and betray it . . . British diplomacy is driving for a reactionary Europe . . . they can't expect the necessary economic help from us, and yet pursue reactionary policies in defiance of . . . the sacred agreements of Moscow and Teheran . . . America must speak up, and out loud . . . The CIO ought to speak out . . ."

December 9

Editorial: Churchill's Hollow Victory. ". . . The only way forward lies in the policy of non-interference with the affairs of liberated Europe, as enunciated by Mr. Stettinius this week . . . Britain must withdraw from Greece immediately . . . And that is what every American trade union, every people's organization must demand . . ."

Starobin: Greece, America, Britain. "Greece becomes the symbol of a new Europe that will not be denied the fruits of Germany's defeat and the fruits of the Teheran agreement . . . And, 'Backward America,' we ought to be proud of it. Mr. Stettinius towers over all these screeching defamers . . . A big businessman, in all the confidence of a flourishing capitalism, understands that only a new Europe is possible, and that only with such a Europe can America and Russia work in harmony . . . Unless the Labor leaders force Churchill to back down, the Labor Party does not deserve to win a general election. . . . Britain—impoverished as a capitalist power—clings to reaction in Europe . . . Greece can never be conquered. Britain is with each day of this stupidity only amplifying the extent of her ultimate humiliation."

December 12

Editorial: The Soviet-French Alliance. ". . . It is a good omen for the future of French democracy that the first diplomatic act since her liberation affirms a new treaty of friendship with the Soviet Union . . . This should . . . make it clear that enemies of this treaty are in fact the enemies of French democracy at home. The new alliance is also a blow against the organization of 'blocs' in Western Europe of a kind that conceal reactionary hopes and anti-Soviet purposes . . . men like . . . Spaak who hoped to draw France into a bloc, anti-Soviet in its foreign policy and reactionary at home, will find the new treaty a real obstacle. And the same can be said for Mr. Spaak's mentors in London . . . The latest act of French and Soviet diplomacy conforms to our best interests and deserves our welcome."

December 15

Editorial: Restating the Issue in Europe. ". . . whereas in the Soviet occupied areas or in France, few or no obstacles have been placed before the people's will, Churchill has inexcusably tried to defy . . . popular will in Belgium, Italy and Greece. The result is disaster."

(December 16, German attack in the Ardennes.)

December 18

Editorial: Churchill on Poland. "Premier . . . Churchill is pursuing a policy toward Poland which is the exact opposite of his tragic course in Greece . . . We applaud Churchill's attitude on Poland just as we condemn its opposite in Greece . . . Polish 'territorial issue' . . . was never more than a symbol of a deeper problem . . . The phrase 'partition of Poland' . . . is simply a red herring . . . Poland is emerging as a great people in command of its own destinies at last . . ."

December 30

Starobin: About Spheres of Influence. ". . . If we Americans are really opposed to spheres and blocs of influence in Europe, we are in agreement with the USSR, which also doesn't want them . . . Soviet policy aspires to a general European influence . . ."

December 31

Allen: Crisis in Greece. None in Eastern Europe. Why? ". . . There is no Greek tragedy in Hungary. It seems simple. Why? Because the Red Army is not afraid of the people and their democracy . . ."
Editorial: New Year's Pledge. ". . . Experience has shown that the active participation of the Soviet Union is required to bring about a settlement of any important world question between Britain and our country . . ."

1945

January 2

Editorial: Our Reply to Hitler's Speech. "Great new political events were ushered in by the New Year . . . the banner event was, of course, the birth of Poland's provisional Government . . . The Lublin Committee . . . accomplished real miracles . . . It would be the greatest mistake for our own public to view this government as a 'puppet of Moscow'; it is as authentic as the unity behind . . . Tito in Yugoslavia . . . As Dr. Oscar Lange points out, it would also be a profound mistake for our own Government and the British to delay recognition to Lublin . . ."

January 3

Starobin: Sources of American Policy. ". . . The United States always enters wars as late as possible and always expects to be arbiter . . . Yes, we are very powerful, but we cannot exercise that power except through a coalition. And our partners in the coalition have the strength of their own . . . the Red Army emerges as the liberator of eastern and central Europe . . ."

January 8

Editorial: The President's Great Message. ". . . in his message to Congress he rose to new heights of leadership . . . he gave significant warning against 'perfectionists' who, no less than isolationists and imperialists, threaten the organization of world peace . . ."

January 13

Starobin: Vandenberg's Hoax. ". . . His real objective is to fool the American public . . . to put the President on the spot, to encourage Europe's reactionaries to hold out . . ."

January 18

Editorial: The Liberation of Poland. "Where shall we find the words to express the power and grandeur of the tremendous panorama which is unfolding this week on the plains of long-suffering Poland? . . . these last 24 hours have a sense of climax . . . which surpasses every previous moment of the war . . . A new fraternity of Poles and Russians and Ukrainians—something historic for Europe—is moving triumphantly toward Silesia and the Oder River. The world stands amazed . . . It is a time . . . for humility . . . there will never again be warfare in Eastern Europe, never again a war that begins in Europe and engulfs the whole world . . ."

January 19

Minor: Cost of Lying About Poland. ". . . The old lie about Poland being a victim of Russia . . . has become one of the world's big businesses . . . it will not stop the Red Army . . ."

January 20

Starobin: Churchill's New Themes. ". . . On the one hand, he wants to make believe that 'Stalinism' sides with him, which is of course mean and evil nonsense. On the other hand, he is beckoning for the support of the most reactionary American circles . . . The longer Britain pursues such a line, the harder it will be for the more conciliatory American circles, represented by the President and the progressive movement as whole, to help understand or help the harassed men of London."

January 21

Sunday Worker. Browder Nails Vandenberg's Attack on Teheran (address at the Lenin Memorial Meeting, January 15). ". . . President's recent messages to Congress . . . mark the highest level reached in the history of American statesmanship . . . eloquent verification of the Teheran Conference decisions . . ."

Editorial: The President's Inaugural. ". . . We are confident the forthcoming meeting of the Big Three will solve many problems of the coalition . . . the situation calls for the widest popular backing of the President's coalition policy right here in America. It was upon our demand that the President is now entering a fourth term . . ."

January 28

Sunday Worker. Starobin: As the Big Three Meet. ". . . the most general problem is whether we are going to help reconstruct productive, going-economics or whether we are going to delay this reconstruction by political interference . . . it would be nonsense to think that the United States can directly un-do the developments which have already taken place . . . No power on earth can overthrow Marshal Tito in Yugoslavia . . ."

February 2

Editorial: Stalingrad to Berlin. ". . . the Soviet Union . . . is actually carrying the war and the world on its shoulders . . . amazing and inspiring the peoples of all countries and . . . welding a brotherhood . . . which will be hard—impossible . . . to break apart . . . The vision of a powerful and friendly Soviet Russia . . . rising east of the mists of the Rhine . . . Our country is fortunate to be allied with this power."

VII

Period from February 11, 1945, when Roosevelt, Churchill and Stalin terminated their conference at Yalta, to July 28, 1945, when the American Communist party, which had ostensibly abolished itself, recreated itself.

February 14

Starobin: The Magic Carpet of Yalta. ". . . This is no simple alliance of victors . . . It has never been seen before. It is pregnant with the most revolutionary possibilities for the future of the

human race . . . A new center of power-harmony has been established in our time . . . The age of isolation is over."
Editorial: The Crimea Decisions. ". . . The world has found a
unique center of leadership for generations to come: such is the
majesty of their achievement . . . the Atlantic Charter . . . can
no longer be used against the peoples of Europe . . ."

February 18

Sunday Worker. Allen: Crimea Accord Spurs U. S. Unity Behind
Roosevelt. ". . . acclaimed as no international accord has ever been
received . . . our foreign policy is enriched . . . Simple humility
would require that we accept the judgment of the Soviet Union
as to what her immediate course in the Far East shall be . . ."

February 25

Sunday Worker. Editorial: Red Army Day. ". . . Towns and ham-
lets in the United States decree that Washington's Birthday shall
also be Red Army Day . . . New and adequate words cannot be
found to describe the monumental achievements of the Red Army.
. . . Today it is the most superior army in the world . . . It is an
army of liberation . . ."

March 2

Editorial: The Nation Must Respond. "It was a genial and heroic
American President who came before Congress and the nation
yesterday to report on the Crimea accord . . . it was an effort to
make Americans grasp the spirit of harmony which exists between
our government and our major allies . . . Let the country rise to
the stature of the President's leadership. Let the labor movement,
in particular, stand fast behind him . . ."

March 4

Sunday Worker. Browder: The US Army Kills the Red Bogey.
". . . This is indeed a great victory for American democracy . . .
Surely the time has come to put an end, officially and beyond dispute, to the fable that 'Communist' is synonymous with 'subver-
sive' . . ."

March 12

Browder: Every American Must Take Stand on Crimea. Report to
the plenary session of the National Committee of the Communist
Political Association. "Our interpretation of Teheran has been
confirmed by Crimea . . . Our own policies and work contributed
essentially to the victory of November 7, and therefore directly to
the consummation at Yalta . . . Our political influence within the
labor and progressive organizations and communities has grown

far wider and deeper than it ever was before. Our own organization is more unified than ever . . . We are gradually breaking down and dissolving the barriers built up against us over a generation by the dominant forces in American society . . . We can confidently look forward . . ."

April 5

Editorial: Synthetic Dust-Storm. ". . . Stettinius debunked all the loose chatter about 'secret diplomacy' at Yalta . . . How then is the impression created that . . . we are somehow battling with the Soviet Union? How is all this distrust manufactured? . . . Powerful interests are operating among us—mostly outside the government . . . These men—like Vandenberg and Hoover . . . —are the chief obstacles for our public opinion to overcome . . ."

(April 12, President Roosevelt dies.)

April 15

Starobin: The New Europe—What It's Like. ". . . Europe today is experiencing the completion of the bourgeois democratic revolution, the burying of antiquated social forms . . . The dictatorship of the working class was a necessity for the peoples of old Russia . . . the path of history does not need to repeat itself but can be different. The dictatorship of the working class no longer presents itself with the same urgency . . . It now becomes possible to consider for the first time on a general scale the transition of many countries toward socialism in a new, and generally peaceful way, through the older state forms . . . Yes, the state will control; but it is already and will be a state dominated by a new configuration of classes . . ."

April 17

Budenz: Catholic Group's Attack on 'Frisco Libels FDR. ". . . The Archbishops and Bishops of the Administrative Council of the National Catholic Welfare Council chose to make public an astonishing document . . . directed against Mr. Roosevelt's handiwork at the Crimea conference . . . What it means, brutally and brazenly, is the initiation of conflict with our most helpful ally, the Soviet Union . . . these people do not speak for America; we can be sure of that . . ."

April 21

Starobin: Poland—Key to Frisco. ". . . The Soviet Union has taken a very firm stand on this issue. One may say that its prestige as a leading power is at stake . . . Unless Great Britain and the United States finally accept such changes for Poland—by way of recognizing a government built around the Warsaw regime—there is no complete assurance that they will accept the whole pattern of internal and external relations in the rest of eastern Europe. At Yalta, this was accepted in principle, but . . . A world organization . . . cannot be expected to function successfully until . . . uncertainties are completely removed . . ."

April 28

Starobin: Perspectives on San Francisco. ". . . The Polish Eagle is missing . . . the Polish people have a government . . . It is not a Soviet government, not a puppet government . . . why are the Polish people unrepresented? It is impossible to escape the conclusion that the Polish people are being penalized because their country was not only liberated by the Red Army, but also insists upon becoming a new kind of Poland . . ."

April 29

Sunday Worker. Allen: Polish-Soviet Pact Bolsters Security of Post-War World. ". . . The 20-year pact . . . ranks among the most . . . constructive agreements of the war . . . On the Polish side, the pact means that . . . the great internal transformations . . . are secured against the threat of aggression . . . Poland . . . the key non-Soviet Slav nation of Europe . . . has been transformed from a base of aggression into a bastion of peace and security. The Polish question, translated into real American terms, is nothing less than the question of American-Soviet friendship, and therefore of world peace. The longer we procrastinate, the worse it is for us . . ."

May 5

Starobin: San Francisco Blues. ". . . let us ask ourselves what will happen tomorrow when two more Soviet republics take their place in world affairs, and later when Finland, Poland, Bulgaria. Romania, Hungary, Austria, Albania, and Italy come into the world organization. When that happens, it is certain that Norway, Belgium, Greece, Iran and France will vote and continue to work with the Soviet Union . . . the world which is now coming out of the war cannot possibly be pro-American at any point where the United States is anti-Soviet . . ."

May 9

Editorial: San Francisco Progress. ". . . Molotov battled for the success of the conference . . . It became clear that Molotov's efforts had been directed all along towards writing a genuine charter of freedom and democracy . . ."

May 10

Lapin: The Case of Senator Vandenberg. ". . . One cannot call this advocate of 'honest candor' with our Allies a liar. That is too simple. It understates the case. For him deception is a way of life, an unfailing political code . . ."

May 16

Editorial: An Anglo-American Bloc? ". . . An exclusive Anglo-American bloc can rest only on a reactionary program. Unity without the Soviet Union tends to become unity against the Soviet Union. It becomes unity to restore Fascist and near-Fascist regimes . . ."

May 17

Lapin: Freedom of the Press for Export. ". . . Freedom of the press as practised in the United States has created enough friction between the Allies already. It has done enough damage in attacking progressive ideas as 'Communist' . . ."

May 18

Editorial: Who Broke the Yalta Concord? ". . . the man who prevented broadening of the Warsaw government was Winston Churchill . . . balked at approving a strong democratic government in Poland . . . Why were the American people told that it was the Soviet Union which refused to carry out the Yalta agreement? Who in the State Department was responsible . . . it is time that the people and their organizations, their trade unions and their churches and their fraternal lodges begin to demand that the foreign policy of Franklin D. Roosevelt . . . be carried out by the Government of the United States."

May 20

Sunday Worker. Browder: The Crisis That Follows V-E Day. ". . . today Roosevelt is not here to play his decisive role . . . Now Churchill has assumed command of both British and American policy in relation to the Soviet Union . . . It is necessary for those who supported Roosevelt now to raise their voices in firm insistent demand for a return to the Roosevelt policies . . . We must raise such a storm around the high official places in Washington . . . that stupid officials will be awakened from their hypnosis under reactionary and British influences . . . Every worker, every democrat should write letters to Stettinius . . . to his Senators and Representatives in the Congress . . . It is time to address this demand also to President Truman . . ."

May 21

Headline: Yanks Gain Slowly on Bloody Okinawa.

Starobin: Three-Dimensional Approaches. ". . . British diplomacy is at the bottom of all nasty goings-on here . . . Some people are talking these days as though the United States does not need the Soviet Union any more . . . This is an illusion for which we will pay dearly . . . Unless the United States thinks it can win the war against Japan alone, we shall need a united and effective Chinese ally, and this involves the Soviet Union's direct as well as indirect aid . . ."

May 22

Editorial: U. S. Policy at Trieste. ". . . The Allied approach to the Trieste issue is a direct violation of the American policy as worked out by Roosevelt at the Yalta Conference and approved by the American people . . . Is the State Department now mustering full support to the Churchill policy, in complete contradiction to the policy of President Roosevelt? . . ."

May 24

Jacques Duclos On the Dissolution of the Communist Party Of the United States. ". . . notorious revision of Marxism . . . by transforming the Teheran declaration . . . which is a document of a diplomatic character into a political platform of class peace in the United States . . . dangerous opportunist illusion . . ."

May 27

Sunday Worker. Allen: Europe's Liberation Tests Unity of 'Big 3' Coalition. Genuine Democracy, Self-Determination Threatened by U.S.-British Stand.

Browder: The San Francisco Conference (radio address on May 24). ". . . Roosevelt's plans for this conference were not carried out by the American delegation . . . If he [Truman] is to make good his pledge to America that he will execute the legacy of Roosevelt's policies, then he must act now and act decisively to reverse the course upon which our country was led at San Francisco . . . America still has a deadly war in the Pacific . . ."

Editorial: Plain Talk About Hard Realities. ". . . In fact, President Truman has virtually admitted this deterioration by sending Harry Hopkins on another mission to Moscow . . ."

May 28

Editorial: The 'Veto' Issue. ". . . This vital principle has been at stake in recent days . . . Only the Soviet Union is left to uphold it. But why should this be so? . . . is there anything peculiarly 'Russian' about desiring a workable world organization? . . ."

May 30

Headline: Anti-Soviet Intrigue by Harriman Alleged [by Johannes Steel].

June 9

Starobin: State Department 'Spy' Case Seen Part of Policy Shift in Asia. ". . . change-over to a reactionary diplomacy in the Far East which may cost millions of American lives . . ."

June 10

Sunday Worker. Allen: 'Veto Power' Vital to Real Peace Machinery. ". . . the Soviet Union is impelled to demand the fullest and strictest compliance with every agreement reached . . ."
Editorial: Danger Signals. ". . . The policies of the last two months must be reversed—quickly and sharply . . . Our delegation at San Francisco must return to the basic principle of the Yalta conference, which envisaged the unanimity of the great powers as the core of future world relations . . . The United States must return to the policies projected by the late President Roosevelt . . ."

June 16

Minor Says Browder is Basically Wrong. ". . . Do not play with the illusion that the American capitalist class, especially the larger elements in it, were materially influenced by the distinction between the Communist support of President Roosevelt as a party and as an association . . ."

June 27

Starobin: European Roundup. ". . . Events have fully proven that the Polish problem was simply exploited by the State Department to whittle down the strength of Soviet-American friendship and to hold the Polish question as a club over the Soviet Union and Europe generally . . ."

June 30

Minor: The People Signed It [The UN Charter]. ". . . the decisive thing in the formation of the United Nations for effective keeping of the peace is the presence in it of Soviet Russia . . . The United States is now by far the greatest stronghold of the enemies of the Charter . . ."

July 4

Starobin: 900,000 Revolutionary Heroes [the members of the French Communist Party]. ". . . France is the last stronghold of reactionary, monopoly-capitalist influences on the continent . . ."

July 16

Editorial: Quick Victory in Asia.—How? ". . . Imagine how much help the Chinese Communists could give us . . . if arms and materials were shipped into the strategic areas which they control! . . . if the peoples of Asia were given a perspective of their own liberation . . ."

July 17

Editorial: Eyes on Potsdam. ". . . As for Asia . . . there will be no real solutions without reckoning upon the strength and position of the Soviet Union . . ."

July 27

Headline: Foster Calls for Return to Party. ". . . reintroduction of 'Leninist democratic-centralism' . . . those participating unanimously reject Browder's position on placing reliance on American big business . . ."

VIII

Period from July 28, 1945, when the American Communist Party resumed its name, to the breakdown of the London Conference of Byrnes, Bevin and Molotov, October 2, 1945.

July 28

Headline: Communist Parley Votes to Reestablish Party. "By unanimous vote . . . With genuine enthusiasm . . ."

July 30

Headline: Foster Chosen to Head Party.

August 4

Editorial: Success at Potsdam. ". . . a practical, business-like agreement which will be greeted with satisfaction by the democratic peoples everywhere . . . all the more satisfying because it comes after the very dangerous tendencies which developed during the San Francisco conference . . . Why has the atmosphere changed? . . . the demand for a durable peace is so very powerful among the peoples of our own country and Britain . . . [also because] From Finland to Poland, to Italy, democratic, anti-fascist movements entrenched themselves . . . what the Potsdam agreement has done . . . is to register the gains already made . . . [also] the British elections . . . [finally] persistent way in which the Soviet Union used its power and prestige . . . But we should not take it for granted that everything will be rosy now . . . some officials make agreements only to break them . . ."

August 5

Sunday Worker. Foster: The Communist Party Convention. ". . . a few of the more important aspects of the Party's new policy as follows: (a) Recognition of the aggressive role of American imperialism on a world scale, which Browder's policy tried to hide; (b) A realization that a progressive collaboration among the Big Three powers will depend primarily upon the role of labor and all other democratic forces in the world, instead of upon the good-will or 'intelligence' of the American big bourgeoisie; (c) A Marxian analysis of the war against Japan which differentiated between the imperialist aims of American big capital in the war and the democratic aims of the peoples of Asia and the United States to maintain the national liberation character of the war in the Pacific . . ."

August 6

Editorial: Potsdam and America. ". . . The United States has now become the principal world battleground in which will be shaped the hope of all humanity for lasting peace . . . The Soviet Union is united to the last man . . . Great Britain has achieved a new unity . . . Throughout all Europe the people are rallying behind progressive new governments . . . It is only in our country . . . that influential politicians . . . are trying to undermine confidence . . . speak for cartelists . . . for the industrial and financial interests which fear a democratic Europe . . . These are the real enemies of the peace . . ."

(August 7, Atomic Bomb.)

August 8

Editorial: Challenge to Humanity—Your Future and Atomic Power. " . . . The war is not over . . . will not be over until the conditions have been created for changing the social structure of our Japanese enemy . . . punishing the emperor, unleashing the powers of democracy in all of Asia . . . there are other peoples who can equal and (for all we know) outstrip our own achievements. The alternatives, therefore, are: competition . . . or cooperation . . . this is the time to fight even more strongly for a fundamental cooperation of the great powers—especially our own country and the Soviet Union . . . The immediate answer is to expose and reject the enemies of the United Nations, the enemies of labor and progress. You know who they are. They must not be permitted to misuse atomic power."

August 9 (Soviets join war on Japan).

Editorial: The Soviet War Declaration. "The atombomb . . . has been followed up by a political and military bombshell of even deeper significance . . . the greatest guarantee thus far that out of what was always a war of liberation there will emerge a genuine peace and a new Asia. We Americans . . . can only rise in humility and tribute to this great Soviet ally of ours. After all they have done . . . this giant family of Soviet peoples is undertaking to help win for us and themselves a speedy and secure peace. Every American must feel a lump in his throat at the grandeur of this solidarity. Let the defamers of the Soviet Union stand up today, and let the wrath of American decency strike them down forever . . . the dastardly plot against both Russia and America—emanating from American reactionaries—has now been dealt a bombshell blow . . . The war is not over, and may yet demand the heaviest sacrifices of our people. Immense landings in Japan and China are altogether conceivable . . . it is essential that the United States take the lead in exposing the arrogant dictatorship in Chungking . . . all American officials committed to past policies must be quickly withdrawn . . ."

August 11

Headline: Japanese Communist Program for Post-War Japan. Epstein: ". . . Soviet Smashed Japan's Hope of Holdout on Continent . . ."
Editorial: The President's Address. ". . . The idea that the United States has to bargain for democracy in Poland or press freedom in Europe is fallacious. The Polish people, with the help of the Soviet Union, know more about democracy than the Vandenbergs and the Tafts . . . If ('to poison' our public with lies and slanders . . . is) going to be freedom of the press, we hope that the democratic governments of Europe will exercise their sovereign right of censorship . . ."

August 13

Foster: The Politics of the Atombomb. ". . . In consequence of the tremendous danger presented by a reactionary use of the atomic bomb, it becomes more necessary than ever to prevent the outbreak of a third world war . . . Capitalism cannot be trusted to handle the atomic power militarily, nor can it apply it industrially. Only Socialism can do these things."

(August 15, War Ends.)

August 15

Editorial: Prevent Civil War in China. ". . . Not a single American gun, soldier, plane or other war equipment must be placed at the disposal of the fascist clique in Chungking . . . American-Soviet cooperation must be maintained and extended . . . The State Department should be bombarded with messages demanding the recall of Ambassador Hurley and Gen. Wedemeyer, and the immediate cleansing of the people in the State Department responsible for this suicidal policy . . ."

Headline: 10 Millions Jobless by December.

August 18

Editorial: Stop the Monkey-Business. ". . . the cease-fire order is being delayed. Russians and Mongolians—our allies—are still dying. . . . how can Chiang Kai-shek dare to fly his troops into Shanghai and Nanking . . . And finally, there is the Herbert Hoover of Great Britain—Winston Churchill . . . Americans today are in no mood to take any wooden nickels. The dilly-dallying with the Emperor in Japan must stop . . ."

August 21

Editorial: Let European Democracy Alone. ". . . big pressure campaign on all the peoples of southeastern Europe. It's a subtle but menacing form of American intervention . . . It cancels the Potsdam decisions before the ink is dry. It is an open challenge to the Soviet Union . . . What is this, if not blackmail . . . Bevin echoes and amplifies the Churchill attitude . . . This is a disappointing start for the Labor government in foreign policy . . . It's clear now that the State Department plans something of a political atombomb on the peoples of Europe . . . that American correspondents, once inside Europe, have orders to prepare the grounds for the 'Byrnes Blitz.' . . ."

August 22

Starobin: Mr. Byrnes and Bulgaria. ". . . [Byrnes'] conception of democracy . . . presumably is God's only kind . . . since he is sitting on the summit of the world, twirling an atombomb, Mr. Byrnes decides to blackmail the Bulgarian people . . . trying to bring about a result which fascism in Bulgaria could not achieve."

August 25

Mr. Byrnes and Romania. ". . . We see no reason for the United States to interfere when a people finally begins to eradicate fascism . . . It seems to us that . . . Byrnes, who manipulated so much anti-Sovietism at the San Francisco conference . . . from behind the scenes, is now managing a similar campaign directly from the State Department. This is nasty and dangerous. It's time it were stopped."

August 28

Editorial: The Soviet Chinese Treaty. ". . . brightens the prospects of peace in the Orient . . . the Soviet Union has set an example of 'non-interference,' and respect for China's sovereignty which we can well afford to follow . . ."

August 30

Editorial: Hands Off Liberated Europe. ". . . Such a policy of blackmail, can bring us nothing but the hatred of the liberated peoples . . . In its insistence upon non-interference in internal affairs of Europe and Asia, the Soviet Union has won the gratitude of the liberated nations . . ."

September 2

Sunday Worker. Allen: Sino-Soviet Treaty Gives China Historic Opportunity. ". . . The main responsibility for averting civil war in China . . . rests fully upon Chiang Kai-shek and his American supporters. The last pretext for . . . civil war has been destroyed." Labor Day, 1945, Manifesto of the Communist Party, U.S.A. ". . . Friendship between the Soviet Union and the United States is the cornerstone of peace . . . The enemies of our great ally, the Soviet Union, are the instigators of the new world war; they must be fought and crushed."
Headline: Bulgar People Resent Foreign Interference.

September 4

Editorial: How Big an Army for America? ". . . Given a correct foreign policy . . . we need a much smaller army for occupation purposes and nothing near the number of troops contemplated for a home reserve . . . there appears to be no need to take up extension of the draft at this time since the present draft does not expire until May 15, 1946 . . ."
Editorial: The Surrender and the Peace. ". . . we cannot continue to do business with an Emperor . . . without leaving the impression that we want to maintain Japan as the watchdog of Asia. Our policy of Coalition must be maintained in the Japanese settlement, also."
Headline: Soviet Genius Conquered the Air.

September 9

Editorial: Byrnes in London. "As . . . Byrnes arrives in London . . . it is well to remind ourselves that the United States has become perhaps the most disliked power in liberated Europe . . . The growing suspicion and distrust arises specifically from the State Department's interventions in the affairs of liberated Europe, the effort to impose democracy, South Carolina style, upon anti-fascist coalition governments . . .

In the pursuance of this policy there is . . . an Anglo-American partnership . . . American Big Business, with the aid of government on the diplomatic level, is reaching out to consolidate and expand its positions . . . The political weapon of recognition and treaty making is backed up by the big guns of our economic might . . . Of course, the apologists for this policy are always great 'idealists,' perfectionists . . . at the same time the foremost spokesmen for 'private enterprise' . . . Theirs is, indeed, a 'one-world' policy of the American Century . . ."

September 11

Editorial: What Peace in Asia? ". . . The policy of the State Department . . . is dictated by fear of . . . democratic forces of Asia. It is directed toward suppressing them. It . . . menaces world peace . . . We have Allies who are sharply opposed to it . . . It must be changed."

September 12

Editorial: The Issue Before the Big Five. ". . . every conference of the big powers is preceded by an artificially stimulated crisis, by a deluge of anti-Soviet rumors . . . the American Government has thus far followed a policy in the Far East which is the very opposite of democracy . . . The issue is the same in Europe as it is in Asia. The issue is democracy. The issue is whether the peoples of Europe are to be permitted to reconstitute their shattered countries along democratic lines without Anglo-American economic and political intervention . . . The course followed thus far by the United States is deeply disturbing . . . it is necessary that we Americans maintain constant vigilance against the schemes of those in high places who think the atom bomb is a substitute for international cooperation."

September 14

Headline: MacArthur Linked to Fascists Seizing Power in Philippines.

September 16

Sunday Worker. J. S. A.: The Issue in Europe. ". . . Power relationships have been basically altered . . . From the Baltic to the Black Sea, formerly reactionary and anti-Soviet states are in the process of transforming themselves into democratic states friendly to the Soviet Union . . . The regimes in these countries are transitional . . . they are neither traditionally capitalist, nor Soviet democracies . . . For the first time in the history of that region, democracy is being established in Eastern Europe. This interferes with the intentions of the Anglo-American monopolists . . . and therefore it arouses the ire of Mr. Bevin and Mr. Byrnes . . . We have the same enemy as liberated Europe."

September 19

Headline: Foster Warns of U. S. Imperialism.
Editorial: Hoover's Economic War Against Our Allies. ". . . He speaks for all those who would fashion the world in the image of a predatory American imperialism, who would build not TVAs but Hoovervilles on the Danube. He speaks for those who would exact huge profits from the suffering peoples of Europe and Asia . . ."
Editorial: Questions About MacArthur. ". . . By failing to root out the feudal-industrialist set-up, MacArthur is helping to perpetuate it. This will cause us dangers of imperialism and aggression for years and decades. Instead of planning a joint occupation with our Allies, as in Germany, the United States is making the job harder and costlier . . . to have a small army and shorten the occupation . . . is exactly what MacArthur fears . . ."

September 20

Editorial: Molotov Scores Again. ". . . on the Italian colonies in Africa . . . On Greece . . . in Romania . . . on the Istrian question . . . The Soviet position will find the same warm reception in this country as the Soviet stand at San Francisco."

September 21

Headline: Indian Communist Leader Exposes Trap in New British Gov't Plan.
Editorial: The Army's Size. ". . . the propaganda from the War and Navy Departments for large postwar armed forces is based on aggressive American imperialism . . . The American people are properly impatient with the slow progress being made in demobilizing our armed forces . . ."

September 23

Foster: On Building the Communist Party. ". . . we must thoroughly cleanse our Party's political line of all traces of Browder's bourgeois liberalism . . ."

September 25

Starobin: The Issue in London. ". . . it's the gloom, just gloom . . . Molotov is a tough customer . . . It seems that our own Jimmy

Byrnes has been outclassed . . . what is American policy proposing? That we impose our conceptions of democracy on the rest of the world? That, my friends, means intervention in other people's affairs. It means to base a foreign policy—not on national interest —but on imperialism . . . it is time American diplomats realized that Soviet Russia is here to stay . . ."

September 27

Editorial: Joint Policy for Japan. ". . . When . . . Molotov now raises the question of an Allied Commission for Japan . . . he is reflecting the desires of . . . large sections of the American public. . . . our people . . . do not and cannot understand why Japan should be treated differently from Germany . . . Only a joint policy . . . can break the backbone of Japanese imperialism . . . "

September 29

Field: The Pattern of U. S. Far Eastern Policy. ". . . immediate aims of American Far Eastern policy . . . to make Japanese military-fascism a junior partner of American imperialism . . . To retain a stunted, American-controlled reactionary government in Japan . . . To maintain China as a semi-colony . . . To form a bloc which . . . will attempt to limit the influence . . . of the Soviet Union and which . . . may be used aggressively against it . . ."

September 30

Sunday Worker. Editorial: Atomic Bomb. ". . . Withholding the secret from some of our Allies became obviously a part of the policy of pressuring the Soviet Union . . . It would be a much needed token of good will if he [President Truman] were to offer immediately to share the secret with the Soviet Union and other United Nations."

October 3

Starobin: 'Big 5' Conference Ends in Deadlock. Reversal of Potsdam Plan by U. S., Britain Snags Pacts . . .
"The United States and Great Britain . . . broke off the Council of Foreign Ministers in London, refusing to abide by the Potsdam decision . . ."
Editorial: Crisis in the United Nations. An Answer to Mr. Byrnes. ". . . It is possible to overcome this crisis, but only if the American people get the underlying issues straight . . . The truth is that the United States and Great Britain are not carrying out the spirit or the letter of solemn agreements to destroy German and Japanese fascism. They are in fact tenaciously encouraging reaction in every form, everywhere . . . Is there any wonder that no sensible democrat will trust the United States? . . . But surely the

American interest is to associate itself with the USSR, to help eradicate the old reactionary interests in Europe and Asia . . . Yet Mr. Truman's administration has . . . conceded to every type of reactionary . . . This cannot go on . . . Let our officials face the anger of an aroused nation, which will not tolerate the betrayal of the peace . . ."

Starobin: Atom Power and Capitalist Morals. ". . . can we imagine what goes through Mr. Molotov's mind as he deals with atom-speculators—Mr. Byrnes and Mr. Bevin . . . the American nation is being placed on record as prepared to bomb the rest of the world to smithereens if it could . . . example of the inherent cannibalism of the men who rule the material power—and so far the minds—of our people. How long, brethren, how long?"

APPENDIX III

A FEW EXCERPTS FROM ONE OF STALIN'S BOOKS

PROBLEMS OF LENINISM (Voprosy Leninizma) by Stalin. Moscow: OGIZ, 1939.

THE TASK OF THE VICTORIOUS REVOLUTION.

The development and the support of the revolution in other countries is an essential task of the victorious revolution. Thus the revolution victorious in one country must not consider itself a self-contained entity, but a support, a means of speeding the victory of the proletariat in other countries.

Lenin briefly expressed this thought in saying that the task of the victorious revolution consists in the accomplishment of the "maximum possible in one country *for* the development, support, and stirring up of revolution *in all countries* (cf. v. 23, p. 385).

THE LONG FIGHT FOR COMMUNISM.

That is why Lenin says that "the dictatorship of the proletariat is the most unconditional and most merciless war of the new class against its *more powerful enemy,* the bourgeoisie, whose resistance is increased *ten-fold* when overthrown," that "the dictatorship of the proletariat is a stubborn fight—bloody and bloodless, violent and peaceful, military and economic, educational and administrative—

against the forces and traditions of an old society" (cf. v. 25, p. 173 and 190).

It need hardly be proved that there is not the least possibility of realizing all these tasks in a short period of time, of accomplishing all this in a few years. The dictatorship of the proletariat, the transition from capitalism to communism, must therefore not be regarded as a brief moment of "super-revolutionary" deeds and decrees, but as an entire historical period, with civil wars and foreign conflicts, of constant organizational work and economic reconstruction, of attacks and retreats, of victories and defeats.

DICTATORSHIP OF THE PROLETARIAT.

The state is an instrument in the hands of the ruling class for the suppression of its "class enemies" resistance. *In this sense* the dictatorship of the proletariat is in no way different, in substance, from the dictatorship of any other class, for the proletarian state is a means to suppress the bourgeoisie. There is a *substantial* difference between the two, however, in that all heretofore existent class states have been dictatorships of an exploiting minority over the exploiting majority, whereas the dictatorship of the proletariat is a dictatorship of the exploited majority over the exploiting minority.

In brief, *the dictatorship of the proletariat is the domination of the proletariat over the bourgeoisie, unobstructed by law and based upon violence, enjoying the sympathy and support of the working and exploited masses.* From this, two fundamental deductions follow:

FIRST DEDUCTION: the dictatorship of the proletariat cannot be "perfect" democracy, democracy for *all*, rich as well as poor; a dictatorship of the proletariat "must be a state that is democratic *in a new way*, for the proletariat and the poor at large; and dictatorial *in a new way*, for the bourgeoisie . . ." (*State and Revolution*).

If, of course, in the distant future, the proletariat is victorious in the most important capitalist states and the present encirclement gives way to socialist encirclement, a "peaceful" road of development is entirely possible in some capitalist countries, where the capitalists, because of the "unfavorable" international situation, will then consider it advisable to "volunteer" considerable concessions to the proletariat. But this supposition deals only with a distant and potential future; for the immediate future these suppositions have no relevance whatsoever.

STAGES OF THE REVOLUTION AND STRATEGY.

Strategy is the establishment of the direction of the main blow of the proletariat on the basis of the specific conditions at any given stage of the revolution; the development of a corresponding plan of disposition of the revolutionary forces (main forces and reserves); the fight for the accomplishment of this plan during the entire period of that stage of the revolution.

Our revolution has already passed through two stages and, since the October Revolution, is starting on the third stage. Our strategy has changed accordingly.

FIRST STAGE, 1903 to February 1917. Aim—Overthrow of Tsarism and utter liquidation of the remnants of medievalism. Main force of the revolution—the proletariat. Immediate reserves—the peasantry. Direction of main blow —to isolate the liberal-monarchist bourgeoisie that was trying to win over the peasantry and liquidate the revolution, by *compromising* with tsarism. Plan of disposition for our forces: an alliance of the working class with the peasantry. "The proletariat must lead the democratic revolution to its completion and attach to itself the masses of the peasantry so as to crush the autocracy's opposition and to counteract the oscillations of the bourgeoisie" (cf. Lenin, v. 8, p. 96).

SECOND STAGE, February 1917 to October 1917. Aim—Overthrow of imperialism in Russia and withdrawal from the imperialist war. Main force of the revolution—proletariat. Immediate reserves—the poorest part of the peasantry. Probable reserves—the proletariat of adjoining countries. Favoring conditions—the long war and the crisis of imperialism. Direction of the main blow: to isolate the petty bourgeois democrats (Mensheviks and Social-Revolutionaries) who were trying to win over the toiling peasantry and end the revolution by *compromising* with imperialism. Plan of disposition for our forces: an alliance of the proletariat with the poorest parts of the peasantry. "The proletariat must accomplish the socialist revolution by assembling around it the masses of semi-proletarian elements of the people so as to break the opposition of the bourgeoisie and counteract the oscillations of the peasantry and petty bourgeoisie" (ibid.).

THIRD STAGE, since the October Revolution. Aim—consolidation of the dictatorship of the proletariat in one country, using it as a point of support for the overthrow of imperialism in all countries. The revolution extends beyond the borders of one country, and the epoch of world revolution has begun. Main force of the revolution: dictatorship of the proletariat in one country and revolutionary movement of the proletariat in all others. Main reserves: the semi-proletarian and petty-peasant masses in the advanced countries and the movements for the liberation of colonies and dependent areas. Direction of the main blow:

the isolation of the petty-bourgeois democrats and of the parties of the Second International that form the main support of the policy of *compromise* with imperialism. Plan of disposition for our forces: an alliance of the proletarian revolution with the liberation movement in the colonies and dependent areas.

Strategy deals with the main forces of revolution and with their reserves. It changes with the transition of the revolution on the basis of conditions at a specific stage of the revolution, while remaining essentially the same throughout any one given stage.

THE EBB AND FLOW OF THE MOVEMENT AND TACTICS.

Tactics is the establishment of the line of conduct of the proletariat for the rather short period of ebb and flow of the movement, of rise and decline of the revolution. It is a fight for the accomplishment of this line through the replacement of old forms of fight and the organization of new ones, through the interconnection of these forms, etc. Whereas the aim of strategy is to win the war, be it against tsarism or against the bourgeoisie, to wage the fight against tsarism and the bourgeoisie to its bitter conclusion, tactics are concerned with the more immediate tasks as they aim not to win an entire war but rather a particular battle; or to wage a particular campaign or action according to the concrete circumstances of the ebb and flow of the revolution. Tactics form a part of strategy, inferior and subordinated to it.

Tactics change with the ebb and flow. Thus, while during the first stage (1903–Feb. 1917), our strategy remained the same, tactics often changed in that period. From 1903 to 1905 the Party followed offensive tactics, the revolution was at a tide, the movement rose, and tactics had to be changed to fit the circumstances. In accordance, the forms of combat were also revolutionary, as required by the tide of the revolution. Local political strikes, political demonstrations, a general political strike, the boycott of the Duma, revolt, revolutionary fighting slogans—these were the successive changes through which the fight went during that period. These changes of forms of combat were accompanied by corresponding changes in forms of organization. Factory and plant committees, revolutionary peasant committees, strike committees, Soviets of workers' deputies, workers' party agitation more or less overtly—these were the forms of organization in that period.

During 1907–1912 the Party was obliged to resort to tactics of retreat during a decline of the revolutionary movement, the movement was at an ebb, and tactics necessarily had to take this into consideration. Forms of struggle as well as forms of organization were changed alike. Instead of the boycott of the Duma we had participation in the Duma; instead of overt revolutionary action outside the Duma, we had speeches and the parliamentary routine of the Duma, economic strikes, or simply a suspension of activity. Of course the Party was obliged to go underground during that period, while cultural, educational, cooperative, social security and other organizations permitted by law took the place of revolutionary mass organizations.

The same is true of the second and third stages of the revolution when tactics changed dozens of times while the strategic plans remained unchanged. Tactics deal with the forms of combat and the forms of organization of the proletariat, with their changes and relations. Tactics may have to change several times during one and the same period of the revolution in accordance with the ebb and flow of the revolution.

GAIN TIME AND DECOMPOSE.

A manoeuvering of reserves designed for a correct retreat when the enemy is strong and when retreat is inevitable, when we are beforehand aware of the disadvantages of engaging in battle which the enemy imposes on us, when, given the ratio of forces, retreat is the only means of preventing a blow on the vanguard and of maintaining the reserves behind it.

"The revolutionary parties," Lenin says, "must complete their education. They have learned how to attack. Now they must understand that it is necessary to supplement this by a knowledge of how best to retreat. They must understand (and the revolutionary class learns to understand by its bitter experience) that victory is impossible without learning both how to attack and how to retreat properly."

The object of this strategy is to gain time, to decompose the enemy, and to assemble forces so as to take the offensive later.

INDEX